IRISH

oral histories of the twentieth century

DAYS

IRISH
oral histories of the twentieth century
DAYS

Margaret Hickey

Photographs by Tom Kelly

Kyle Cathie Limited

For my beloved father, Jim Hickey,
who tells his story in these pages.

First published in Great Britain in 2001 by
Kyle Cathie Limited
122 Arlington Road
London NW1 7HP
general.enquiries@kyle-cathie.com
www.kylecathie.com

This paperback edition published 2004

ISBN 1 85626 521 8

Project editor Caroline Taggart
Designed by Robert Updegraff
Text edited by Catherine Blake
Map by Hilary Evans
Production by Lorraine Baird and Sha Huxtable

The image on page 110 is reproduced courtesy of Mansell/Timepix/Rex Features

Margaret Hickey is hereby identified as the author of this work in accordance with Section
77 of the Copyright, Designs and Patents Act 1988.

A Cataloguing in Publication record for this title is available from the British Library.

Printed and bound in Great Britain by Biddles Ltd, Guildford

Contents

A note on the map
The map opposite shows all the places in Ireland mentioned in
the text. Four of the storytellers came from the same part of
Galway and the inset map gives more detail about their locality.

ACKNOWLEDGEMENTS

I count myself very fortunate to have met the men and women who appear in these pages. Although we are of different generations, through them I have come to understand that old age does not quench the spark within. So many societies today seclude old people in caring ghettoes, but, like Shylock, they might plead to be treated differently: 'If you prick us, do we not bleed? If you tickle us, do we not laugh? If you poison us, do we not die?'

I have always relished the vivid, at times poetic, use of language by many of the old Irish people I met, both in Ireland and in England, where I was brought up. Many and many a Sunday I listened with delight to the debate, diatribe and repartee that took place in my father's kitchen between him and his brother Jack. It was through being in their stimulating company that the penny dropped – people older than oneself are not necessarily dry old sticks. Listening to Jim and Jack being at times all of these – wry, comical, incisive, preposterous, contentious and profound – gave me to understand what younger people are missing if they are not exposed to the company of a lively-minded older generation.

When I came to live in Ireland, Mary-Kate Slattery welcomed me unconditionally into her life and looks after me as if I were one of her own. Her place is at the heart of her loving family and her late husband, John Slattery, the cousin with whom my father and Jack were reared, is greatly missed, not least because his knowledge of local history was unrivalled. His untold story is a loss to us all.

But the stories that I did collect came about through the kindness of many people. My good friends Michael Carson and Liz O'Donnell were most encouraging, and it is through them that I came in contact with Kevin Barry, Taylor Carson and Mona Henry. The bold Ken Crampton and his wife Susan introduced me to Patrick Mackenzie and their friend Nyall Speirs put himself out to introduce me to members of the hunt in Co Wexford. Phyllis Molloy was marvellously helpful in my various contacts with her father Kevin Barry, while Claire Maher and Millie Larke put me in touch with Charlie Coughlan. My cousin Anne Costello seems to know everyone in Galway city and she put me in touch with St Francis's Nursing Home, where I met Bridget Dirrane and also Tom O'Donnell; my thanks to Rose O'Connor, the Matron there. My cousin Mary Ryan put me in touch with Sister Carmel Walsh at Moore Abbey, and I met Jimmy Murray in Knockcroghery thanks to Merrily Harpur and Fionnuala Hussey. My neighbour Willie O'Toole arranged for me to meet his father Austin, and it is through my father that I met his old schoolmates Michael-Joe Tarpey and Tommy Hanley. My thanks to Mrs Hanley for the open welcome to her kitchen and to her daughter Mary-Jo Dermody for lending me the wedding photograph of her parents. I first met Eddie Mulvihill during a visit to Woodford in the company of my cousins Tome and Pat Slattery and I thank them for the introduction.

While travelling around to interview my storytellers, for the most part in their homes, friends and family offered me all kinds of encouragement: in particular my cousins Bernie Hogan, Theresa Doocey and Margaret Burke, and my friends in Dublin, Denis Cahalane and Grainne Murphy.

For sound advice on the Irish words and phrases in the book, my thanks to Elizabeth Cleary, Eamonn O'Hara and, again, Denis Cahalane.

It must be every unpublished writer's dream for a publisher to invite them out to lunch and, out of the blue, ask them what they would write about if they were to write a book. Kyle Cathie, that most unconventional and inspired publisher, did just that, and when I told her I should love to put together a book of verbatim conversations with Irish people over the age of eighty or so, she said, 'Well, why don't you do it?' She put me in the careful and sensitive hands of my editor Caroline Taggart, who was patient and encouraging.

I cannot thank Tom Kelly enough. He agreed to take on a project which must be one of the most difficult for any photographer – to take a series of portraits of people whom he did not know, and people whose great age demanded sensitive treatment. To compound the difficulty of the assignment, he had to accomplish it at great speed and most of the portraits were taken in the dead of a harsh winter. A dedicated lover of the motor bike, Tom travelled Ireland in every kind of weather and in the shortest time imaginable would establish contact with his subject, take photographs on several cameras, changing from one to another almost imperceptibly, monitoring the light, the background, the mood of his subjects with seeming casualness. Fred Astaire once said that if you couldn't make it look easy, you hadn't worked hard enough. Tom is of that school of thought. His portraits add significantly to whatever merits this book has.

Last of all I salute most gratefully the men and women who are the storytellers in *Irish Days*. I appreciate their generosity in telling me their stories. Some tales are more personal than others, but all were offered with an open hand and an open heart and I hope they will be received with equal generosity.

Note to the paperback edition

Some three years after this book was first published, many of its storytellers are still alive. Those who have died live on, at least, in these pages.

Introduction

The men and women of Ireland who tell their stories in these pages are all rich in years, rich in experience, doyens and doyennes of life. They are not, however, all of the same vintage – decades separate the youngest from the oldest, whose life has spanned three centuries.

These, their stories, are rooted in a largely agricultural Irish world scarcely recognizable from the Ireland of today, a world of the ass and cart and the horse-drawn carriage, of well-water and turf fires; where nights were dark and starry, undisturbed by electric light, and where, in the absence of any outside entertainments, people had to amuse themselves. Card-playing, dancing, the music of fiddle, flute or whistle – these were all cherished diversions. But the most universal and most magical way of recreating the soul was the spoken word. The chance to sit around a fire in the evening, take a pull on a pipe and converse was a treat keenly relished, and those who could tell a story were welcome across any threshold. As the poet W. R. Rodgers has it, these were people 'unlettered but not unlearned', and many were masters of the art of the wordsmith.

Although several of these storytellers have travelled abroad, and a small number of them grew up in a city, most come from rural Ireland, a good few from west of the Shannon. Some whose lives took them on to a wider public stage have chosen to tell of their careers and achievements. Others recount their life stories on a more personal level, reaching back for memories that stand out in high relief on the map of a long journey. Yet others engage in conversation, where anecdote, comic story and reminiscence give way to commentary and speculation on current events. In every instance, they have been generous enough to reveal intimate thoughts and attitudes, and have done so with a simplicity and unguardedness that is most affecting.

A few of these people are well known to each other, and we are the silent listeners to their conversations. Most have no connection with one another, and none has followed the same walk of life. I came across these men and women in a variety of ways, mostly through personal acquaintance, sometimes by serendipity. In each case I was gripped by their stories as they unfolded, told in their own words and with their own individual take on life. The modesty with which they gloss over their achievements, the fortitude they have shown in the face of hardship, the humour that allows them to knock a spark of laughter out of the grimmest situation, and the simple, open expression they give to both indignation and sorrow – all these qualities I found in full measure.

These stories not only shed light on individual lives; they also illuminate many of the most important strands of Irish life: religion, politics, sport, music, farming, the pub, the legal profession, Dublin city life, horsemanship, both fine art and the performing arts, and the poignant story of the emigrant. They start with the family, and the world within which our storytellers grew up, where life for the most part centred on kitchens smelling of turf smoke and lamp oil, a soft light shed on sparse furniture. Water for cooking, cleaning and washing clothes came from rain barrels and buckets from the well; much clothing was handmade, and shoes often knew the cobbler's last.

In the grand houses, life was conducted far more comfortably, but theirs was a narrow social orbit, and those acquaintances who were deemed suitable company often lived far afield. While the peasantry had no difficulty filling their time, the leisured classes often knew hours of ennui and constriction. Musical evenings, balls and dinners lifted the tedium, and many threw themselves into a sporting life, where tennis and croquet had a genteel following, but where the shooting, fishing and equestrian pursuits prevailed. In those early days horses could canter across a countryside innocent of barbed wire and roads were largely empty – glory years for the hunting brotherhood.

As I gathered these stories together, the warp and weft of the fabric of Irish life in the early decades of the twentieth century became visible. In those days, scarcely a village or townland lacked its musicmakers. Schoolchildren were commonly taught how to play a musical instrument, and today, at céilís, wakes and weddings, hulking farmers and labourers with thick, work-worn hands play fiddles, flutes and accordions with a nimbleness that belies their looks. A relatively recent phenomenon in Irish cities and among expatriate Irish communities abroad is a strong revival of interest in traditional set dancing, while there has long been a flourishing scene for traditional music. And whether you played or not, you danced. Up and down the country, social gatherings still see scores of couples of all ages, sizes and shapes taking the floor with no self-consciousness, and when called on to give the company a song or a recitation, there are always people ready to oblige after only a token show of reluctance.

In some of the houses I visited I was privileged to listen to some grand music, rich and varied in tone and tradition, from Michael-Joe Tarpey playing, at different times, fiddle, whistle and bodhrán (the Irish drum), to Sister Carmel with her fine singing voice. Others could recite poems, long poems at that, without hesitating or stumbling – all learned by heart a lifetime ago by people whose formal education ceased before they were fourteen years of age.

Meeting Eamon Kelly reinforced my respect for the wealth of dramatic talent that Ireland has produced and continues to produce: great directors and producers, actors of breadth and versatility. And although there have been fewer painters and sculptors, Robert Taylor Carson's story made me look afresh at art in Ireland, including the extraordinary, visionary canvases of Jack B. Yeats.

But the Irish genius has its finest flowering in the word, both spoken and written. The way that language is loved and exercised in Ireland is unparalleled, and happily the popularity of the Irish language seems also to be rallying amongst younger people, after a dangerous decline.

One of the very greatest delights for me, whilst compiling this book, was listening to the poetry of expression that so often cropped up in these oral histories. Little phrases of colour and freshness would leap out at me, and at times I felt a pang of envy at the kind of mind that could mint them with so little straining. The door of education being closed so prematurely deprived many of those once-young people, but it deprived us, too. Who knows how many mute inglorious Yeatses and Heaneys there have been?

Sometimes words are spilled out impetuously in a torrent of wild exaggeration, usually with comic intent. This outpouring of loquacity may or may not be accompanied by other more liquid outpourings;

certainly, the pub has long nurtured the fine arts of conversation and diatribe. At other times, words are used with an exquisite delicacy, and this poetry, never committed to paper, is simply spoken in company, gloriously squandered and destined to vanish into the air.

It happens again and again – a mundane conversation suddenly catches fire, the dry sticks of banalities kindled by a sudden, thrilling simile or startling image. This spontaneous combustion can be encountered anywhere – in pubs, at wakes and weddings, in a waiting room, or simply standing by a ditch, looking at nothing much. I am not equipped to comment on the richness and poetry of the indigenous language of Ireland, but it is manifest that the Irish took on the language of the stranger and mastered it. Some of the curiosities and quirky turns of phrase that Irish people use when speaking English can be accounted for by their being a literal translation from the Irish. Most often, however, it is a lively imagination and a native verbal exuberance that stitches the poetry into the speech.

The storytellers need, in a sense, no introduction; as with any work of art, the tale that each has woven stands for itself. But a few words about each, at this point, may be of help to the reader.

Eamon Kelly is internationally recognized as one of Ireland's finest actors, and has a special place in Irish affections for his role as *seanchaí*, the oldtime storyteller. His distinctive, deep Kerry voice, his impeccable sense of timing and his wickedly sly humour equip him admirably for this part. But he has made his reputation in a much broader field as a versatile and intelligent actor. He created the role of the seemingly curmudgeonly father in Brian Friel's *Philadelphia Here I Come!* to great acclaim, and has been an ambassador for Irish acting, most notably when he travelled with the Abbey Theatre Company to perform in Russia.

Michael-Joe Tarpey worked for most of his life in the Forestry, where his quick eye once spotted a Stone-Age axe at the bottom of a drain. In what spare time he had, he engaged in building (he built his own house virtually single-handed), thatching, barbering, making bodhráns, dowsing for water, bee-keeping, mending clocks and playing both the fiddle and the tin whistle, and he still does most of these. The sight of him on his bicycle, his cap pulled down 'on the Tipperary side', is a familiar one around where he lives in his neat little house, with its symmetrical avenue of twelve clipped trees leading up to the front door.

The song 'Kevin Barry' is one of the most popular in Irish gatherings, and any modern history of Ireland lists the name of Kevin Barry, a young student who was caught up in the struggle for independence; his execution in 1920 prompted hundreds to kneel outside the prison, saying the rosary and waiting for news of his death. The Kevin Barry, both publican and Republican, who tells his own story here, shares the same name and is, indeed, related to the young man. He gives a riveting account of the prisoner's last night on earth. In telling his own life story, hardships are touched on lightly and his essentially romantic nature is revealed.

While it is true that Jimmy Murray was also a publican, he was, in his own words, 'stone cracked on football', and the heart of his story centres on his life as a player. A contemporary remembers him simply waltzing round anyone who came to tackle him. As the captain who led the Roscommon team to two consecutive victories in the All-Ireland Football Finals at Croke Park, Dublin, his name is in all the record books, and the walls of Murray's pub are lined with photographs of great sporting endeavours, including one of him being carried off the field on the shoulders of his team-mates – the proudest moment of his life.

During his working life, Patrick Mackenzie, for all his soft-spoken authority and incisive intellect, was surely one of the kindest and most humane of judges. He gives us a remarkably frank insider's view of what goes on in the courts, particularly on the unfashionable circuit where he began his career. A cultured man, with a connoisseur's taste in art and an appreciation of architecture, he has very much the common touch and clearly relishes the eccentricities and casual lunacies he came across in his many years practising law. A High Court judge with a fine sense of the ridiculous.

Jim Hickey's is a very Irish story – he is one of hundreds of thousands who was forced to emigrate. But although he left Ireland at the age of eighteen, some seventy years ago, he is as Irish today as the day he took the boat to England to meet a father he scarcely knew. Having served his time as an apprentice, he became a joiner and spent much of his life in the building trade, where he was not the only Paddy by a long chalk. He pays tribute to the decency and wit of those lads who made the motorways of Britain, dug the tunnels and rebuilt the country out of a landscape of post-war devastation. And he makes special mention of the Irish diaspora further afield, who drove the railroads through America, who helped to settle Australia and New Zealand, and who ensured that on 17th March, Saint Patrick's Day, there's some corner of every foreign field, no matter how far-flung, that will be celebrating.

Mona Henry grew up near Dublin's Phoenix Park, on the north side of the city, where they say the true Dubs come from. She paints a marvellous picture of the capital city at a time when most Dubliners would know virtually everyone by sight and be prepared to pass the time of day with all. She has very happy memories of her Dublin childhood, and hers is the gift of finding happiness, no matter what her circumstances; her generous spirit is infectious. Her house, which she shares with Ben, her little white poodle, shines like a pin, and although there are no trophies for her prowess as a camogie player (camogie is the female counterpart of the sport of hurling), there are plenty that testify to her skills on the golf course.

You might not immediately guess that Tommy Hanley lost his sight late in life, because he steps out to greet visitors with confidence and the raised, interrogative face of one who is weighing you up. He delights in demonstrating his talking watch, which literally tells the time, but otherwise he passes no remarks on his condition, preferring to quiz you on your news and views. A lifelong Pioneer (teetotaller), Tommy, who made his living dealing in cattle and driving the roads of Ireland, is no killjoy, but loves to engage in banter and enjoys a good verbal scrap.

Sister Carmel Walsh is just the person to dispel the notion that nuns are either other-worldly and ethereal, or else embittered misanthropes. An immensely capable woman, she has the qualities that would have equipped her to become a captain of industry or a politician, instead of which she has devoted her energies to caring for the needy, specifically epileptic women and then mentally handicapped people. She has also thoroughly enjoyed herself doing it, and her good humour and common sense are invigorating.

The painter Robert Taylor Carson is someone who gives the impression of really belonging in his own, artist's world. Softly spoken and seemingly taken by surprise by all that life has offered him, he combines an artistic sensibility with a wonderful pragmatism. A Protestant born in Belfast, not a trace of sectarian feeling has lodged in him. Rather, he is dismayed by the bitterness that is to be found on both sides of the main divide in the north of Ireland. Nor is there anything highfaluting about his artistic temperament, and no false modesty in his assessment of his own work, either. It is as if he believes that fate singled him out to be the channel through which a talent for painting must be expressed, a fate he accepts with gratitude.

Charlie Coughlan is the pride of his local hunt, as he has been riding to hounds since he was a boy of eight. Tough as the leather of his well-worn saddle, he makes no great deal of following the hunt still, in rough country and in all weathers – 'Often got a wetting, never caught a cold.' His wife accepts that his heart is divided, and horses remain his passion. When the Ormond Hunt meet in County Tipperary, his tall figure makes as fine a sight as it ever did.

Eddie Mulvihill is an actor manqué. With his love of poetry, especially that of Lord Byron, his declamatory style of conversation and his easily tapped emotions, he could have taken to the stage with aplomb. Instead, he drove cattle round the country and took part only in amateur dramatics, along with his friend Tommy Tuohy. But his devotion to verse and his respect for Irish history are deeply felt and evident on the briefest acquaintance.

It has been an ineffably poignant experience to catch these glimpses of a world that has all but vanished for ever – a world to be regretted. In the first half of the last century, there was poverty for the mass of the people and great wealth for the few, but sometimes hardship can act like the refiner's fire, strengthening what passes through it. Tommy Hanley, whose story appears in this book, told me a story of a tinker woman he saw by the side of a road one cold day, bathing a small child in an icy stream. 'What are you doing? You'll kill the child!' 'Yerragh!' said she, 'What do you know of tempering a tinker's child?' She well knew what she needed to do.

Although rich and poor had relatively little contact, certain attitudes and values permeated all strata of society in Ireland in those days. It was considered important to live in the present and not be pushing at time. Many would agree with the old Irishman who said, 'Sure, when God was making time, he made plenty of it.' Wealthy people, with their unlimited leisure, occupied themselves in a variety of ways, and apart from engaging in sporting activities, they set in train great building schemes, and most entertained widely and generously. There was plenty of scope for eccentricity, too, and it was felt among their English counterparts that the Irish gentry were rather wild.

The poor worked long hours, so they, too, had a strong sense that you should take your pleasure where you could. They did so with a will, sometimes melding religious observance with an occasion for social life, other times improvising entertainment from the most meagre ingredients – dancing at the crossroads being a famous example. (Eamon de Valera's vision of an Ireland free from British influence was one wherein Irish men and women could lead lives centred on a truly Irish culture, a country of 'comely maidens dancing at the crossroads'.)

The practice of helping one another out was commonplace, and highly valued. The rural tradition of 'coring', whereby neighbours contributed their labour to one another on days when big tasks needed many hands (such as saving the hay) is just one instance of co-operation working to everyone's satisfaction. Within the urban setting there was an equally vital tradition of neighbourliness and sharing. In little houses and tenements, neighbours often took on responsibilities for each other as if they were members of the same family. Allied to this was a deeply rooted sense of hospitality. The poorest peasants would offer refreshments to the visitor, even if that meant depriving themselves, and the impulse was just as great amongst the gentry. The novels of Elizabeth Bowen and Molly Keane give a vivid account of such traditions in their portrayal of life in the big houses of the day. And William Trevor, whose work offers great insights into the lives of a wide range of Irish characters, is a particularly acute observer of the small band of Irish Protestants living in the twenty-six counties who were not the wealthy Anglo-Irish, but respectable shopkeepers and such like.

The sincere religious fervour of Irish people in those days had the most profound effect on Irish life. Among the most devout Catholics in Europe, the Irish sent priests and nuns to every corner of the earth; few were the families that had no one amongst them involved in the religious life. While most of the Establishment were Protestant, a certain number of affluent and influential people were Roman Catholics, sharing the faith of the vast majority of the population. The faith of the men was as strong as that of the women, and it informed daily life in countless ways: crossing yourself as you passed a church, the family rosary, fasting before Mass on Sunday, abstaining from meat on Fridays and the frequent invocation of the names of God and the saints in a way that was half prayer, half expletive.

Sadly, many priests in those days, conservative by nature and driven by a narrow, wrong-headed interpretation of Christian teaching, fostered a climate of guilt, repression, ignorance and hypocrisy that blighted lives. Not only the waning of popular faith but also the outright rejection of organized religion in Ireland by large sections of the population are now deeply established and the decline seems set to continue.

But a genuine, popular devotion to the Sacred Heart, and especially to the Virgin Mary, was the source of much compassion and highmindedness, and a great deal of charitable and necessary work was done by religious organizations and enlightened priests and nuns.

Wayside shrines and calvaries are still to be found in rural Ireland, but so, too, is plentiful evidence of the survival of an older worship: so-called 'holy wells' that wear their Christian dress rather unconvincingly; certain trees to which rags have been tied in supplication or in thanks for a favour granted; sheila-na-gigs which are often found in old churches, and many other testaments to the ineradicable strain of pre-Christian Celtic belief that lies below and is strangely mingled with Roman Catholicism. Although it is hard these days to find people willing to confess a belief in pishrogues, the faerie world and the supernatural, such things were very much part of the Ireland in which the storytellers grew up.

Times were bitterly hard. 'My mother was a very hard-working woman' is a sentence that recurs again and again in these stories. Poverty and privation were the lot of working peoples and peasant classes all over Europe, but added to this in Ireland was the spectre of mass starvation, not to mention forced emigration and pitiless eviction – all within living memory. With the strife of a very precarious political situation, Ireland was a 'most distressful country' indeed.

Yet you will find much gaiety and merriment in these stories, too. Confined as life was, there were compensations. If a river cannot grow wide, it will cut deep. The intensity of release into religion, politics, music, sport, dancing and poetry was fierce. And when life is grim, the Irish answer is to sing and dance in defiance.

Although old people in Ireland are, for the most part, living in greater comfort and security than they have ever known, they nevertheless live on the margins of society. Almost all of us in the so-called developed nations enter into a conspiracy of silence about old people, for we dread the day when we too will face diminishing powers and failing health. And even if we push that to the back of our minds, we of the lively tread and the rising sap are impatient of the slower pace of old people and their occasional tetchiness.

But as the year moves inexorably from high summer into autumn and eventually winter, so do our lives, and the human challenge is to find those fulfilments and pleasures that are the rewards of each season. The winter landscape, stripped down to its very skeleton, can be the most compelling and truthful of all. I hope that these oral histories will demonstrate by their truthfulness, liveliness, humour, wisdom and humanity that we should be seeking out the company of old people, not out of pity but out of self-interest. We have much to learn from them and so many of them prove to be delightful and inspiring companions. From them I have learned the lesson of the nobility of old age.

ESSENTIAL NOTES

Seeing the storytellers Thanks to Tom Kelly's masterly, sensitive photographs, we can see each of the principal storytellers, but it is you, the reader, who will animate these stories by tuning in to each individual voice, and sensing when the mood shifts or a memory flashes in. The more subtle your reading, the more these stories will come alive and the brighter will their colours shine.

Hearing the storytellers There are a handful of English words which have a specifically Irish cast. For example, it is quite common for the word 'height' to be pronounced 'heighth', which seems fairly logical, given the sequence of related words all ending in 'th': width, length, breadth, depth. Similarly – and I have touched on this more fully in the Glossary – certain constructions of grammar and syntax in English spoken by the English differ from English spoken by many Irish people, which is largely influenced by a parallel construction in Irish. 'He used go Mass every Sunday at nine o'clock' would be a perfectly common sentence, and the absence of the word 'to' nothing remarkable. 'David came round to have the dinner with ye, and I after telling him to come home to me for the dinner' is a similar example. When seemingly curious constructions such as these occur, therefore, it need not be assumed that there is an error or an omission.

Pronunciation It will help to note that the two letters 'ea' in a word is very often pronounced as it is in 'break' rather than in 'steal'. For further examples, see the Glossary on page 23.

True identities of people and places Although I imposed a rule on myself from the outset never to reinterpret or otherwise 'tidy up' the storytellers' words, I have, on occasion, suppressed a name, giving only an initial, and sometimes I have changed a Dan to a John or a Biddy to a Molly. This has been done to preserve the privacy of those who cannot be consulted.

The intricate art of storytelling In the days when these men and women were growing up, people did not always prize brevity and speed in the way we do in our fast-moving, fast-talking world today. Before the multi-distractions of television, radio, video, computer games and more, a good story was worth eking out, with all its embellishments, every aspect of it to be explored, and little grace notes added now and again. Many cultures across the world share in their storytelling the almost hypnotic ebb and flow of a narrative, like waves breaking on a shore, advancing or retreating almost imperceptibly, wherein a phrase can recur several times, almost as a chorus, and the basic structure gains accretions of detail and illustration. In the ancient oral tradition, which long predates *Beowulf,* the storyteller might depart from the strictly linear approach and begin in the middle of the action – *in medias res* – and work forward or backwards as seems fitting. Sometimes a vital piece of information is withheld until almost the end of the tale, casting a different light on the whole thing and forcing us to reassess it all and revise our opinions.

For example, when Michael-Joe Tarpey is telling of Biddy Earley, the wise woman of East Clare, he tells of someone who visited her wearing a coat which was not his own. Michael-Joe tells us she immediately informed him he was wearing a neighbour's coat. At the time, I didn't think this all that impressive. It wouldn't be too difficult to guess that an ill-fitting coat could have been borrowed for the occasion. It is only further into the tale that Michael-Joe drops in the extra piece of information that makes all the difference – that Biddy Earley named the neighbour from whom the coat had been borrowed, although neither her visitor nor the neighbour were known to her.

For these reasons, I urge the reader to enter into the spirit of some of these tales and not to be infected by an impatience that is impertinent to what is being offered. The world we are living in spins ever faster, it might seem, but here we are invited to step back into a slower, older, some would say more gracious time.

GLOSSARY

Why include a glossary in a book written in English? Simply because Irish people speak an English so indistinguishable, it seems, from the tongue of English people that any differences that crop up in the course of writing – and yet more in speaking – are perceived as mistakes, grammatical and syntactical errors, ignorance. The charitable have them as Irishisms, of the sort that the stage Oirish would spout. 'Begob and bejabers, but never a wink of sleep he had at all, at all', and such like.

In fact, even a cursory glance at history tells us that the mass of Irish people were speaking their own language, with its own distinct and sophisticated grammar, syntax and vocabulary, until the British government decided that it would be to their benefit if everyone could speak English, the language of the establishment. The Penal Laws (1695–1727) had already made it difficult for Irish people to keep to their own language and culture, including their religion, and this was profoundly felt. The introduction of primary-school education in English in 1831 continued the attempt to erase the native language and culture and replace it with one that would make for greater control and render the native Irish more biddable. (For a coruscating examination of this, and the way that British cartographers came in and changed the place-names of Ireland to suit the authorities, I urge you to read or re-read Brian Friel's fine play, *Translations*.)

There exists, therefore, a language which might closely resemble Standard English, but which the distinguished scholar Terence P. Dolan has termed Hiberno-English. According to Dolan, in his book *A Dictionary of Hiberno-English*:

'Much of the vocabulary of Hiberno-English...consists of words in common currency in standard English, but an appreciable proportion of the word stock of Irish people is not standard and may be misunderstood, or not understood at all, by speakers of standard or near-standard English. ...Categories include Irish loan-words, sometimes respelt (e.g. 'omadhawn', fool, from Irish amadan); words whose use has become restricted in England because they have fallen out of general use (e.g. 'to cog', to cheat in an examination); hybrid words derived from both Irish and English sources, most notably English words attached to the

diminutive suffix -een (Irish in), as in 'priesteen', 'maneen', etc; English words reflecting the semantic range of the Irish equivalent (e.g. 'bold', from Irish dana, 'intrepid' or 'naughty'); local words…; colloquial vocabulary…; English words that have taken on meanings developed from an Irish context and remain restricted to that context (e.g. 'hames', in the phrase 'to make a hames of' and 'yoke', something whose name one cannot recall, etc.). The Irish contribution to American speech is also recorded (e.g. 'slew', 'slug', etc.).'

Ireland has given the world a number of world-class writers hugely out of proportion to its small population, and a moment's thought will provide any number of names to support this. Wilde, Yeats, Beckett, Joyce and Heaney are only a very few of the brightest stars in the Irish literary firmament. And it has been said that when an Irish person *speaks* English well, he or she speaks it better than the English themselves. The cultivated Irish, for example, pronounce the letter 'h' in words such as 'where', 'why', 'when', 'whisper' and so on. But when they use an expression unfamiliar to speakers of standard English, it may well be a direct translation from the Irish. An uncle of mine commonly used the expression 'he's on the pig's back, now' meaning 'he's well off', and this is a translation of the common Irish expression *ar mhuin na muice*.

The great Irish patriot Daniel O'Connell, known as 'the Liberator' (not because he liberated Ireland from England, which he failed to do, but because he liberated the mass of Irish people from the political limbo in which they had existed hitherto), urged the Irish people to learn English to lessen their disadvantage; he did not envisage them losing their native tongue. (Nelson Mandela, in his long years in prison, taught himself to become fluent in Afrikaans, driven by a similar impulse to understand and be understood by those who exercised power.)

Cultural references
Aside from the actual words and grammar used by the storytellers in this book, certain other words, inextricably tied in with the culture of the country, are listed. Some of the tales include references to 'missions', 'stations', both of which were essential parts of life in rural Catholic Ireland years ago, and which still survive today, even if their role is somewhat diminished. And there are many other words and expressions which refer to the rites and dogma of the Catholic Church, a major influence in the lives of the Irish people who are telling these stories. The native Gaelic games and the GAA, the Gaelic Athletic

Association, which was set up to foster those sports, furnish us with another set of words. And there is a certain vocabulary relating to the political system in Ireland, especially that set up after independence.

Pronunciation

I have not made a serious attempt at a guide to pronunciation, but it should be borne in mind that 'ea' commonly gives the sound heard in 'great' rather than in 'heat'. President Ronald Reagan made sure his name was pronounced this way, and other surnames, such as Keane and Treacey, follow this rule. Very many everyday words, such as 'beat', 'treat', 'heap' and so on, are also pronounced thus, and, perhaps by association, words such as 'decent' – which becomes 'dacent' to rhyme with 'adjacent' – often share this pronunciation, too.

above: over, up. 'The Currans live above at the crossroads.' 'He got himself a grand job above in Dublin.'

abroad: outside. 'If you're looking for the bucket, I saw it abroad in the yard.'

after: used to form a kind of perfect tense. 'He's after posting the letter.' ('He has just posted the letter.') 'If you don't like gravy, why didn't you say so, and I after pouring it on your plate?'

again: another time, later. 'He hadn't any money on him, so he told me he'd give it me again.'

amn't: the logical negative inversion of 'I am'. As in 'Amn't I after doing it?' The standard English 'aren't I?' seems less 'correct', but I note that Irish people are being discouraged from using this little phrase.

anseo: present, here; the response to the calling of the school register. Pronounced, approximately, 'unsher'. 'The master would call out your name and you'd answer "*Anseo!*"'

asthor, asthoreen: my dear, my dear little one.

ax: ask. 'Ax him yourself why he's late.' A common instance of metathesis.

aye: yes. 'Aye, that's the truth I'm telling.'

bacon: almost invariably a joint of bacon or ham, and not a thin slice of bacon, as this is known as a rasher (see below). 'You can't beat the bacon and cabbage, I don't care what you say.'

báinín: the type of undyed wool, with none of its natural lanolin removed, that was traditionally used for sweaters, especially those of fishermen of the Aran Islands. Pronounced 'bawneen'. 'These days they sell so-called Aran sweaters, but they're nothing like the real bainin gansey.'

Ballybunnion: a seaside resort with a famous golf course, in County Kerry (not far from Listowel).

banbh: a piglet, a small pig. 'Last night the sow had her banbhs, fine healthy ones, all of them.' Pronounced 'bonnive', to rhyme with 'son of'.

banshee: from the Irish *bean si*, woman of the fairies. 'She was wailing like a banshee.' The story is that a woman of the fairy people knows when a death is to occur in certain families, and begins to wail and lament as that death

25

approaches, or when the death occurs. Sometimes the lament happens at the time of the funeral. Occasionally the cry is one of triumph, if an enemy dies.

Benediction: a short service in the Catholic Church, often with music and hymns, in which the Blessed Sacrament, displayed in the monstrance, is shown to the congregation and the sign of the cross made over them by the priest, as a blessing. 'Will I see you at Benediction tonight?'

beyant: beyond, as pronounced in rural areas; over. 'He's beyant in the yard, if you want him.'

Black and Tans: a British force of Auxiliaries deployed by the British government in the early 1920s, to help put down the IRA and civilians suspected of being sympathetic to the Republican cause. Many of them wore some part of army uniforms left over from World War I, supplemented with other uniform-style clothing, hence the name. There is also a famous pack of hounds of the same name. 'We'd hide under the table until the Tans went by.'

Blackrock College: a secondary school of some repute in the Dublin suburb of Blackrock.

Blessed Sacrament: a host of unleavened bread and a chalice of Communion wine, which, in a belief central to the Catholic Church, are transubstantiated into the actual Body and Blood of Christ at the moment of the consecration, during the Mass. 'Bow your head when the priest lifts up the Blessed Sacrament.' Sometimes just referred to as the Sacrament, usually the Host, or transubstantiated bread, only.

bodhrán: a circular wooden frame on to which is stretched a single skin, to make a musical instrument; a drum.

'Every fool thinks he can play the bodhrán.' Pronounced 'bowrawn'.

bog: a piece of land which can be of varying size, where the soft ground consists of decomposed vegetation. From this land, people would cut sods of turf eventually to be used as fuel. (There is an entire culture of the bog in rural areas, which cannot be entered into here.) 'Daddy used to take the entire family down the bog and we'd be there all day working until our backs were breaking.'

bogman: someone who is well versed in the work of cutting and dressing turf in the bog. 'John, now, he's a real bogman.' Also a pejorative term, similar to *culchie* (see below): 'You should see the cut of him – a real bogman.'

bold: naughty, and not the usual meaning of daring. 'Now, then, Seán, don't be a bold boy.'

bonham: a piglet, a young pig, a suckling pig. 'I was bringing a load of bonhams back from the mart, when th'ould lorry broke down.' Pronounced 'bonnum'. (See also *banbh*, above.)

book: a book, a magazine or a notebook. 'He got out his book to write down my address.'

boreen, bohereen: a country lane, a narrow track. 'She lives down that little boreen.'

bould: bold. A humorous, affectionate epithet. 'My bould McCarthy stood up and ordered another pint.'

brack: a fruited bread, also called a barm brack, from the Irish *bairín breac*, speckled loaf. 'Will you have butter on your brack?'

bright: pale in colour. 'If oak floorboards are too dark, you could have deal or ash, because the wood is nice and bright.'

bring: to take or to fetch. '"Twould cost a fortune to bring the whole family to the match.'

but: a common way of ending a sentence, usually spoken in a slightly interrogative tone. 'It's a lovely day, but.' 'She's a very pretty girl, but.'

butt: the end or the bottom. 'He lived at the butt of the hill.'

camog: a stick used in playing camogie.

camogie: a game played by women, very similar to the men's field game of hurling (see below). 'My brothers and I were always mad on hurling and my sisters played camogie, too.'

ceád míle fáilte: from the Irish, meaning 'a hundred thousand welcomes'. 'I went in and straight away it was *Cead mile failte*.' Pronounced 'cade meela fawltya'.

céilí: an informal visit or an informal party for song and dance, more recently an occasion for organized music and set dancing. 'What are you going to wear to the céilí on Saturday?' Pronounced 'cayley'.

cipin: a twig. Pronounced 'kippin'.

Clery's: a well-known department store in Dublin.

clock: a black beetle. 'He looked down and there was a clock on the ground.'

cod: a joke (as a noun) or to hoax or tease (as a verb). 'Sure, he said he was married, but 'twas only a cod.' 'Are you really going, or are you coddin' me?'

codology: mock-scientific term for the practice of teasing, or codding. 'Don't give me any more of your ould codology, I've heard it all before.'

cog: to crib or copy (as a verb), or illicit notes taken into an examination (as a noun). 'He was leaning over me, cogging off my paper.' And 'Mary went into the test with a cog up her sleeve.'

cot: a small flat-bottomed boat. 'We crossed the Shannon in a little cot, and went over to Terryglass.'

country: a particular area or locality. 'I know that part of Kerry, now, sure me mother was from that country.'

craic: fun, entertaining conversation. Pronounced 'crack'.

Croke Park: a sports venue in Dublin, where the GAA All-Ireland Finals are played.

culchie: someone from a rural area, with the implication that they are gauche and unsophisticated. Possibly from an abbreviation of 'agricultural', or from the name of a small place in Mayo, Kiltimagh, which is put forward as the epitome of all that is remote and backward. 'Oh, in Dublin, we stood out like the pair of culchies that we were.'

deas, clé: right, left: the orders for marching. 'We'd line up and then it was *deas, clé, deas, clé,*, into the school.' Pronounced 'desh, clay'.

delph: crockery. From the town of Delft in the Netherlands, known for its glazed earthenware (often blue and white). 'She was putting the delph in the press when he walked into the kitchen.'

Deputy: a member of the Irish Parliament (cf *TD*, below).

destroy: to damage. 'She has me destroyed, going round all the shops in Galway, looking for a pair of shoes to fit her.'

ditch: not, as in standard English, a trench or drain, but an earthen bank, usually with a hedge growing on top of it, and sometimes a drain or small stream to one side of it. 'If you watch the cattle, when the wind blows cold, they get in behind the ditch.' 'He put the horse at the ditch and it flew over with feet to spare.'

do: a way of indicating that an action or a state of being is habitual. 'I do be going to the mart every week.' 'He does be very often visiting them; they're like family to him.'

DMP: Dublin Metropolitan Police.

eat: shout at, be angry at. 'Look at the time! Mammy will eat us when we get home.'

eccer: an abbreviation for exercise (school exercises to be done at home); homework. Particularly common in Dublin. 'As soon as we got home from school, Mammy sat us down to do our eccer.'

eejit: someone foolish. Often said in exasperation, and not as cutting as the standard English 'idiot'. As in 'Why did you do that on your own, you eejit? Didn't I tell you I'd help you?'

e'er: a common contraction of *ever* (see below).

ESB: Electricity Supply Board.

ever: a way of softening a request. 'Would you ever shut the door? There's a fierce draught coming in.'

famous: wonderful. 'She was a famous baker. She makes lovely cakes, so she does.'

feathers: A humorous way of referring to bed. 'He's only just up out of the feathers.'

feile: a gathering at which music, poetry recital, etc takes place. Pronounced 'failer'.

Fianna Fáil: a political party founded by Eamon de Valera in 1926, whose name was taken from the band of warriors who followed the legendary hero Finn McCool. The party remains one of the major political forces active in modern Ireland.

fierce: mighty, very. 'Oh, 'twas a fierce frost we had that time.' 'Don't talk to her just now, she's fierce cross.'

Fine Gael: a political party formed in 1933 by the Cumann na nGaedheal and the Centre Party. From the Irish, meaning 'the Irish people'. A major political party in modern Ireland.

fire: to throw. 'We used to wait for them coming from school and fire stones at them from behind the ditch.'

First Holy Communion: a ceremony for a child who receives the Blessed Sacrament (see above) for the first time. Often an occasion of family celebration.

fleadh: a festival, a celebration of Irish traditional music. Pronounced 'flar'.

flying it: going well, succeeding. 'Once we'd got on to a straight stretch of road the pedals started going round like spinning tops and we were flying it.' 'Oh Colum's up in Dublin, working in the bank. He's flying it.'

football: Gaelic football. 'Ger was great at football and hurling.'

fornent, also **fornenst**, **forenent**, **forenenst**: in front of, facing. 'He lived in a little house fornent the chapel.'

for to: an intensified way of saying 'to', in order to. 'She took him to the doctor for to get his leg seen to.'

fry: a fried meal, usually consisting of fried rashers (see below), black and white pudding, egg and maybe mushrooms. 'When you've come back from Mass on a Sunday morning, there's nothing can beat a fry.'

GAA: Gaelic Athletic Association. 'If you want to see a game of hurling, you have only to go along to the GAA ground.'

gansey: a jumper, sweater or jersey. Probably a corruption of Guernsey. 'It's about time you washed that ould gansey, it's all stink.'

garda (singular), **gardaí** (plural): a member of the Gárda Síochána, or police force. 'You never see a garda when you want one.'

Gárda Síochána: the national police force, from the Irish, meaning 'guard of the police'.

gas: fun, both as a noun and as an adjective. 'God, she's great gas, that one, she'd make a mouse laugh.' 'Brendan Behan, he was a gas man, all right.'

give out: to scold, complain, criticize. 'Holy God, give it a rest. You're always giving out about something.'

goban: a person who is a jack of all trades. Pronounced 'gubborn'.

gossoon: a stripling, a young boy. Some people speculate that the word is a corruption of the French *garçon*.

haggard, haggart: a yard where hay is stacked, or a kitchen garden. 'We left the bales beyond in the haggard.'

hairpin: a disagreeable or bad-tempered woman. 'He had no peace with her – she was a right hairpin.'

hedge school: a makeshift, illegal school, operating from around the late seventeenth century until the nineteenth century, where schoolmasters taught Catholics (not necessarily children) at a time when it was forbidden by the British authorities for them to be educated.

hokey: Used in the phrase, 'be/by the hokey'. An exclamation or interjection. Perhaps 'By the Holy…'. 'Well, be the hokey, I wouldn't stand for that, so I sent him packing!'

hurling: a Gaelic field game played with hurleys or hurls, and a small, hard ball called a sliotar. One who plays is a hurler. The same game played by women is called camogie (see above).

in it: there, present, existing. 'I called in to see how ould Healey was doing, and the doctor was in it.' 'Nothing would surprise you, the times that is in it.'

IRB: Irish Republican Brotherhood.

is. Since both the singular and the plural form of verbs usually remain unchanged in Irish, the singular of the verb 'to be' is often used after a plural subject. 'Times was very hard' 'Get over to your own side of the bed, your feet is freezing'.

jarvey: the driver of a jaunting car (see below). 'We climbed up and the jarvey set off and drove us right round the park.'

jaunting car: a horse-drawn open vehicle, usually for hire, with the driver seated on a bench in front and the passengers seated behind. The benches for the passengers may be arranged facing one another or they may be placed back to back, the better to allow people to take in the view.

jig, in jig time: quickly, as fast as you'd dance a jig. 'Oh, she's very good at it; she'll have it done in jig time.'

keen: to lament, to cry. 'I heard he was dead, and from the house I heard the lonesome sound of the women keening.'

killed: in context, to be punished, possibly beaten. 'Jasus! I haven't done me lessons and when the master finds out, I'll get killed.'

lift: to steal. 'You couldn't leave anything down for a moment in that place, for fear it'd be lifted.'

lilt: to make music by singing nonsense words or syllables, such as 'diddle-idle-eedle-idle', etc. At gatherings, when no instrument was available, music for the dancers could be made by people singing the airs or tunes. Lilting is also called 'mouth music'. 'They were a very musical family, and the uncle was a great man for whistling and lilting.'

lock: a quantity, usually a large quantity. 'I sent him out foddering, so he gave the beasts a lock of hay.'

lonesome: a more commonly used word than lonely. 'Sure, she'd have to be a very lonesome woman to look at him!'

mam, mammy: mother. Much more common in Ireland than 'mum' or 'mummy'. The Irish is *mamai*. 'When I get home I'll tell Mammy what you said.'

más é do thoil é: the Irish phrase for 'please'. 'Close the door, *mas e do thoil e*.' Pronounced 'moss eh though huller'.

Mass: the principal service of the Catholic Church, in which Roman Catholics believe the bread and wine are transubstantiated into the Body and Blood of Jesus Christ. Although people are said to attend Mass or go to Mass, there is also the phrase 'to get Mass'.

master: a male schoolteacher. Usually given as a title. 'Master Delaney was a very strict teacher. The least thing you did wrong, he'd beat you.'

matchmaker: someone who arranges or brokers a marriage. 'My own uncle was the matchmaker who arranged for him to marry her.'

mavourneen, ma mhuirnín: my dear one.

Maynooth: site of a great Irish seminary and college.

messing: to confuse or else to tease, to joke. 'Don't go messing in the bedroom, I've just straightened it!' 'Oh, don't be cross. I wasn't serious, I was only messing.'

messages: errands, shopping. 'Every Friday she brings the messages from the shop.' 'I have to go to town for the messages or there'll be nothing to eat tonight.'

messer: a joker, an ineffectual person. 'Take no notice of him, he's only a messer.'

middling: moderate, fair (as an adjective); tolerably, reasonably (as an adverb). 'Do they pay you well?' 'Oh, only middling.' 'Her health has improved and she's middling well.'

mighty: wonderful, exciting, intense. 'The game was mighty.' 'The night John Reagan got married was only mighty.'

milling: teeming, pouring (rain). 'Nothing would stop her cycling to Mass, even if it was milling rain.'

mise le meas: a formula, used at the end of a formal document, meaning 'yours respectfully', from the Irish, meaning 'I am with respect'. Pronounced 'mish eh le*mass*'.

mission: a visit (usually annual) to a parish from one or more priests who specialize in such things, designed to strengthen the faithful in their religious ardour and to bring back into the fold those inclined to waver. A time for spiritual renewal. 'Next week there's a Mission on and they'll be looking to see the church packed every evening.'

musha, also **maise, mhuise**: well; indeed; really? 'Musha, Tim mavourneen, why did you die?'

national school. To replace the hedge schools (see above), the authorities introduced, in 1831, a network of schools given over to primary education, in which the lingua franca was English.

no. Since there is no separate Irish word for 'no' (nor for 'yes'), a question is often answered more formally, giving a negative or positive of the verb as in the question. 'Did you take the bucket out?' 'I did.' 'Have you boiled the kettle yet?' 'I have not.'

novice: a probationer in a religious order. 'There were three novices of the Notre Dame order in the chapel last week.'

novitiate: the state of being a novice (see above); the period during which one is a novice; the part of the religious house where the novices live.

oighear: Ice, chapping or chafing by exposure to the wind. Pronounced 'ire'.

oighreach: Chapping of the skin, caused by exposure to wet and cold. 'You'd get the *oighreach* in the winter, going to school in short pants.' Pronounced 'ire-och' with the ch as in 'loch'.

only: used as an intensifier, meaning really, absolutely. 'We had a great time and the dinner was only beautiful.' 'He was only gorgeous.'

ould, also **auld**, **oul'**, **aul'**: the Irish pronunciation of 'old', but often with a softening, maybe even affectionate sense to it. 'Would you ever have an ould shovel you could lend me?' 'Listen to that ould fool spluttering away!'

peg: to throw. As in 'We were behind the ditch, getting ready to peg stones at Duffy as he came past.'

pet day: a fine day after a spell of bad weather. As in 'It's been fierce wet but today's a pet day, thank God.'

Pioneer: a member of the Pioneer Total Abstinence Association. This Catholic organization was set up to prevent young people from ever taking to drink. A white badge bearing a red Sacred Heart image is worn, usually in the lapel or pinned to a coat. Once hugely influential in Ireland.

pishrogue, **pishogue**: a piece of folklore, a superstition, a charm or a spell. 'She would always refuse to let may blossom into the house, but I suppose that was just a pishrogue, wasn't it?'

press: a cupboard. 'The sugar's in the press on the left hand side.'

postulant: a person who makes a request to enter a religious order. 'I never suffered from any true doubts when I was a postulant.'

Pro-Cathedral: St Mary's, Marlborough Street, Dublin, now fully a cathedral. When it was to be built on O'Connell Street, there was much opposition from the Protestant community and it was therefore built on the street behind, running parallel, between 1815 and 1835.

quare, queer: sometimes this means strange or odd, other times it refers to someone or something singular, outstanding in some way. In Brendan Behan's *The Quare Fellow* the eponymous fellow was in prison, awaiting the death sentence. 'He's a quare kind of a farmer; doesn't get up till ten o'clock in the morning.'

quench: turn off, extinguish. 'Quench the fire before you leave the house' 'Quench that tape machine till I tell you something, now.'

rasher: a slice of bacon or ham for frying or grilling. 'Throw a couple of rashers in the pan, now, I'm famished.'

RIC: Royal Irish Constabulary.

rosary: a string of beads with five sets of ten beads divided by other single beads and groups, as a guide for saying a sequence of prayers. An act of devotion to the BVM, or Blessed Virgin Mary, consisting of these prayers. As in 'My godfather gave me a lovely set of rosary beads for First Holy Communion.' 'Every evening in the month of May, the whole family would kneel down and say the rosary together.'

rose: the past participle of the verb to rise; risen. 'How are you, Ciarán?' 'Oh, not so bad. I'm still keeping the smoke rose, anyway.'

RTE: Radio Telefis Eireann, the public radio and television service.

sally: willow, especially in the phrase sally rods, sticks of willow cut by schoolteachers for disciplining the pupils. 'The master sent him out to cut sally rods and we knew what was coming next.'

seanchaí, also **seanachaí**, **shanachee**: a traditional storyteller. 'You'd be waiting for the *seanchai* to fill his pipe and start his story.'

shantyman: the singer who sings the lead line in a sea shanty. In all worksongs, one singer takes the lead line, setting the rhythm for the work, while the group sing the response.

shebeen: an illicit drinking house. 'He told me he knew of this nice little shebeen the other side of the mountain.'

show: pass, hand over, give. 'Show me those scissors while I cut this out of the paper.'

slane, also **slan**, **slean**: a sharp-bladed tool specially designed for cutting turf. 'Just as he was going mighty, didn't the handle of his slane break!'

sliotar: a hurling ball. 'It's hard to get hold of the sliotar when the field is all mud.'

so: often meaning, 'in that case' or simply as an intensified affirmative. 'I told him I was going, so I did.' And 'Sheila's having a chocolate, and I'll have one, so.'

soccer: the name given to association football, as opposed to Gaelic football, which is what is commonly referred to as 'football'. As in 'Jimmy was mad about football and hurling, but Brendan was really into soccer.'

start: a while. 'A start ago.'

station: a custom prevalent in rural areas. Every so often (maybe every few years), the priest comes to a private house in the parish to say Mass, which Mass is attended by all the neighbours. Generally, a meal and drink is provided afterwards. 'She was painting the house and getting new carpet down in time for the station.'

Stations of the Cross: a set of fourteen images (sculpted or painted) depicting scenes in the progress of Christ to Calvary, his subsequent death and burial. It is a practice in the Catholic Church to say a set of prayers at each of these images, especially during Lent, the period running up to Easter.

sure: a common way of opening or closing a sentence to give extra emphasis. 'Sure, I've been going there for years!' 'If he told you that, he's a liar, sure.'

Taoiseach: leader of the government, the Irish post equivalent to that of the British Prime Minister. pronounced 'tea-shock'.

TD: *teachta Dála*, member of Dáil Éireann, the Irish parliament. A TD is often known as a Deputy. As in 'Who's your local TD? Oh, it's a guy from Fianna Fáil.'

thrauneen, **thrawneen**, from the Irish *tráithnín*: a blade of grass, hay or straw. By association, a thing of no importance.

tinker: a member of the travelling community. A term somewhat frowned upon today as being pejorative, it was once an accurate description of the way many travelling people made their living – by plying the tinker's trade. 'It was a tinker mended this pot for me.' 'There was a crowd of tinkers camped outside the village.'

traveller: a member of the travelling community, as well as the more general sense of the word.

true: as in the expression, 'it's true for you', meaning 'you're right'. 'It's true for you, he was never any good.'

UCD: University College, Dublin

uilleann pipes: a highly sophisticated form of bagpipes, in which air is squeezed through a bellows operated by the arm, and the note is thus produced, not by blowing. 'Of all the instruments, the uilleann pipes are what I like best.' Pronounced 'illian'.

vocation: a call from God for someone to become a priest or a nun. By extension, a call to do some other altruistic work, such as nursing. As in 'The nuns were always looking to see if any of the girls would show signs of having a vocation.'

wake: the tradition of keeping watch over a dead body. Often, when many gather for the wake, drinking and merriment take place, too. 'He would never miss a wake or a wedding for miles around.'

wet: as in the phrase 'wet the tea', meaning 'pour boiling water on it'. 'The first thing we'll do when we get in is wet the tea.'

whiskey: the Irish spelling for the Irish version of *uisce beatha*, literally 'the water of life'. 'Irish whiskey is triple distilled, as opposed to Scotch whisky's being twice distilled.'

woeful: terrible, great. 'Yesterday was woeful rainy.' 'She's a woeful liking for the drink.'

Wren Boys: a group of musicians who would travel about from house to house on St Stephen's Day (26th December) playing music and expecting some entertainment or money in return. The name derives from the custom of carrying a dead wren, or effigy of one, and any money collected is supposed to be for the funeral. It was believed that St Stephen was hiding from his enemies inside a bush, and was betrayed by a wren flying in and out of the bush, drawing attention to it.

yes: the word does not exist in Irish, and so questions are answered more formally than with just the affirmative. 'Is this your book, Peter?' 'It is.'

yoke: anything which is not given it proper name, a thingummy, a whatsit. 'Show me that yoke over there, will you?' 'Did you see Mary's new car? A fine yoke, now.'

your man: anyone, that fellow. 'Tell your man to come over here a minute.' 'D'you see your man in the corner – that's the one I was telling you about, that has a daughter in the bank.'

Kevin Barry

born 22nd February 1906

Kevin Barry is a tall man with a fresh complexion and a full head of hair, much of it dark, despite his great age. His namesake was a young Irish patriot who was hanged by the British authorities, and whose death is commemorated in a famous song.

When he was sitting for his photograph, he asked his wife to come and perch on his knee. He was full of praise of this, the most beautiful girl in the world, and he'd marry her again if he had his time over.

I COME FROM CASTLEDERMOT, I was twenty-eight years in the bar trade, twenty-eight years I held the place. It was called Barry's Bridge Bar. My mother said she would leave it to me on the condition that I got married.

And did you?

I did. I've been married fifty-six years. But working in the bar trade, it was a tough life. I wouldn't do it again. A pint of stout was 7d. in 1943. It was mostly just men came in drinking. There was a private room where women could be. They'd come in with their husbands...I remember the pint at 4d.

My mother, God have mercy on her, ran the pub and brought up five children on her own. I lost my father at four. That was in 1910. I was born on 22nd February 1906. But my mother, she would close the pub when she wanted. She had her money made and she preferred to close the doors in the evening. It was a rough life. It was a harder life then than people have now, but food was cheap – food was natural.

We had a quite a time in that bar, in the middle of the town. There'd be cattle events, and open fairs. There were five fairs in Castledermot. Christmas, January, June, August and one in the autumn. And there were horses. We children were sent out of the house when there were fairs on, because there'd be horses anywhere and everywhere. It was safety first. My mother sent us away; we were popped off out into the country.

Did you mind that?

Oh, no! It was a new life in the country. Making the hay in the summer. And we'd be after rabbits and foxes and hares. Hunting.

I never thought of the bar trade. My mother was head of the house – my father was dead through an accident. He died in 1910. He was a Pioneer.

It was St Patrick's Day one time. The Church didn't like heavy drinking – the clergy used to come out into the streets where there'd be trouble and they'd make peace. There was so much trouble with drinking on that holiday that the government made it a black day [*the pubs were not allowed to open*].

School? I was at boarding school. My mother and Tom, my brother, and myself, we took a bus to Blackrock College...or maybe we went up to Dublin by train. It was a big excitement. You'd stick your head out and see the smoke. I was delighted with it. Blackrock College, they had great results on the field. And in education. Some of the greatest scholars going were there. I was one of the worst. My mind was on football – rugby and Gaelic football. In 1920 and 1921, my mind was all on sport. My brother Tom, he was all study – he went for the priesthood, went on to Maynooth. My mother was very proud of him.

Well, I'm sure your mother was proud of you being in the team.

She was NOT!

I played for Kildare Juniors and I played in two All-Ireland Finals at Croke Park, one against Cavan, and one against Kerry. We lost by one point on each occasion. I played right half-back in Gaelic football.

Two years before there had been a shooting at Croke Park. British troops fired at the crowd. Two nights before that, a lot of British spies had come over. Twenty-one were shot in their beds by the IRA. Then the soldiers came to Croke Park, British soldiers. They called them the Black and Tans.

My brother Mike was the eldest of the family. He was in Blackrock College from 1916 to 1920. He came home and got involved with the IRA. That time we had the RIC in every part of Ireland. It was run by the British government. The RIC – one of those men came into the shop – he was fond of a pint – and he told my mother, 'Get your son out of the country. He's on our list to be shot dead.' So Tom got out; he went away and we never saw him again. My mother sent some money on to some place in Australia ahead of him. That was complicated, then. And in Australia he was conscripted by British troops

(Australia was an ally of Britain). He was badly wounded and his regiment came back. He was wounded and treated out there, and he died in Australia and is buried there.

There wasn't much welcome for the RIC. People were all Sinn Féin.

Did they raid houses?

Yes – they'd warn you, though.

Did your mother ever hide any Sinn Féiners?

She was brave. She wasn't afraid of the police. She painted the bar the colours: green, white and gold. The Tans got on to her. They said, 'You have your colours up.'

She shut early. She could have kept going till twelve for travellers, ten for locals.

My mother had a lot to bear. She was a great person for Ireland to become Fianna Fáil and suspended from England – not to be dependent on England and not having our annuities going over to England every year. The annuities were sent over twice a year. Then de Valera decided to hold them back. My mother was unusual for her time, because women didn't follow politics so much at that time. At that time every little village and every big town had an RIC barracks – police stations – and they were paid by us.

When did we become a republic? I forget now what year. Well, yes, the treaty was signed in 1922 and the Republic was set up in 1936. Before then, we were under England. Yes, England had recruiting for the British Army. Bands playing and speeches to get us to join the British forces. Then we were the front line men. When we were drilled and ready for war, they put us in the front and the British soldiers behind. I saw it as a young fellow. A band playing in Castledermot, a band playing and a recruiting station. What the lads signing up didn't know is that they were for the front line. We were a divided country.

You have a famous name. Are you related to the Kevin Barry of the song?

My father and Kevin's father were second cousins. A distant relation, you might say.

I was at Blackrock from 1920 to 1924. I was there when they broke the news to me. [*Kevin Barry was captured on 20th September 1920 at Church Street, Dublin and executed on 1st November. He was eighteen.*]

But I know people in 1916 were not allowed home for Easter – there was shooting on the streets. Anyone who had to go by train – Howth and places – people were kept in college for the Easter Rising.

Kevin Barry on two wheels.

Kevin Barry wasn't at Blackrock, though. He went to Belvedere. And then he was a medical student at Trinity College. I was in school when he died. Father MacDonald was the science teacher – a great man from Grangegorman, County Carlow. He called me out of class and said, 'Your relation was executed this morning by the British troops.' Andy Mac, we called him. He said, 'I'm very, very, very sorry for him.'

We weren't allowed to the funeral. But later I went to Kilmainham Jail where he was interned – no, it was Mountjoy Jail. I got in, somebody brought me, and I saw the room where he was imprisoned before his execution. We had a photograph in the family. It was given out the night before he was hung. Somebody asked him to sign it, and he didn't have a pen. So then they found a pin, and he scratched his name on it. K. G. Barry. I remember feeling it with my fingers – a pin scraped on the photograph. He said, 'I've no pen. I've nothing here only a safety pin.' And they said, 'Well, use that.' I was terribly impressed when I went to the cell. It was very emotional. He was eighteen years of age. Kevin Barry. He came from Tullow, County Carlow. His statue is there. He died on 1st November 1920.

English people were shocked that he was hanged. Hanged like a dog. 'Shoot me like a soldier, do not hang me like a dog.' The song goes as such:

In Mountjoy Jail one Monday morning, high upon the gallows tree
Kevin Barry gave his young life for the cause of liberty.
Just a lad of eighteen summers and no one can deny
As he walked to death that morning he proudly held his head on high.

Just before he faced the hangman, in his dreary prison cell
British soldiers tortured Barry just because he would not tell
The names of his brave companions and other things they wished to know.
'Turn informer and we'll free you!' Kevin Barry answered, 'No!'

Calmly standing to attention, while he bade his last farewell
To his broken-hearted mother whose sad grief no one could tell,
For the cause he proudly cherished, this sad parting had to be.
Then to death walked, softly smiling, that old Ireland might be free.

Another martyr for old Ireland, another murder for the Crown
Whose brutal laws may kill the Irish but cannot keep their spirits down.
Lads like Barry are no cowards, from the foe they will not fly,
Lads like Barry will free Ireland, for her sake they'll live and die.

My mother left me the place on condition I got married. My mother was elderly at the time and didn't want much work at the bar. We'd close at six or seven in the evening. We were entitled to close. She'd go into the kitchen and say her prayers. Then have tea and go to bed early.

We were a very good bar. She bottled her own whiskey. People came from near and far. The whiskey was always a bit stronger. She wanted me to mix the whiskey, but I wouldn't. I said, 'I wouldn't do it as good as you. Let Jamesons do it.' We got on great. It was a rough life, though. The pub was known as 'Mrs Barry's'.

When I took over, I worked like a Trojan when we got married first. My mother gave me very little money to carry on. She said, 'I'm handing over a good business, if you carry on as I did.'

We were entitled to open till ten o'clock. She'd close at seven. We had a housekeeper, Kate Lawlor, and when my mother had had her tea she'd go to bed between eight and nine.

She handed over the bar to me. I said to Mother [*his wife*], 'We'll make a job of this, now. Which we did do. I bottled all my own stout and ales. We had a big cellar, all shelved, and I used to bottle ahead of myself to get the beer into condition. Oh, we had a terrific sale. But I'd always leave some to mature. After the bar was closed I'd go down to the kitchen to have something to eat and then I'd wash bottles until three or four in the morning, sometimes, and usually until 2.30. Then I'd be up at seven. All the bottles would be dried and turned upside down. I made my own Guinness. It took eight weeks to come on and mature. All that work, it never affected me. I kept going. We had our own label on the bottles. 'Kevin Barry, Bridge Bar and Hotel, Castledermot.' And we had our own glasses, too. I have one of the glasses still.

I thought it was called the 'Bridge Bar'?

Well, my mother kept people, so it *was* a hotel. But it was really a bar.

My mother, she was a hardworking woman. She made a great success of it. She turned away, she *turned away* business. And she had an apprentice in the shop to mind it.

My first car. Well, it was Alfred Smith's car. It cost £90. He paid £112 for it new. I bought it for £90. The tyres were hardly dirty on it. He sold it because he'd been told, 'The Germans will be over in no time, and cars will be confiscated.' Alfred thought he'd better get the money while he could.

And you weren't afraid the Germans would invade?

I never thought of it.

And how did you get the money together?

Well, I was three years an apprentice in a grocery. It was £13 for the year. And the place was a bar and a grocery, and we sold oil and coal and paraffin. It was called 'Cope of Castledermot'. I was up at eight. There were five vans to be packed and on the road and out at nine. I went training in Cope's for the first three years.

Was it all work?

No, we went to dress dances. Tynan's ballroom in Carlow – a great centre for dances. We went in February – so many years ago. I came out in the morning at three, and snow had the ground covered. To that depth – five inches. All the crowds who came down from Dublin, they had to leave their cars and get the train. The cars were later vandalized and wrecked.

And other dances we went to. Kilkenny, Graiguenamanagh, Lawlor's Ballroom in Naas. Tynan's Ballroom. We went for Easter, Christmas, New Year's dances, farmers' dances. I had my own dress suit. £14 it cost. Tails. It was tailored for me. I'd go with the hackney man – Harry Giltrap or someone. And the women. Some of the girls had beautiful long skirts, streeling the ground. I'd love to see them.

I remember I had a pet fox. There was a farm at the back of the pub. There was a man minding the farm. They had sheep, a lot of sheep. And they had a person on the land to keep out dogs, keep them from tormenting the sheep. You'd get an odd fox on it. This man came into our pub in Castledermot and said, 'There's a fox on Mullaney Hill, trapped by me. There are sheep over there.'

Now, the fox was in a burrow. He was caught by his leg – yes, Mr Fox was there. I got him out as best I could, and I filled the hole behind me. I got him into a sack and took him home and settled up the leg. I put bandages on it, and after that the fox was a real pet of mine. A man and two or three lovely ladies heard about this, and they'd come for a loan of the fox. No, I wouldn't give him to anyone. He was flying it. I had him for a year or so after.

The fox knew my step when I was coming near, and started barking. I had to chain him up, and I kept him for two or three years. Then a woman complained to the authorities that the fox was smelly. So I moved him to the top of the yard. Then a Mrs Crosby, she started complaining, too – 'The fox is smelly.' In the end, I gave him to someone to let him out in the wilds. Put him in a car and brought him two or three miles: Lacey's Hill, beyond in Grange. I let him out there, where there was a fox's cover. He followed me for a couple of yards and then he went. I got into the car and drove home, but he came back. So I decided to take him five or six miles, and put him in the middle of cover. I called him Gyp, and he had a lead and a collar. I got him as a pup. Mr Allen of the DMP [*Dublin Metropolitan Police*] came to me and said, 'Have you a pet fox?' 'I have.' 'I'd love to see how you get on with him.' 'There's a stable over there. Look through the window and see how I get on with him.' I let out, 'Gyp!' and he galloped and ran to me and was up on my shoulders, licking my ears and licking the back of my neck. Let out Mr Allen, 'That's marvellous.'

The biggest changes I've seen? Well, they wouldn't be able today to do what we did. I used to go after the fox hunt. I followed it from Macey's to Milford, County Carlow. Clothes, socks, boots would be all torn off me. And nothing to eat. I'd keep going all day.

Jim Hickey

born 18th December 1912

Jim Hickey's is a very Irish story, a story of emigration. After his father had emigrated to England, in time it was Jim's turn to go, too, at a young age. Both father and son were driven to leave Ireland to look for work when there were no prospects of any at home. In his long life of exile, Jim has paid warm tribute to the fine qualities of English working people, particularly people from Lancashire, but he has always remained Irish to the very bone. Full of humour and a boundless enthusiasm for life, Jim Hickey loves to engage in conversation, especially on his favourite topics of politics and sport – football above all. A strong man who would not hurt a fly.

NOW, FIRST I want to talk about the small town of Woodford in East Galway, how it became world news back in the 1880s, when the Earl of Clanricarde, who owned vast estates in East Galway, was an absentee landlord living in London, gambling and drinking his money that he was screwing out of the peasants in Ireland, and if they didn't pay their rents, which were rack rents, really, he would evict them – regardless of the weather or what time. And he got away with it for a long time because nobody resisted.

But in this particular case it was a farmer called Saunders, and he resisted. His place – they were to be evicted and the house knocked. My Uncle Joe Slattery and my Uncle Davy Hickey were both involved in this campaign, called the Tenants' League, to resist being evicted in the townland of Woodford in the 1880s. Uncle Joe and Uncle Davy would be young men in their twenties. So Saunders' Fort (as it was called in the newspapers at the time – 1886), it was big news. A group of about twenty young men decided to barricade the house.

Portumna was the nearest town, and it was managed by a barracks, with the Somerset Regiment there. A big force of police, they would come to the house to be evicted, they'd come with battering rams and smash the walls and the roof down, and set fire to it, and throw the people out on the roadside, and this had been done hundreds of times. But in this case, they decided to resist.

So these twenty-odd young men barricaded the house and prepared to resist arrest. The usual crew came out with battering rams – police and bayonets. They attempted to – but they were beaten off with resistance from inside the house. Ladders were put up against the house and were immediately thrown down again. They climbed on the roof and tried to break in that way, and boiling water'd be chucked on them. So the police, they gave it up. They gave it up. And they come again the next day and had another try, and all day long, and resulted in failure again. So the following week, they brought an army – a small army. As one man said, it was less an army for the Spanish invaders – they took Peru with a smaller army. There was 500 police and 200 Somerset Light Infantry, cavalry and a mile-long string of carts. The roads around – bridges had been blown up, trees had been felled and placed across the road, all to delay them. They had to bring logs to make new bridges across to get to the Fort. The people were there, but made no resistance, because the police removed them. The police surrounded the house and at the back of them was the army with fixed bayonets to stop anybody coming through to help them. So the twenty-odd men in the house had to do the best they could, and they did.

It was over a week before they succeeded. And this time they did succeed. They broke through the roof, and the people inside threw hives of bees out at them, and lime water – anything – pushed the ladders away from the walls. But in the end, before the day was out, the police came into it. The police, up to then, had just remained outside and it was the bailiff's men that was trying to break in. But if the police took part, the men inside would be arrested. So that's the way they had to do it. The police put ladders up front and back and gable ends as well, and mounted them with drawn swords and forced their way in and arrested twenty-two young men that was in there.

That was known as the Battle of Saunders' Fort. My uncles, Uncle Joe Slattery and Uncle Davy Hickey, they were amongst that twenty-two men that were arrested and sent to jail. But it was evictions like that and the resistance to them that broke the landlord's grip on the peasants, and in time things changed, and for the better, and we seen the back of the landlord class. He was a disgrace to his name and his country.

And since then, most of the families round there, they still have it in their memories of the time they were evicted and forced away from their properties and everything. Planters were brought in. Whenever these people were evicted, planters would be brought in from the North of Ireland. And they were boycotted. People wouldn't serve them in the shops and wouldn't help them in any way, making life very uncomfortable for them. But in the end, the Land Commission, the government, they bought the land and in time it was given back to the people where originally they owned it.

And to this day, names are still here – people that was helping Clanricarde, names of people who resisted Clanricarde. Yeah, they were bad times and people suffered a lot and starved. The name of Clanricarde is very, very low in East Galway. They were a Norman planter, who had been planted there several centuries before. So the little town of Woodford became know as the point where the evictions were finally defeated. That's all I can say about that.

Now, I'll tell you a bit about myself. This is the story, and I might as well give it you from the start. My father, Tommy Hickey, came from Rossmore. A big family of them, there was – about ten or twelve of them. Most went to America, but my Uncle Davy stayed farming and married my Aunt Brigid – I think they had ten or eleven. I'll get to that later. My father, Tommy Hickey, he was a carpenter who was living in Manchester (he'd had to go over there to find work), and he married a girl from Fermanagh – Enniskillen. Her name was Mary Maguire. And in 1910 my eldest brother was born. Jack. Jack Hickey, born in Manchester, in a place called Fallowfield, which I'm sure isn't a field now, but it was a field then. Anyway.

Then war broke out in 1914. Up to then my father worked away as a carpenter. I was born myself then, in 1912, the tail end of 1912 – December. The year the *Titanic* went down. So I don't remember much about Manchester at all. It was all very vague to me. One time during the war there seemed to be no lights and the people used to be talking about the Zeppelins, whatever that was – I remember that.

But the thing was, my father was conscripted into what they now call the Royal Air Force. I think it was the Royal Flying Corps, and the aeroplanes of the time were made out of timber. My father was recruited into that job of making and repairing 'planes, so we didn't see much of him.

In 1918 this is what happened. There was a 'flu epidemic and it took over Europe and Britain – other countries, I believe so. My mother, God rest her, she was one of the victims. She died in Manchester in early 1918 and my father was left with four lads: Jack, myself, Dave and Joe. Joe was only just a few months old and my father was left stranded. It was poor times – poor conditions and no help of any kind. So my father got in touch with his brother Davy in Rossmore, who already had ten in the family. Would he be able to take two of us sons? And my other uncle then was Joe Slattery. He was married to Mary Hickey, who was a sister of my father. *And* Davy Hickey in Rossmore. *They* were brother and sister, too.

So the upshot was that the Slatterys, my Uncle Joe and my Aunt Mary, took the two eldest ones – me and Jack – and we was brought up at the Slatterys', and reared with their own son, John. We were brought up there and went to school and accepted into the family as just one of the family. Of course, they were called Slattery and we were called Hickey – that was the difference. But down at Rossmore, Davy Hickey with his ten – two more Hickeys was drafted in – that was Davy-Gerard and Joe. They mixed in with all the others. All had the same name.

It was very, very good of them to do that. If they hadn't have done that, we would have been slung into some children's home in Manchester and looked after by the council there. God knows what would have become of us at all. Probably finished up drafted into the army as boy soldiers. I'll always be thankful to the Slattery family. I've always kept in touch with them ever since, and you couldn't wish for finer people.

We went to school then. National school, six or seven miles away. Down all the roads, rocky old roads. There was a man by the side of the road and he'd have rocks brought to him. He'd sit there for weeks on a sack and a pair of goggles on him, and a hammer and a sledge, and break up rocks into small pieces and then hammer them into little pieces. Stonebreakers. Yeah. That stuff was shovelled on to the roads.

From the end of April, anyway, we'd be going in bare feet. No tarmac, no nothing. Stony roads that cut the feet off you. That's how you had to walk all the way. We had shoes on from November until the end of April – otherwise, it was going barefoot. We couldn't get our shoes off quick enough, but we'd have to walk them damned roads and we'd have stone bruises and cuts and *oighreach* – a kind of frosty cold wind that would get your shins – that was called *oighreach* – very painful. But that was what we done. We had to get used to it. We would set off for school, but before we'd go we'd have jobs.

We had to get up early then, because we had a mixed farm – growing things and hens and pigs and what have you. Not like they are now, just with a few cows in the fields, and milking. No, we had a few cows that had to be milked by hand, then the cream brought in and put in the coldest part of the house till it was creamed off, and then it was churned into butter. We had a modern kind of churn with a handle to it and dashes inside. (The older kind had a single handle that you'd move up and down.) So cream would be poured into it. The churn would be scoured out absolutely clean, and then everyone that came in took a turn at swinging the butter, even the postman, who was a man from Yorkshire, John Harris. He had an old bike, a Pierce bike. Oh, they were heavy, strong yokes. Had to be, because he was weighed down with ould parcels and boxes and letters. He had to cycle out from Portumna to our post office, Power's Cross. A very famous place, that was. Its name went all over the world, as part of the address and on maps, too. Well, John Harris, he'd come down to our house and leave in some rashers and eggs. Then he would carry on through the village delivering. On his way back, then, he'd have time to have a breakfast. My aunt would have it ready for him – he'd sit in the parlour, as we called it, and we used to look at him through the window. He'd have the newspaper propped up in front of him and he'd be as happy as Larry there, eating away there. That was the best part of the day for him, there.

I remember one story about John Harris. He was very English, but he got engaged to a local girl, but she wouldn't marry him unless he took instruction in the Catholic faith. So, he didn't mind and he went along to the priest. And after a while, the priest was examining him and asked him to make the Sign of the Cross. So John began, 'In the name of the Father, and of the Son and – by Jove! I've forgotten the name of the other chap!'

Well, before we'd go to school, we'd have a lot of work to be done. We'd have to go to the well for drinking water. Other water was in barrels with pipes leading into them – for washing potatoes or washing anything. And there was turnips and mangels to be put through the grinder – that also had to be turned by hand. So each one of us got jobs to do. Another one might be feeding the calves before breakfast, which would consist of porridge, or stirabout as we called it, soda bread and home-made butter. Then for school, we'd take some cuts of bread and butter and maybe a cut of sweet cake as well. All wrapped up with a bottle of milk.

We had to be at school for half nine, so it would take us, oh, an hour at least to cover that distance – six or seven miles. Anyway, scholars used to come down from the next village, higher up than us. They had another mile more to walk, those from Derryvunlan. Every house we came to, we'd pick up another one or two. We'd go along the road, sometimes slow, sometimes fast. There were dogs along the road would chase us. Aggressive dogs, people had. Guard dogs. If you wandered into his territory, you'd be chased out of it. And we'd be pegging stones at them. I remember one mother had to deal with about three different kids, and they didn't want to go to school. Every road they come to, they'd run up. She had a hell of a job. The eldest lad, Willie, was the worst of them.

We all used to go across the fields to torment Maggie Donnelly. She was a lady who lived in the bog, quite near the bog. Past Stanny Burke's house, an old cottage in the bog. She had dogs in there as well, geese and all that kind of thing. They used to make it a thing of going tormenting her. One time we were in there, Keane and myself and Frank Fahy and she came out with a scythe, shouting, 'Hould young Fahy while I mow him to the ground!' She had no more chance of catching us than... How did we torment her? Throwing stones and chasing the hens and the geese round about. That would torment her. Why her? Because she was the only person to be able to be tormented.

Then we'd go on to Porters, and Katy Porter was a crippled person, and she was always by the fire, and her greeting every morning was 'Anything strange or startling?' Because she never moved from there. There was no television, nor radio, no papers. To her our passing was something strange, and we'd always call in there. She was much older than us. That was another calling place. We never took anything, no tea or nothing. Just calling in on the way – just a custom. There wasn't many places where we called. It was on the side of the road, so handy. Then we'd carry on. We'd be picking nobody up from there. We'd have to hurry then, because time was going on. We'd be coming up near the school. We could hear them from the school there – from Shragh. So we'd make a hurry then as if we'd been hurrying all the way. We used to arrive in a hurry.

The teachers would form us up into classes and call the roll in a national way [*in Irish*], as a protest, you know, against the British way of life. Sometimes an RIC couple of men would cycle by and they'd be taking notes of what was going on. Reporting the teacher, I suppose, for nationalistic tendencies. Then, in 1918, 1919, 1920, there was a lot of guerrilla fighting going on, ambushing and burning of houses by the Tans. The RIC used to patrol the roads on these big police bikes, the same as the postman's. They were strangers, the RIC men. No one bothered with them locally, and they came from other parts of the country. They were the eyes and ears of the British government, because they knew every house in the villages, and knew the young men. If any young man was missing and an ambush took place, they would be suspect and have to go on the run. Sometimes a stranger would come to the house – no questions asked. Stay for a night or two nights and then go again. It was only after that we found out that they were men on the run.

But, to get back to school. The teacher, in his own way to show patriotism, would call the roll in Irish. He called your name and you'd answer *anseo*, 'present'. Then we were lined up and he played the gramophone – a march like 'O'Donnell Abu', and our favourite one was 'A Nation Once Again'. We marched around the schoolyard into school, *deas, clé, deas, clé*, – right, left, right, left. Sometimes the RIC would be passing and get off their bikes and take notes. I don't know if the ould teacher ever got into trouble....

We got into all kinds of trouble at lunchtimes. We used to go rambling round and there was a castle a few miles away, a deserted castle. Dates back to the Norman times, I believe. We used to go down there – run all the way down and climb up the staircase, a spiral staircase. It was overrun with crows, and when you got to the top the crows would all be flying up. That's all we could do, was look down and wonder how it was built and why it was built and all this. Then we'd come back for the afternoon. One day, one of the lads, he captured a young crow, so when he got back to school he hid it under his jersey, under his gansey. The teacher was very strict and he banged on his desk with a stick. Well, Larry, he let the crow out from under his gansey and the crow was flying all over the room. The teacher was shouting and roaring at us. Sure, we did more damage getting it out of the room. He never knew who done it, never knew who was responsible.

He was a good teacher, Master Canning. Not these days, of course. He'd get jail for what he did. He'd send a lad out to the hedges to cut sally rods and pare them and then bring them in. He'd have a stock at one side. You'd hold out your hand and you'd get two across the hand and maybe two on the other hand. That was the way of it. And if you was at the blackboard and not doing what you should be doing, he'd knock your head off it and give you a kick up the backside. 'Come here, Hickey, and answer this,' he'd say, and when you couldn't, he'd go *Bang!*, and your head would be ringing. 'You're a genius, Hickey,' he used to say. And then there was another lad who couldn't say 'shadowy'. He'd say 'shaddio' and he couldn't get the other one. He ended up some big priest in California, I believe.

The lads that was leaving school, they all put contracts out on the master – they was going to kill him. Then they never got to him. He never got attacked in any way. (His daughter, Mary Ellen, was teaching the girls at the other section of the school, which was a long, low, bungalow-type, with just a fireplace at each side. The teacher would heat that – I think turf was allowed – but it was a cold place for the rest of us.) At the same time, he turned out some very good scholars – some of them turned out to be priests and schoolteachers, so he couldn't have been all that bad. I was never very good, myself, except I could read English and I could spell and could remember things, you know. What I was remembering, though...ould dates and that.

But coming home from school was a different thing in summer, spring and autumn. You had to hurry home because there was so much work to be done. There was no delaying at all, except on special occasions. But at weekends we used to go fishing down in the Shannon for perch. The equipment would be a pole – the natural branch of a tree. Cut it from a straight sapling, tie the line to it, hook and a bait on the end – in a primitive kind of a way. Line up along a bank and throw it out into the river, which was the river that goes down by Clarke's mill. The Benown, it was called. We thought it was a big river. And it was big enough, too. There was plenty of perch in it and pike and bream. But perch was usually what we angled for. We used to bring them home.

You couldn't catch a pike. We didn't have the tackle to catch a pike. You had to catch a small perch and put that on a strong line with strong hooks and use that perch as the bait. Some people did do that – they'd leave that stuck in the bank and sometimes the pike would take it, but he'd be too strong. There was some huge pike in the Shannon. One caught was nearly 50lb weight.

At that time the Shannon was very much used for fishing. Most people along the Shannon would fish. There was a form of rowboat – a cot – that let water in. It wasn't by any means watertight! You'd come to the cot which was moored and it would be half full of water before you'd start. Two seats in it. It was very, very dangerous. The Shannon is a deep river and gets rough at times. There has been cases of boats being wrecked on rocks or overturned, quite a lot, but people didn't think of that. We'd go out fishing for perch and when you'd got out so far you'd stop rowing and cast your lines out.

John the poacher had lines set on the lake. Posts driven in a line across, the line with hooks on. When he examined it in the morning – the early hours – there'd often be as many as ten or fifteen. Which was his livelihood. He'd sell them in Portumna to the shopkeepers. He'd take them in with a load of turf. Also with rabbits which he'd snared or trapped. He'd sell the rabbits to the butchers. They'd get rid of them. And the skins he would sell, too.

My Aunt Mary cooked them. Rabbit stew smelled very good. My Aunt Mary had been in America as a cook-housekeeper for many years, and she was acquainted with the American way of cooking. So was a lot of women. My Uncle Davy had been in America, along with many more. They all got a knowledge of how things were in another country. There was absolutely no communication in other ways.

I could tell you a few stories that show how out of the way it was here. When the radio came, it was a wonder. The story goes that several of the neighbours were invited to come over to a house where one of these new-fangled things was installed in order to hear the news at one o'clock. One old farmer met another: 'Are you coming over to Tuohy's to listen to the news?' 'I am, I am, begod, but I've to go over to Kelly's first. Don't let them start till I get there.'

When the radio first came out around here, the farmers used to listen out for the weather report. One old farmer, if it wasn't favourable, he used go down to the neighbour's house to see had they got a better one.

I remember my brother Jack telling me of an old man who heard on the radio that Wilson had devalued the pound. In those days, the Irish currency was very much tied in with the British, so when he heard they were devaluing, he jumped in his ould jalopy and raced into Portumna to the bank. When he got there, he told them he wanted to draw all his savings out in cash. Not wanting to pry, nevertheless the bank manager asked him if he had maybe a big purchase in mind. 'No!' he said. 'I'm taking my money out. They're not going to devalue my money!' And nothing would do him but take it home and put it under the mattress for a couple of months, then bring it back. He wasn't going to have them interfere with his savings, by God!

Another time, I remember old K. was at home and an insurance man came to see if he could persuade him to take out a policy. It wasn't so common in those days. Anyway, this lad talked to him and put the case to him, but K. didn't bite. So anyway, the lad came back to try to clinch the deal and this time he brought his boss with him. The boss started to put forward all the arguments again, but old K. put up his hand and stopped him dead. 'No, no, no, no. Your accomplice has already told me all that.'

Well, anyway, we got a paper only once per week – the rest was all hearsay, gossip and travellers. A travelling man used to come twice a year to Slattery's – Paddy Murphy. He would bring himself and his goods, his belongings. He had nothing to sell, only news. He travelled the thirty-two counties, walked everywhere. He might have had a lift, but he never mentioned it – walking was his main thing. He didn't stop in hotels; he stopped in farmhouses everywhere. He told tales to them of how things were. Paddy was a storyteller. He'd have stories to tell in Donegal which would be about Galway and Mayo. And he'd also tell us stories of Donegal and how they depended on fish and rock – rock oyster or whatever the hell they are – crab, everything like that. Herrings. They used to eat a lot of herrings, which was very scarce down here. Maybe once a month at a fair someone would come selling herrings from Galway. They'd be two for a penny. They used to get eaten – picked over. They were very cured. A different taste altogether to what we were used to. Red herrings, they called them.

We'd go catching eels as well, with a primitive method again. Put a circle of wire on the end of a pole and a flour bag attached to it. You could see the eels – the Shannon that time was clear. You could see the stones along the bottom. We'd go anywhere right from Crawford's, past Shiel's. We'd go along the Shannon. The only part barred to us was the minister's, Crawford. But from there on it was open. ('We' meant us, the Kennedys and Patrick Gorman and them.)

Other times it would be nuts. There was a big copse, or wood, belonging to Connells down near the Shannon. There was land extending from the house to the Shannon and at the far end there were all hazel trees. They never objected, the Connells, at all. They came from far and near at the season and it would be an army there, collecting hazel nuts. Climbing trees, shaking trees. It wasn't our property at all, but Connells never bothered about it anyway. (People would now, of course. It would never be allowed now, climbing fences and breaking trees.) We could save the nuts up for Christmas. Kennedy was good at that. He was a big, tall, rangy fellow. He could climb trees and he had bags with him and he'd fill the bags up, hanging under his coat. He'd climb the trees and pick all the best nuts and bring them home and put them in jars. He'd have nuts sometimes in the spring. He never moved with the times, never altered. Old-fashioned to the end of his days. When everybody else got machines, he still persevered with the scythe, the pitchfork and rake. He didn't cut silage. No machines, just save the hay in the old-fashioned way. Cut the turf with a slane and a barrow.

We'd go swimming, too, in summer. Coming home from school, we'd make our way down to the Shannon and have a dip. We used to catch eels and swim at the same time. It wasn't all slavery. With no books in your way, you could do that. Go swimming, fishing, setting snares for rabbits. It was simple enough. There was plenty of rabbits in those days. The fields were full of burrows. Through the hedges, the ditches, you'd see the paths where the rabbits would go, and you'd drive a stick into the ground with a wire attached to it and with a noose, where the rabbit would run into it and put his head in the noose, and it would choke him, wouldn't it? And you'd come round in the morning and pick them up, if you were successful. You might get one.

In winter, we'd make cribs to catch birds. With a twig we'd make a beehive with a filed stick to hold it up. It'd be propped up in the snow. A filed stick just resting on something, very shaky. If a blackbird came – you'd put berries down, or bread – if a blackbird came, and seen that, he'd disturb the stick and the cage would fall down on him. They called them cribs. Aye, we were cruel little bastards.

Most people had a shotgun, men of course, had one for shooting. They'd go up the bogs. That time there were geese, snipe and there was plenty of pheasants knocking about. Another bird called a partridge – they were in wild ground. Then there was the deer as well. Sometimes a farmer would shoot deer. It was not allowed to do it...they'd have to get rid of the evidence. Have to be divided up amongst the farmers, you know. I never tried it, venison. I believe it is strong. There's plenty of deer now in the ould forest. I suppose they cull them sometimes to keep the numbers down. At that time the demesne was a guarded place.

At the time there was ambushes and burnings and reprisals of all kinds going on, which, as there was no radios, no television, no phones, we had to depend on people who used to call at the house, and tramps bringing news. And there was a newspaper on a Saturday called *The Freeman's Journal*, and by the light of an oil lamp that paper would be read from cover to cover – not only read all week but debated on and studied and talked about so the people were well equipped there for getting news. But, of course, the news would be censored about the war and about all the people getting killed. We didn't know that.

Then of course there was the Rising in Dublin in 1916, which was also talked about. So it went on until the 1920s – it got more and more violent and up and down the country there were ambushes and people raiding for shotguns. Farmers used to have shotguns and licences for them, and gangs of whatever side would come looking for them. I remember the time leading up to the truce – there was talks of a truce between Britain and Ireland. It was brought about, and the Border was divisioned off. A lot of people were so fed up with the war and glad to accept the twenty-six counties as a Free State and try to bring the other six counties in later. But the Orangemen at that time were very, very strong and powerful and they had the British Army to back them up.

The man at the time was Michael Collins and another one was Arthur Griffith. We didn't know much about them at the time. From what we could hear, they went to London and had to accept the terms of the Free State – that there would be a Governor General and they would have to swear allegiance to the King of England, which wasn't very well accepted.

On the other side, Eamon de Valera and his crowd went up against them. They were called the Irregulars, I believe. They were attacking the Free State troops and barracks and blowing up bridges and causing as much damage to the government as they could. It was very, very bad, the Civil War was. Very hard. Worse than the war against the Tans and Auxiliaries and the British. But eventually in time it died out and they came to some agreement and formed the Dáil.

At that time I'd be twelve or thirteen – time for leaving school and looking for something, but there was nothing. Poverty-stricken times. People were finding it hard. At that time there was no public transport of any kind, so we were really stuck in our own villages and not able to get about. You wouldn't call us travellers. Bicycles was about the only…if you was lucky enough to get a bike. The other means of getting about was an ould ass and cart, which I would have to go to the nearest town on the ass and cart to the shops to get the messages. A board across and the reins and a stick, and away you'd go. It was a long way and a long time. Eventually you'd get to Woodford, our nearest town, a one-street town on a hill – built on the side of a hill. You'd eventually get there and the young Woodford lads, they'd be sat on the wall on the corner and as we'd come up on our ass and carts we'd have to go through the jeers:

> *Country gawks, country gawks*
> *Threw away the potatoes and ate the stalks.*

We'd have to retaliate with:

> *Woodford town, it is no town,*
> *A church without a steeple*
> *At every door you'll see a fool,*
> *Looking at the people.*

Anyway, we'd get to the grocer's, John O'Reilly's. You'd hand in blocks of butter, fresh country butter. The women used to make it into little bricks or boxes with patterns on them. Your butter would be well known. The grocer would weigh it and allow you so much for groceries then. He would also count the eggs which you'd bring in. There'd be hen's eggs, there'd be duck eggs and they'd be graded and counted and weighed and all this, then the grocer would know how much groceries you'd get in the line of tea, sugar, salt, soap and bread – tea, mostly, and perhaps a bit of tobacco as well, if it would run to it. Other groceries, too, but mostly we had stuff at home ourselves. We had all the vegetables you could need at home.

But then you'd have about maybe twopence left over to get your-self something. We'd be up and down the street of Woodford from one end to the other, looking to see where we'd get the best value for a penny or a halfpenny. It'd take a long time before we'd finally settle on some Bluebird toffee, Peggy's leg, liquorice fountains. There was all kinds of gadgets. And mints. It would take a lot of picking. But, anyway, we'd get off home then, and do the long journey home again with the ould ass and cart, bringing the messages with you. Aye.

Then another thing we had to do – we'd have a thrashing every year for the corn because we'd grow our own oats and barley and wheat. We'd work all harvest time – we'd put the corn in stooks till the machine would come. The first machine I saw was drawn by horses. There was a big drum and shafts out of it and two horses were tackled to the shafts and they'd go round in a circle, and that was driving the machine for threshing the corn. Big belts were attached to it. You could hear the hum of it through the village. The men from every house in the village would come and work for a day – it was called 'coring'. Everybody was busy and everyone had their own job to do. We'd be up on the stacks, untying the sheaves because they had to be thrown down on to a big table, from where a man would be feeding the corn into the beaters. The man doing that had to have a constant supply of sheaves to keep him going. He was the only man allowed near the beaters because they'd take the hand off you.

In the meantime, straw was going down one chute and chaff was going somewhere else. Corn would go down the chutes into the bags that were hooked on. The men would bring them away into the barn while there was others making a reek of straw which was getting bigger and bigger.

When we'd have the stacks done, the machine would be stopped and all would be cleaned. The next threshing would be wheat, which was very valuable. And last of all, we'd do barley, which was, oh, terrible stuff – all fibres and whiskers on it, and the air used to be full of it and your hands would be all... but everything would get done, and there'd be a big meal for all who worked on it. There'd be lashings of food for everybody and maybe a barrel of porter. The men would all go back then to their own houses, carrying rakes and forks and whatever they brought with them. Then the machine would move on to the next farm, which might be a bigger farm and would take all day to do, or it might be a small farmer and he would have to move again. 'Twas a great day out.

The thing was, there was a flour mill about maybe five mile away, driven by a big water wheel. It was called Rourke's Mill. That was another job for us. The donkey and cart would be brought out again, the ould ass and cart, and there'd be a sack of wheat. You'd have to take that to the mill and when you'd get there, there'd be a line of people all waiting and your name would be put down, but you might be there a good few hours before your corn would be ground. It was a big stone mill, with grindstones, as they call them, driven by the wheel. The water would be dammed further up and then the water let go to do the day's grinding. The wheat would be ground up between these stones and then dropped to a lower level and ground again and so on. You'd have two bags going home. You'd have one bag of flour, pure flour, and the other bag would be what we call bran – the outside of the wheat kernels. That was a great day out. The mill, also, it drove a sawmill. Timber would be cut up and sawn. It was all a very interesting day out.

But as time went on and there was no work, my brother, my eldest brother, Jack, he found an apprenticeship in the next biggest town near us, Portumna. There was a man there, Jim Gorman, who had his own tailoring business. Now, in those days a tailor, he had big rolls of cloth: brown and blue serge mostly – all dark stuff – and farmers'd come in and have a suit made. So they'd have to pick the suit that they wanted and the colour and all that, and then they'd be measured and all them measurements would be jotted down. They'd have to come in, then, in a few weeks, for a loose fitting. The suits'd be just pinned together with threads and the tailor would give them a fit and any little alterations that needed doing. Then after that the suit would be made complete with trousers, jacket, of course, and the waistcoat, which was also part of the suit. And that would take a long time to do that. I think he had three besides himself, the tailor. His own son and Jack, and he had another. It was all done by hand – there was very little machine work there. So that was how Jack come to be a tailor.

Now, in the meantime, there was talks of me being put to carpentry, but there wasn't many carpenters about, so I just took up a job, a job with the council, to put me over. There was bogs round there and they had to be drained, and the council, they organized a group of lads and me, and paid us. I don't think we were killed with wages, but it was all shovel work – spades and wheelbarrows, and they'd cut big trenches through the bog to drain the place.

While this was going on, my father, still in Manchester, he was a carpenter, he was a carpenter working in the building trade there, which was very slack at the time, because England was depressed as well. It was Whit Week, I know that, and it must have been 1928 or 1929, and he sent word over that he'd be able to get me on as an apprentice where he was working. I hadn't seen him for years and I'd never been anywhere – not Dublin, not Galway, even.

A coach – a bus, you might say – went up once a day from Portumna to Dublin and my Uncle Joe, he came with me and he took me up to Dublin. I'd never seen anything like it before. There was buses and trams and trains and Lord knows what, and I was completely lost. I was supposed to catch the boat at Dun Laoghaire, at that time called Kingstown.

When we got to Dublin, two students from our village, schoolteachers learning the business, were to meet us. My Uncle Joe had to go back. The coach went back at six. But the boat didn't go from Kingstown until nine o'clock. So the two lads, they took charge of me and took me round Dublin on the trams. They showed me the zoo and the Phoenix Park and St Stephen's Green – all sights to see. Then they took me down to where they were lodging, and we had something to eat. Then they took me down to Kingstown on the tram, on top of the tram, and it was all new to me. They dropped me off, put me on to the boat with a little bit of a suitcase with me. I might as well have been going to the moon, because I was a greenhorn, absolutely.

The next crack was that the cattle was loaded on to the boat. They was superior to the passengers – they got better treatment. We were down below in the holds. There was no such thing as fancy lounges like there is now, and bars and all this carry-on. You were down below and you sat on your ould box, and people was being sick, and the ould boat was rocking all over the place, and it was at night. I don't know how many hours it took to get across. There was a man there got talking to me, and I told him I didn't know where the hell I was going. I said it was to Manchester, and he said, 'Oh well,' he said, 'I'm going on to Leeds,' which I found out since was further on in

Yorkshire, and Manchester was in Lancashire. So when we got off the boat, we took the train and after another long journey we landed in Manchester and he put me off there. My father was there to meet me. I only knew him from photographs and he only knew me from photographs, but eventually the man who I was with, he got us together. My dad took hold of me right away then, he warned me about talking to strangers. He'd turned. He'd been that long in England, he'd turned into an Englishman, you might say. He read English papers and he voted Tory. He was a real Tory man. He wasn't at all what I thought.

He was a good carpenter, and he was well respected on the job. I landed there in Manchester on the Saturday, I think it was, and he had me working on the Monday, up on the job. Up early in the morning and out. We had to catch a tram before seven, because if you done that, you'd save a penny. You can laugh at it now, a penny, but the wages were very small, very small, and every penny and halfpenny you could save was valued, so to get this seven o'clock tram you had to be up and out. That would give you a three-halfpence return ticket – a workman's ticket, whereas if you didn't get that, it'd cost you twopence return.

Then we had to get the train out to the job, to which we was going. At that time the building trade was very slack, especially the private building trade, which is what my father was in. They were spec builders – speculative builders. They'd buy some land and build a pair of semis and do a really good job on it. People would come out at weekends to look at them and if they fancied a house, well built and all that, they would put a deposit down on it, and once that deposit was down, the builder would decide to build another two houses and as he sold them, he would build more. When we seen people coming round, buying them, we knew that the job was secure for a bit longer. But the houses was built to the best. The best of materials went into them, and the best of workmanship as well. No cowboys in them days. Everything had to be done right. The bricklayers, they depended on the carpenters and the carpenters worked in with them. We had to leave everything, if we was laying the joists, clean and right after us.

There was the ground work to be done for the carpenters, then there was first fixing, which meant laying floors, putting in staircases and putting all the frames and windows in, and all that was first fixing. Then, after first fixing was done, we had to leave everything right for the plasterers. We had to leave everything spot on. Then as soon as that was done, there was a gang of roofers who were experienced. They had their own ladders, they put wooden scaffolds up, and they used to do a very fine job. But we couldn't do any fixing inside until the roof was on, the tiles. So every trade had to work in with every other trade. That was the beauty of it. And by doing that, the plasterers would leave it tidy for the carpenters going in. Then the carpenters would put on the skirting boards and the moulds around the doors and there was also picture rails.

Electricity was in its early stages then, too. We had to work in with the electricians. Plumbers, of course. We also had to be careful not to nail any of their pipes or cut any of their cables. The bricklayers, too, they had to keep the floor clear of mortar, and so they would get up to the wall plate heighth. Then we had to put the wall plate on. But the roofers then took over. They were a gang of their own. I think they were self-employed. They would put the ceiling joists across and all the rafters up, all the hips and valleys and that. Very, very interesting work.

It was out in the country. A lovely country place, it was. At that time, there was no airport in Manchester. They were just going to start building one. I remember well it was a councillor called Flanagan. It struck me, like, being an Irish name. He was the leading man – he suggested this airport. The land where they were building this airport was the finest land there was in Cheshire – all nurseries and allotments, supplying Manchester markets with everything – potatoes, carrots, parsnips, even tomatoes, eventually. People there were making livings off it. It had to be the government that got permission to confiscate all this land. There was great uproar at the time, I remember. Since then, I can see they were really looking ahead to see what would be. If they hadn't bought all that land, they wouldn't be able to do it.

Manchester Airport today has grown out of all knowledge. Instead of one terminal, there's four now. You'd get lost in the place. But I'm going back to them days, when aeroplanes were very few and far between. People would go out to the airport to look and marvel at it, and the 'planes coming in.

Altogether, the 1930s was a bad time in England – great depression everywhere. The building trade was going in fits and starts. In the summer, it would be busy and then in winter there'd be nothing doing. There was nothing for it but the dole. The only thing was, the food was very, very cheap. Even though people were living on the dole, there was plenty of good food. Fish and chips was the big diet. Fish and chips and peas – you'd get them for next to nothing. Rabbit was very common then. Plenty of butchers. The food was very good, considering. Other things was bad. Millions of terrace houses with chimneys, like you'd see in *Coronation Street* now, all fuelled by coal. In the winter, in November, it would start. The fog would settle down on the city like a big blanket, and outside your own front door, you'd be lost in seconds. If you was at work, it could take you ages to get home again. You wouldn't know where the hell you'd be. You'd have to be wearing a handkerchief over your mouth. No wonder people in Lancashire have bad chests. I've had a bad chest all my flipping life. I blame it on that.

But there was football. In them days, Manchester City was the main team in Manchester, and we were living right beside it, so I used to go there. We used to work Saturday morning, mind you. We had to work five and a half days – finish at twelve. Then I used to go and watch Manchester City. They had a player there called Peter Doherty. He was an Irishman from Derry. If he was playing today he'd be a superstar, but in them days the players were on very poor wages. We thought they were on good wages – £5 a week. The most a tradesman then could get was £3 after working forty-eight hours, and we thought footballers were doing great. I talked to some of them afterwards, and they knew they was being exploited. There used to be crowds of 60,000 at Maine Road. There was a military band and they'd play tunes. In the meantime, the lads would come up the tunnel and look out and see 60,000 at a shilling a time and there might be another 10,000 at half a crown a time. They'd go back to the dressing room and say, 'There's only eleven of us here. Eleven fives is fifty-five. Where's the rest of the money going?'

One man was sent in as a spokesman for the rest to try to get a bit more money, but he didn't succeed. All he got was, his name was taken and he was blacklisted. I think there were ninety clubs in the country and he was blacklisted as a troublemaker. Things were bad then. I don't think they had managers. From what I can gather, it was the secretary who was the boss. Trainers were not very important in those days. But it was something for people to go and do. They used to love the football. On Saturday afternoons, the streets were jammed with thousands of people walking to the ground. No one had cars them times. They'd come on buses so far, then they'd let them off to make their own way to the grounds, and the same on the way home. Ah yes, them clubs have come a long way since then. We had a man called Matt Busby recruited to City in the 1930s. He turned out to be a great star and a great manager for Manchester United. United had a poor record in the thirties, until 1939.

I remember well, I was in a pub on the Sunday morning, I think. It was eleven o'clock and Chamberlain gave a speech on the radio and said we were at war with Germany. The pubs were jammed with people who never had a drink before, all so excited on it. People were falling over each other to join the army. That was the first day, when they were drunk. There wasn't any great military activity at all. That was 3rd September. Just the odd 'plane would come. Then we had a very, very severe winter – seven weeks of frost between November and December, and the building trade was completely wiped out. You couldn't move anywhere, the ground was so hard. Everybody was on the dole. They had to open up schools and empty places to form labour exchanges to cope.

In the meantime, myself and another young carpenter, we were that broke – we didn't have the price of a Woodbine between us. So we walked miles and miles looking for jobs. We heard about a big firm that was looking for carpenters – hundreds of carpenters. They were going to build a big hutting scheme for the army and the air force. They were going to have thousands and thousands of huts put up. We were waiting for them, and they didn't come, with the frost. Then, suddenly the frost thawed and there was more work. You could cope, then. Oh, this hutting scheme, you could work all the hours you wanted. Seven days a week, until it was rushed up. All them huts, they were filled up with footballers, mostly, and cricketers and athletic people of all kinds. They were converted into physical training places – PT. I met Peter Doherty there, the Irish chap. He could run all day, yet he was a heavy smoker – pipe and cigarettes. That confused me, that, how he could do it, because he was noted for his stamina. Anyway, that hutting job finally came to an end. It took us a good few months, then they transferred us to a munitions factory.

It was twenty-eight miles around, all underground. In them days the machinery wasn't as good as it is now. It was mostly done with primitive stuff. The roads and tunnels all had to be excavated. They recruited 20,000 people from Ireland – workers – big strong navvies, used to hard work. They got great conditions, mind you. Free travel over on the boat, free accommodation round the sites, all the hours they could put in. They were allowed home every month for a free weekend, you know. They got great work out of them – without them it would never have got off the ground. These men dug tunnels and laid railway tracks, built big roads, so in the end it took eighteen months or more – all underground. On the top, anybody flying over it, it was just hills and trees and the odd dummy farmhouse, to look to a German plane as if it was just part of the country. Underneath it was all tunnels and entrances. That's where the munitions were made, down there. All the fittings we had to put in was all brass, so there'd be no sparks. It cost – oh, millions. I think it was supposed to cost £11 million at the start. It finished up more like £11 billion. All kinds of roguery going on. The big firm that had the main contract, they had a lot of tackle, and the sub-contractors come in and they had no tackle. They used to thieve the other tackle. Plenty of small firms became big ones. That was what you called a deferred occupation. While you was working on those schemes, there'd be no chance of being called up, although hundreds of thousands of people were being called up.

After the war, I went back to Ireland, whenever I could. I remember being in Dublin and I saw a bus, and I said to the conductor, 'Do you go to Ballygar?' 'No,' he said, 'Ballygar is in Mayo. We don't go that far.' 'Well then,' I said, 'What kind of gars have you got?' 'We've got a Rathgar.' 'That'll do.' They're very, very witty, Dublin people. Another time, I was a right eejit, as green as grass, I saw a bus as I was walking along and it was going very slowly in the traffic, so I said to the bus conductor, 'Do you go as far as O'Connell Street?' 'We do,' he said. 'Hop on.' So I hopped on to the platform. 'Now,' he said, 'you can hop off again. That's O'Connell Street right there.' And it was only a few yards away! As I walked away, I heard him saying to the other passengers, 'Holy Mother Ireland, she's rearing them still.'

I'd like to talk a bit about how Irish people had to emigrate and how they did their bit and more for countries like America, and for Britain, too.

Now, at the time of the Boer War there was very little work in Ireland because that's the way the country was run by the government of the day – the British government. They were using Ireland for recruiting labour, both for military purposes and also for construction. Both my uncles had been forced to emigrate to America, along with thousands of others, and there they were mostly employed in New York, doing the underground in New York, and bridges and roads and highways and docks and jetties and airports. All that kind of hard, heavy, badly paid work. But they had to do it.

They passed through Ellis Island and there they were given a very, very strict examination – they didn't want anybody that was ill or suffering from any ailments – they wanted fit, strong young people. They did not want huddled masses at all – they wanted workers. And Irish people, they had the same language and that was a big asset to them as regards the Italians, or Europeans.

So the Irish and the Scots too, for that matter, they were – well, I think they were exploited and that's why there's so many Irish regiments and so many Scottish regiments. But they were recruited against the Boers in the South African War, and the Zulu Wars and, oh, praised highly for their gallantry and bravery. Eejits!

Both my uncles eventually came back from America because they'd inherited their farms, but more stayed over there. The thing was, there was no work in Ireland. And then the First World War broke out, with all the propaganda, and Lord Kitchener, who was an Irishman, was the recruiting man. He was from Kerry. Well, the idea was to recruit huge Irish regiments fighting for the freedom of small countries.

On the political side, they were promising they would give them Home Rule if they joined up in the forces. John Redmond was one of the nationalist leaders, and he believed the British government of the day, Lloyd George's promise that Ireland would receive its Home Rule after the World War was finished. It was to be a government with a Governor General ruled from Britain – you'd be in the Commonwealth. Northern Ireland, the politicians up there, they did not want that. They resisted and the British army backed them, and was going to withdraw. They were going to fight, the two lots.

So, anyway, John Redmond's party believed, and they encouraged thousands of Irishmen to join up, with the hope that they would get

Home Rule at the end. On the other hand, Sinn Fein did not believe them and they said they would resist conscription. Sinn Fein objected to recruiting and such.

In 1916, they formed a rebellion, as it's known in history. And they took over the Post Office in Dublin and other big buildings, and resisted for a week against very big odds. And that then led to four years' guerrilla warfare with Britain. The Black and Tans, the Auxiliaries, were called in. In the background, political moves were being made, so in 1921, the British government gave them the Free State of twenty-six counties. The six northern counties were disordered and still ruled by Britain. This led to civil war. De Valera, who was one of the Sinn Fein leaders, wouldn't accept this position of only the twenty-six counties being free, but Michael Collins and Arthur Griffith *did* accept this, by a small majority, and as a result there was civil war.

For about a year and a half the Irish guerrillas was fighting each other. It caused a lot of damage and a lot of bitterness, and families were split up, and, as everybody knows, even though Britain and the Allies won the First World War, the people, the soldiers, came back to Britain to poverty and distress and unemployment, and all their fancy promises came to nothing.

Ireland then, from 1921 to 1922 onwards, the Free State, it had to run its own affairs and had to provide armies and navies and merchant ships and everything, to continue trading with the world. And then in the 1930s, the German threat started. The 1930s was a very, very bad decade. There was poverty, unemployment, and you could see it was leading up to a big war with Germany. A lot of British politicians and aristocracy, they were favouring Germany at the time and trying to make a political agreement with them. The Prime Minister was called Chamberlain and he was trying his best to avoid a big war, and try to come about some way out, but the German leader, Herr Hitler, was determined to increase Germany's powers which they'd lost in the First World War, and he wanted to bring them back into a big nation again. And so he did, from huge armies of well-trained men and started taking over land which had previously belonged to Germany, in his opinion.

Now, this started the Second World War, and Ireland, under the leadership of President de Valera – he would not take part in the war while his own country was divided by the border. That was the point where he couldn't agree to join up fighting Germany. Because they were fighting for the freedom of small nations and his was a small nation and it was not free.

But even so, even though there was no conscription in Ireland, still thousands and thousands of Irishmen – because there was no work, no prospects of anything – for excitement and a living and that, thousands and thousands joined the British Army. They would go up to the North of Ireland, up to the Six Counties, and join up there, because that was under British rule and then they were distributed around in the British Army.

I was in the British Army myself, and I seen it. There was thousands of Irish people, both native and second-generation Irish. My brother Dave was in the Merchant Navy in the 1930s, as ship's carpenter, which was a very, very risky business, the Merchant Navy, when the war broke out, because they weren't in convoys and they were liable to be torpedoed any time, which he was. He was torpedoed in 1940, and after four days in an open boat out in the North Sea, during which ten of his mates died, they were rescued by some Scottish fishermen. And in the next couple of years he was torpedoed – he was torpedoed a *second* time, and a *third* time he was bombed, so he had a rough, hard action there.

But most of them Merchant Navy men were also Irish or Irish descent, and those people never got the credit they deserved. And another brother, he'd just emigrated to New Zealand in 1939, and when the war broke out, he joined the New Zealand navy and completed five years with the New Zealand navy. They were manning a battleship called the *Duke of York* up in Scotland, Rosyth and that, and after the war he was demobilized in New Zealand and remained there, and my other brother, Davy also, when he left the Merchant Navy, he went to New Zealand and remained there also. And they take great pride in being members of the Anzac group of servicemen.

So Irish people, although Churchill called them for not taking part in the war, they did their part and much more than their part, too. Like they always have done. I always thought the Scottish and Irish peoples were used very badly by the British governments at the time. All the years down, they kept them poor and poverty-stricken, and gave them no options but to join up, and gave them a bit of notoriety, making them into famous regiments…. Aye.

A gang of building trade workers at a job in St Helens, circa 1957. Jim Hickey is second from the left in the back row, next to the foreman.

Now, I, afterwards, worked in the building trade in Britain and partly during the war, when tradesmen were very, very scarce. It was a reserved occupation to be engaged in building big hutting encampments and then munition factories. And then I got on to the ships, in Manchester, converting cargo boats into troop ships – they were carrying provisions and goods and trucks and jeeps, everything. And also carrying troops, as well. That was another reserved occupation. There again, I found there was a lot of Irish labour or Irish descent in amongst the dockers and crews who were working there.

Now, the big munitions factory I was working on was called Risley, between Warrington and Manchester on the main rail line, and it was huge. I mentioned this before. It was twenty-eight mile around on farmland and bogland that had been taken over by the government to create that into an underground factory. And that took some doing. The machines they had then weren't so good as what they've got today. But they had to get men in, so they recruited from Ireland. They recruited thousands – perhaps twenty or thirty thousand – of young construction workers. They provided them with passage over and accommodation and work all the hours they could – they needed that – otherwise, they'd never get the munition factory done. All the tunnels

*Jim Hickey and John Slattery in front of Portumna Castle,
the seat of the infamous Earl of Clanricarde. John is also
mentioned in Tommy Hanley's story.*

and roads and underground factories. After a couple of years, when that
was finished, it looked from the air as if it was just farmland, with roads
and dummy houses and trees and cattle. As if there was no factory
there. And yet that factory was going day and night, turning out arms
and shells for the armies before D-Day, before they attacked France and
made the landings. Yes, the Irish certainly done their part.

The Germans, which they were bombing Britain, sometimes
unloaded – whether deliberately or by accident – they bombed Dublin,
even though the lights was on, and in Britain everywhere was blacked
out. But the German 'planes came in anyway and bombed Dublin.
Done a lot of damage and killed many people. Then another time, they
carried on up the coast to the Six Counties and they bombed Belfast,
which was a target, of course, with it being under British rule, and they
were building aircraft up there, and ships. But it was a bit far for the
German bombers and they didn't carry on with it very much.

So after the war, when the Allies won and Britain was bankrupt,
the Americans stepped in with Marshall Aid, and Britain had to be

built up again – all the factories. Steel. Steel and coal and roads and transport had to be built up. There again, the Irish labour force came in and the advantage of an Irish labour force was this. On the motorways, the job was in construction all the time – day and night – every day. And you couldn't have a fixed force. You had to have a flexible force of men that would move with the motorways. They would be in huts or they would be in caravans and all this. But they would be working and moving. That's how they motorways of Britain got built, and the bridges and.... Yeah.

So in this respect, the Irish done very good. They built drains and tunnels. Wherever the work was. In the most outlying places where they couldn't get labour or labour wouldn't go, the Irish would go, and take chances.

So I took myself. Yes, I worked in the building trade all over Britain. And wherever I went, the building workers in Britain was as fine a lot of men as you could wish to meet. Wherever we went, whatever we were working on, there was never any trouble, all working together and helping each other, and a good comradeship and friendship amongst us. You could leave your tools anywhere – if you was off sick for any length of time, when you come back, your tools would be there. They were honest amongst...there was comradeship amongst them. They might rob the builders and the government, but they certainly wouldn't rob their workmates.

I don't know if that exists today amongst them. Because somehow I don't think it does. Because the building trade is made up mostly of privatized cowboys. Not at all the same spirit as the miners in Britain. They put up a great fight to rescue their livelihoods in the 1980s, when Thatcher, the Prime Minister at the time – an evil woman, I call her. And she threw everything at the miners. For eighteen months they struggled and fought and they were starved into defeat in the end. Yeah. Yeah. She done more damage to Britain than Hitler with all his bombing. And she done huge damage to Ireland, too. She has a lot of deaths on her conscience, in my opinion.

Michael-Joe Tarpey

born 8th September 1913

Two rows of expertly trimmed trees stand in front of the house in which Michael-Joe Tarpey lives, a house which he designed and built entirely by himself, save slating the roof. Hugely skilled and accomplished and profoundly modest, Michael-Joe retains, for all his years, a youthful air, and can be seen still riding his bicycle to and from the post office at the cross and puffing away at the odd cigarette. The following includes conversations with Jim Hickey (JH), who also tells his story in these pages.

MJT I'll tell you about the stone axe I found. I'm not able to give the year exact. 'Twas about thirty year ago.

JH I seen the axe up in Dublin.

MJT You've seen it?

JH I seen it. It's there on public display – where it was found and who found it.

MJT 'Twas over thirty year ago anyway, maybe thirty-five. Anyway, we was making a drain, myself and the timekeeper – it should be in the harvest – and I scooped this out. 'Twas about a foot and a half down at the bottom of the drain. And I scooped out from the side of it with a shovel and I took up and looked at it. O'course, I didn't know what it was, so I showed it to all the men that were working with me. 'Twas ten inches long and 'twas about four inches on one end – the shape of an egg, now. 'Twas flat, but lovely finished, and 'twas pure green stone. So, I dug it up anyway, and no one knew what it was, so I brought it home and I had it here a week and I showed it to a lot, and no one knew what it was, and I didn't know myself, so I acquainted my boss about it and he wrote up about it. And he come down to me and he says, 'Give me that yoke you found,' he says. 'I have to send it up. They're doing nothing but writing for it.'

So he did and when it went up, anyway, they found 'twas a stone axe. It had an edge on both ends. One end, now, the edge was like a lance. It could chop timber out of it. So they turned around and sure,

71

'twas between two and three thousand BC. That's the age they give of it, like. So, anyway, they turned around and they sent me down £2 of a reward for the finder, and 'tis above now in th'museum. And if you went in there – 'tis in Marble Hill wood I found it, that's in the parish of Ballinakill – if you want to see it, you'd have to ask for the Marble Hill axe find. 'Twas in a wood called Marble Hill and they'll show it to you and they'll show you a map of the wood and there's a cross on the spot where I found it.

And after a couple of months after that, they sent word. We had to stake it, where 'twas found. There was a white stick peeled and druv down in th'exact spot where I found it, like. So they were to search it, like. Whether they ever did or not I couldn't tell you that, now. I don't know. So if you were to go in, you want to look for the Marble Hill axe find, and you'll get the finder's name on the sheet.

What really happened was the Forestry, they presented it to the museum, and I was only the finder, d'ye see? And they sent me a reward. I knew 'twas something, you see, when I picked it up, you see. 'Twas finished – 'twas as fine as that tile [*pointing to the tile surround of his stove*], now, d'you see? Pure finest green stone. Them all, o'course, laughed at me. And I brought it down anyway, and I was eatin' my lunch. I put it into my lunchbox and I brought it home. You're supposed to – anything that you find in the forest, when you're working, 'tis their property, like, and you're supposed to give it up. I give it to me boss. My name is there as the finder.

Another time, something strange happened in the forest. Well, this'd be about half-past eight in th'morning. We were working that time at eight o'clock. And myself and the timekeeper was edging a saw and I was holding one end of it, you see, and he was edging th'other end, you see. And next thing we heard the axe working, and the next thing we saw a big oak tree falling. About twelve or fourteen yards away from where we were edging the saw. And down it goes and you'd hear the crash of it and all. The two of us went in to see who was it, and there was no one there at all. And there was no tree there, but y'see, we saw the tree split up the whole way and it falling! We saw the white part of it split, and when we went in there was no tree at all in it! I told the boss about that, too. He said things like that could happen. Well, that really happened at half-past eight in th'morning. And every one of the men – the men that was gone in to work on th'other side, you know – they heard the noise of th'axe as well, d'ye know, and away goes the tree. Y'know, 'twas a big tree falling and it split up the whole way. We were twelve yards from it or thirteen and we went in and there was nothing there at all.

Sure, they claim, sure, there was fairies out long ago; anyway, they do. Oh, there definitely was. Well, in them days there was lots of things seen. Lots of people was frightened, like. And whether they saw things or not, I don't know. I've heard things myself, at night, when I used to go when I was young, and 'twasn't natural, either. I heard a big press one night – like a big press dragging along th'road. And I came right up to it and went back th'road again, and th'night of it was fierce, a starry night. And yet we saw nothing.

Oh, they were out long ago. But I'd say since th'electric light came.... There was no electric light in them days. I have th'impression it brightened up. But fairies long ago, 'twas terrible. Ye'd be afraid to go into a house. Ah? There'd be fairy stories. They'd be talking about fairies all night. Ye'd see some gathered in kitchens all night – pulling up the chairs – pulling them near the fire and looking up at the door for fear one'd come in. They'd be feared of going home.

JH Yes, we'd be feared to go home. If we was up at Kelly's in Derryvunlan, they used to fill us up there with stories and then we had to walk all the way home down there at night. And you'd be jumping, you know. There'd be cobwebs across the roads and you'd walk into them in the dark. Bats flying about.

MJT They were definitely out in my young days, fairies, there's no getting away from it.

JH You'd hear movements behind the ditches. Groaning. Might be cattle, you know. You'd be feared, I tell you.

MJT You'd be afraid. We were afraid going out to visit anyone at night until we were thirty years of age. Fairies were drummed into our heads. Th'ould people talking about them. They were out all right in them days, like.

JH Especially at All Souls and All Saints – that was in November, th'beginning.

MJT You heard about the banshee, too, didn't ye? Well, I heard her twice in my time. I heard her crying from the point o' the wood, off down along the road, down across the bog there. There was a woman that must have come from Dublin that night. The funeral passed up here from Dublin around nine o'clock – 'twas dark as a bag. And I happened to go outside the door, like. Cripes, before it came. Watching out for the funeral and you heard the lonesome cry of her down along the bog. And I heard it in Easterfield another night. She cries for the Nevins and cries for Carthys and...cries for a lot of people. She cries only for certain families. Oh, she cries only for certain families. No, she wouldn't cry for the Tarpeys.

JH She'd cry for landowners mostly, that go back hundreds of years. O'Briens and families like that.

MJT Oh, a terrible sad cry. Oh, terrible sad to listen to her, and she cried down along the bog. She came from the point o' the wood, inside in the bog now and went down along. I'd say 'twould be about nine o'clock in the night – the funeral was late coming down from Dublin. I think of that the same as yesterday. 'Twas a long time ago, though.

They make out, like, some saw her. She was a little, small woman with long hair, long teeth. That's what they made out in them days. She was definitely out them times, but you'd get people that wouldn't believe, wouldn't listen to that at all. But because they never saw her, she didn't cry. I never heard her, only them two times. I was very young that time, so that just tells you that there was quare things out.

Biddy Earley lived up in Feakle. She could tell you anything. One man went to her anyway, and she told him he had a neighbour's top-coat on him. And he had. She could tell anyone anything, she could. A Dr Loughnane done up her cottage one time.

JH Dr Bill Loughnane. He was a great man.

MJT He done up that little house one time.

JH He was trying to revive all th'ould Clare stories and music and that. He was a great man. He was a TD [*member of the Irish Parliament*]. John Slattery used to go up and see him. He was always there for advice or anything like that.

MJT But several went to Biddy Earley from down as far as Tynagh. There was a little lake near the house, or some sort of pond outside, and they made out she had a blue bottle and 'twas fired into the lake. They say 'twas lost, anyway. She made cures for people.

JH The priests didn't like her. They condemned her.

MJT No, they didn't like her. And I wouldn't like to go to one of them, either, the same. Would you, Jimmy?

JH I wouldn't. No, I wouldn't.

MJT That she could know a man that he borrowed a topcoat. 'You've such a one's topcoat,' she said. Told him straight. He said he had.

Ah, such a lot of things happened long ago. They used to take the butter, too, long ago. That time, cows, people hadn't many. You could be churning all day and you'd have no butter. You'd have only... They could take the butter. And May day. There was often people caught milking other people's cows and that was for the butter. Did ye ever hear that?

JH I often heard that, yes, I did.

MJT And that's the truth.

JH Yeah, but round this part, if you was churning, whoever come in had to take a hand.

MJT They had. You had to do that at John Power's now, and Bridgie Goonan's now, below, as well. She lived to be 104, she did. And any time she ever was churning – she had a little dairy, you know – and she'd get the tongs and she'd have them ready to go start, and she'd bring a little coal out of the fire and she'd put it under the churn, d'ye see, for fear anyone would bring the butter. A small little bit – just put it one side of the churn there. To protect it. Well, there isn't a word about things like that now. I mean, they'd laugh at you now, like.

JH They say the number thirteen is unlucky.

MJT I always heard any odd number was unlucky.

JH But thirteen especially. There was the Last Supper. There was Christ Himself and the twelve apostles – that was thirteen.

MJT 'Twas.

JH You know how th'Last Supper finished up. That's why people think it's unlucky. And you don't bring may blossom into the house. The hawthorn blossom, you don't bring that into the house.

MJT But that's all gone now. What? Sure....

There's a stream, 'tis somewhere one side of Craughwell, now. Between that and Ardrahan, and 'tis crossing the road, like, a gullet, we call them. A small little gullet over it – 'tis a byroad. And you can boil the water that side of it – you can rise it up and you can boil it. And if you live for ever, you'd never boil the water once it passes that gullet th'other side. They hang rags there [*a sign of supernatural presence*] – up till very lately, now... rags up where they couldn't boil the water. 'Tis back between th'road and Ardrahan. I think 'tis Monksfield, they call the place. And if you were down that country, like, you'd get the history of it there, like. But they used to tell me the water can not be boiled once it passes under the gullet. You can boil it from th'other side. 'Twill boil away for you. They put rags on the bushes there. 'Tis strange, all right.

There's a statue, 'tis below in the parish of Eyrecourt – no, 'tis below where Father Walsh is buried – Clonfert. Well, the statue is there on th'altar. They were knocking a tree one time and the statue was hidden in a tree and they didn't know. They cut off that arm getting it out. I don't know is the arm missing or not. Anyway, they cut th'arm off. After a time they brought it up to the chapel in Eyrecourt, and when they put it up in Eyrecourt it turned around when they left it and it turned – it faced around from where it came from and they had to bring it back again.

JH I think that statue was put in a hollow tree to protect it from the Cromwellian soldiers, you know. I heard when they were cutting the tree the statue cried out. That's how they knew it was in there. When they cut the arm, they heard it cry out.

MJT That's it now. Our Lady of Clonfert.

Sure, wasn't there a witch below in Tynagh there? Wasn't that the same as Biddy Earley? Ye heard of her, Jimmy?

JH I did. I heard of her.

MJT Well, she used to haunt the priest. The reason why she haunted the priest – she wasn't a good-living woman, ye see. And anyway, it turned out that she haunted the priest and they went down to where she was buried and abrought her funeral back into Ballycorban graveyard. Ye never heard that? They dug a bit of clay, ye know [*to reinter her in consecrated ground*], and they brought her back into Ballycorban and buried her, and that's what it is. Oh, she'd haunted the priest for years. Not just the one priest but every priest. The story is that no priest would live any length of time after getting Tynagh parish. About seven of them died that time.

JH The priests are always against people like that, that claim to be witches or healers or anything like that.

MJT That's the only thing I have about Tynagh, now. John Slattery knew every inch of all that.

JH Michael-Joe, you never left this, did ye?

MJT I was up in Dublin several times and Galway. I have every county in Ireland visited except in the North.

JH What took you there?

MJT Tours! I was playing music in the buses and everywhere we went. I was in – the nicest place of them all I counted it – the Glens of Aherloe. The Glens of Aherloe – the nicest part of Ireland. In Tipperary. 'Twould pay you if you were to go there some time. You're driving up to it and when you land, like, you don't know whether you're going up a hill or not, but when you come to it, when you come to this spot, ye'd be afraid to look down. And there's a full country below beneath. Hundreds and hundreds of feet down and 'tis straight down. The best of land and a house isn't the size of that [holds thumb and forefinger as if holding a matchbox]. 'Tis a big place. There must be more than a parish in it, like, and the grandest scenery I ever saw was that. When you go down to the very end there's a singing pub there and they're dancing in the daytime in it. Oh Lord, 'tis an awful drive to get there, though. Through Tipperary town and miles beyond that. 'Tis a fierce drive!

I was in Avoca and Glendalough – nice place, too. I was in the Achill Islands, off Sligo direction. I went up there, halfways up the hill that's there on the bus, and them all got panicky and the busman had to stand and them all got out and they walked the rest of the way. When you're above on top of this hill and look down straight, 'tis surely forty feet down to the sea, and then back to your right, 'tis all little houses – callowish-looking land, you know. Hard living there. Ah, what!

I have all the Aran Islands done. I have the big one done twice and I have the small one done that you cross above Lisdoonvarna. The Cliffs of Moher. I went from the Cliffs of Moher to one of th'other islands. I think there's three of them in it. I went to the small one in an ould boat – could be drownded, too. 'Twas about a mile and a half. 'Twasn't big at all, the boat. I'd say 'twould be twenty feet long and an engine and a bit of the top of it covered. But there's a bigger boat going from Galway. Oh, 'tis like a ship, and I went on that twice.
JH You'd be safer on that, too.
MJT Oh, you would, you would. 'Twas like a house, th'other one. I done a bit of travelling round in my time, anyway. On the Aran Islands, sure all the houses is built on one side of it, like, you know. All in a cluster. Then you go out along on it, like, and ye'd see a garden and there'd be a wall built round it and you might see a beast in it and you mightn't. That way, they might have a cow fenced in, and if they were to bring out the cow there, they'd have to knock the wall with their hands and build it again when they're after driving it in there. And 'twould be only as big as a garden. 'Tis all a mass of stone walls on the

islands I was in, in it. Little roads on them, only just barely there. Little pubs in it, nice pubs, too. Jarveys there to hire. Bicycles, too.

JH When we were there it was covered with fuchsia – wild fuchsia everywhere. Everywhere you looked and turned, there was the fuchsia, and the people was talking Irish, you know.

MJT Talking Irish! Now!

JH We went across and Margaret went up the hill up to Dun Aengus. 'Tis a long way up and me and John Slattery stopped down below, and we were talking with the Aran Islanders, you know. They could talk English and they could talk Irish. Amongst themselves, they were talking Irish.

MJT There was a publican owned the pub in the Aran Islands and I'll never forget it, like. You go on up and 'tis there to your right. In th'evening around three o'clock. Well, there was hundreds sitting on the walls, you know, everywhere round about, see, and Timmy Bugler was with me and the wife, and he could tell you about it. We went in for a drink and this lad, he comes in and he says, 'Does any of ye play music?' And Bugler says, that I do. But I had nothing with me but a tin whistle, so he got us to play a tune. Well, lookit, I filled the pub in a few minutes and 'twas the best hour that was ever spent in th'Aran Islands, was that hour. Well, he couldn't keep pints filled! He never stood a drink to me, that brought in the crowd for him. D'you know? Well, we made a haul for him. Bugler will never forget that.

''Tis you,' Bugler says to me. And 'twas nothing only the bare tin whistle and they went mad for it. Now! Isn't it easy draw a crowd? I ended up, I was playing for about an hour in it and them all got out and danced. Nothing only the bare tin whistle. The landlord hadn't time to get me a drink and they were dancing and lepping and hoisting round about, y'know. That's the last time I was in the Aran Islands – not so long ago at all.

A fiddle is contrary. Carrying it, you know. That's why I had the tin whistle. I just stuck it in my pocket. No, I had not it in my pocket. The lad got one. I had no music e'er at all with me. The D is a whistle concert pitch. You can tune a fiddle to it, then a flute will go with a D and all th'other instruments will go with a D. But there's a C, but ye can't tune to them. If you don't meet a great accordion player – if he has the notes on the wrong scale – there's wrong scales on an accordion, and the same applies to the fiddle – and if you haven't it on the right scale, you'd play it no whit, you see. If you get the right scale, you'll keep going right, d'ye see?

Well, the fiddle I'd rather, because it's easier – you've no blowing to do, ye see. The fiddle is different, like, but a tin whistle is nice, too, like. But I'd prefer it if I was playing for an hour to be playing the fiddle. Ye'd want great puff for the whistle.

I can make the sound – you can imitate the sound of the [*uilleann*] pipes with the pipe, like. The trick on the fiddle with the pipe. You lay the pipe under the bridge and 'tis just like the sound of the pipes. I learned the trick to a man in Clare – his name was Dillon, Danny Dillon. He was a great fiddler and I went one summer to him on a bike. He lived this side of Whitegate. I went a full summer to him on a bicycle from here. I was a young lad, I was. Kept at it, you know. You can't learn a fiddle in twelve months. You'll be a long, long time at it.

JH It's a great county for music, Clare.

MJT 'Tis. Best in Ireland, sure.

JH The east side of Galway, as well.

MJT Did ye ever see a jew harp?

JH I could play one of them!

MJT Wait till I get it, then. They're a very scarce instrument, now, though.

JH They're not in the menu at all now, but the tin whistle and the jew harp was common.

MJT You never saw a jew harp? This is a jew harp, now.

[*JH is twanging away and humming into the little metal jew's harp.*]

MJT 'Miss McLeod's Reel'! You got it there, what!

JH You got it. That's the one we used to start on.

MJT I'm not able now, indeed I'm not. But Jimmy, ye're letting out the tongue too much that way, like. Ye're to guide the tongue with those two fingers. [*He starts to twang away.*] That's the way 'tis played. You hum into it.

JH You see, if there was no other instruments for dancing…

MJT You can get plenty of volume out of it.

JH I wonder why they called it a jew's harp.

MJT They're a very scarce instrument, now. You guide it, the tongue of it, with your finger. Don't let your finger touch it, though. Ye've to leave it against your teeth, mind.

JH When you played the tin whistle – as soon as you picked it up, could you play it? We all used to have them when we were going to school – people would have tin whistles. Ye'd get them at Christmas in your stocking. A jew harp could be in your stocking and some people would pick them up and others couldn't.

[*MJT plays*]

JH 'The Geese in the Bog' was one tune.

MJT I get breathless for a while. If your fingers isn't down right on the hole in the whistle, you get a deaf note. That was happening me there. Once you have made a deaf note, ye're caught. If I practise at it. You mentioned 'The Geese in the Bog', and people used to call it 'The Kid in the Mountain' or 'The Geese in the Bog'. I know the one ye're talking about. I'll play that for you.

JH If there was no music and no musician, somebody would play the tin whistle or somebody would play the jew harp, or if there was nothing, they could lilt, you know. [*JH gives an example.*] Well, they could dance to that. That's it. Aye. [*MJT brings out fiddle and tunes up.*] That's a nice tune. [*MJ plays 'Toss the Feathers'.*]

MJT Now, this is 'The Geese in the Bog'.

[*JH is tapping away with his hands on the edge of the chair.*]

MJT That was an ould hornpipe. Another one is this. [*MJT plays another air.*] 'Radney's Glory', they call that one.

JH I wonder would that be anything to do with British music at the time? 'Rodney's Glory'. Rodney was an admiral. In the Oranmore [*a Galway pub*], the man played 'The Blackbird' and 'The Stack of Barley', 'Rodney's Glory' and 'The Foggy Dew'. That was an English tune, I imagine. [*MJT plays on.*] Good man, Michael-Joe. Good man! [*MJT plays one more air.*]

MJT That's what they call 'Wallop the Protestant'.

JH 'Wallop the Protestant', aye! [*Laughs.*] How old is that fiddle, now?

MJT It came here from America in 1928, that fiddle, now.

Now, I'll tell you how I make the bodhrán [*the Irish drum*]. First and foremost, you have to get the timber and get it sawn and get it planed for the rims. You have to turn the rims – it must be ash – and you have to steam that to get them round and then you have to put them together and prepare them for the skin. Well, then, about the skin. You turn around and when you get the skin you have to spread it out and put roast lime on it and whiten it, just. Whiten it and fold it up tight and then you'd put it in a container and fill it just over the skin with water. The skin can be goat or deer. You fold it up and put it into the container of water and you have to leave it steeping there for eight days, and when you come up, you take it up, 'twill clean off for you. And you have nothing to do then, only wash it and prepare it to put on th'rim.

Then, the next thing is, that's the principal part of it is putting on the rim. You have to know the tension – the skin it wants. If you make it too set, 'twould be too hard. You put it on criss-cross from cant to cant. You cross the bodhrán first then you cross it again and tack it on the cant, round about. And then you turn around and when you have that on, you leave it up to dry. And you can't go finish it, like, until 'tis well dry. It depends on the weather, how long. You have to dry it outside because if you dry them inside, they'd be always getting slack. You have to dry them outside. And if you get a good day or two, that way they'd be dry, then you can trim them up then, and that's nearly all the making of a bodhrán. To know the set, to put on the skin, is the principal thing.

I learned from an old man in the parish of Portumna – he was eighty years of age, nearly, at the time. He was John Ash. 'Twas he showed me how to make the first bodhrán, and that's over sixty years ago, maybe sixty-five. And I made them down along from that up, so I did now, like.

JH You're a gifted man, Michael-Joe.

MJT Ah, indeed I'm not. No harm to know how to do all those things, like. I was interested in all that, you know. And if you're not interested in a thing, you can't do it. Sure, that's all now, like, I could say about the thing. Oh, the animal that you make a bodhrán with wouldn't want to be any more than two year old. If they're older, the skin gets thicker and you won't have as good a sound. A lot of things to think of, you see. They make them in factories now, they're what you call th'artificial ones. They have no power – no power like th'other ones. They look fancy. They're too tinny. The skin – ye'd get that stuff to buy, ye know. You'd get that in Galway. But 'tis too tinny, like. You could call them a bodhrán and they charge fierce prices for them.

'Tisn't so long ago since I made the last bodhrán. I made one, 'twas this year. 'Tis above in Dublin. 'Tis in a hairdresser's saloon. The man that came for it, he has a hairdressing saloon. I don't know what he wants it for after that – to hang up in the kitchen, or what. He has seven or eight working in there. And then I sent one to America last year and lots of them gone to England, too. But there's lots of them gone to France and every country. They buy them for souvenirs. I made more bodhráns for foreigners up around Whitegate in my time. I often had ten or twelve of them here at one time. They're a big help to a musician. They are, to be sure.

Michael-Joe was once a linchpin of the local mummers, or Wren Boys. In times long ago, a wren used to be caught and killed and its corpse paraded from house to house on 26th December, St Stephen's Day, as the mourners collected money for its funeral. (It seems the bird deserved this fate for, when St Stephen was lying hidden in a field, the wren betrayed his presence to the Roman soldiers intent on hunting down all Christians.) In Michael-Joe's time, it was an effigy that the Wren Boys carried round.

MJT They used set out from this house, Coen and John-Joe Watson and Timmy, Paddy and Ralph Kelly. And myself – I'd maybe play the bodhrán. You've no business going out for the wren without a bodhrán. Two, preferably. 'Tis the bodhrán makes the thing.

We'd walk in the door of the neighbours, without them saying whether you're welcome or not, and set to. We'd start early and finish late – up to twelve o'clock at night. And at some house or other you'd have a few sandwiches or a leg of the goose.

But you finished on St Stephen's Day. You could be fined to go out after that. They were great times. I remember John Kennedy and them with big strong shoes on them. They used to tear the floor out of it, dancing.... The song we sang was this:

> *The wren, the wren, the king of all birds,*
> *On St Stephen's day got caught in the furze.*
> *Although he was little, his honour was great*
> *So stand up, good woman, and give us a treat.*
> *'Tis up with the kettle and down with the pan*
> *And give us a penny to bury the wren.*

A musical evening with Michael-Joe, his wife Betty, and Jim Hickey

In the cosy kitchen of their little house, Michael-Joe and his wife Betty, now sadly passed away, entertained their old friend Jim Hickey. As the five clocks ticked away, Michael-Joe brought out his fiddle and his tin whistle, and after tuning up, set into a lively reel.

MJT No one ever heard that reel before. I have the real old reels no one knows. 'The Sligo Maid'. I could be playing different tunes from now until two o'clock in the morning.

I had a terrible lot of tunes. I was here on my own, playing tunes for four hours. Didn't I have a terrible lot of tunes? Here's one: 'The Pigeon on the Gate' – a great reel. I must play that one. [*Jim joins in.*] And here's 'The Ship is Sailing'. A great reel. You're a lot of help to me, Jimmy. I haven't played three times since you were last here. 'The Shannon Breeze'. A lovely reel. [*Michael-Joe plays another.*] You ask me what's the name of that reel? I don't have the name. It hasn't got one.
JH Why don't you give it one?
BT Call it 'The Sack o' Spuds'.

MJT I used to hate the uilleann pipes. [*He crosses over to the wall, takes a pipe from the bowels of the clock and shoves it in under the bridge of the fiddle. He plays and, sure enough, you get the impression of listening to the uilleann pipes.*] I learned that trick from a fiddler. You bring two strings together.

Now, did ye ever hear there were highwaymen roamin' the highways and roads of Galway years ago, sixty or seventy years ago, like? Well, a man and his wife were going to the mission in Ballinakill in their pony and trap. And a highwayman halted them and they got out. He searched them, but he found nothing, so he drove away in their pony and trap. 'What'll we do now?' said the man. 'We've no money or anything.' But lo and behold, the wife opens her mouth and she had the money hid in it! 'Sure, 'tis a pity we hadn't your mother with us,' he said. 'She'd have fit the pony and trap in her mouth.' The mother was a fierce talker, you see.

New Year conversation between Michael-Joe and Jim Hickey

JH Happy New Year. There's not so many of us left, now.
MJT I'm going on eighty-seven. The 8th of last September I was eighty-six.
JH I'm just that bit older – I was eighty-seven on 18th December.
MJT Are you older than me then?

Michael-Joe holding the pine marten which he captured and delivered to Dublin Zoo. It was once thought that pine martens were extinct in Ireland.

JH I'm about nine or ten months older than you. You know, I was in Connell's and they have the old school rolls from 1920 to 1930. With Margaret Mullen.

MJT I'm in that photo!

JH No, this is the school rolls, what the master had every day.

MJT They have a photo of the whole group at school.

JH I wasn't in it.

MJT Weren't you? How was that?

JH I wasn't in it, and neither was John Slattery, and neither was Jack, and John Kennedy wasn't in it. I don't know. It was after we moved from the old school.

MJT Will you ever forget the evening you took Master Canning's leg under your arm? Will you ever forget that?

JH He drew a kick at me.

MJT I'll tell you what happened. He kept us in in the evening after hours – for what I don't know. Something about lessons. But to punish us he wouldn't let us home. And whatever he did it for – he wouldn't do it now! – we were put marching around the school in a row, and he began kicking us. Every lad he met, he'd up and he'd give him a kick. Begod, he came on to Jimmy and he drew the kick at him and Jimmy clapped the leg up like that and he held it under his arm, and he hopped the master round the school! He had to roar for mercy. D'ye think of that? It took a great lad to do it! The minute he drew the kick Jimmy sidestepped him and caught the leg and hopped him round about.

JH He got his own back after. At the blackboard, you know. He'd come behind you and he'd hit your head onto the blackboard.

MJT Oh, he would, he would. Oh, cripes, he was fierce. I think of him well.

JH They have the rolls down there – every day, who was in and who was missing. Very valuable, them. All the names are in there. All the names come back to you. The Rossmore crowd was in: Lyons and Hickeys and Tullys and Morans.

MJT We used to go to school, we used to walk it from here. We used to have our lunch ate before ever we got there – it's a long way. And we'd fast all day. And we'd steal turnips in the evening, steal apples – we were doing any kind of mischief. In bare feet. Once the month of March would come in, you'd be in bare feet. The roads weren't tarred at that time. Big, rough lads would be putting stones on the road. We'd often a sore toe or a sore foot.

JH Oh God, many a time. Stone bruises. We got used to it.

MJT There was no such thing as shoes that time. We had them in the winter and we'd be mad to get our shoes off – often in the month of March. We'd go along the road, a cluster of us. We were late a few mornings and got beat for it! What!

I was born up the road from here but our place was divided – there was no will made. That must be forty-five years. I was married nine year the first time, and my wife died. And I was a year and three months on my own and then I married again and we were married thirty-four years, just exactly.

Now, if you go below to Slattery's and you see a house running the whole way down, 'twas I put the roof on that. You didn't know that.

JH I didn't know that, but I was looking at it, and it's a very good job, a strong job.

MJT You know yourself. You're a carpenter. There was a difference between the front wall and the back wall. The front wall was a foot wide and I never forget the back was only nine inches. I cut the roof across to suit the three inches, to get the right roof.

JH You done the hell of a good job of it.

MJT John Slattery came up to me here and asked me would I do it. And 'twas I cut the roof of John H.'s house and I felted it. I didn't slate it, but I got permission out of the Forestry to do it. You couldn't go out and work for anyone when you were working in a council job. I got permission from, I think Duncan was his name. He told me, 'Why not?' I spent eight days on John H.'s house, and that time 'twas a handsaw – there was no other thing. I was down the same time as we worked at the council – eight o'clock. And in eight days I had it up – purlines and everything. John and Michael was helping me. When it was done, he asked me would I stop and slate it with him and I said, 'I'm eight days at home at the job, and I have to go back to work.' 'Cause you'd break your time, if you're too long. I went back to work and I said, 'Wait till I work a week or a fortnight,' says I, 'and I'll give you a few days again.' But he hadn't patience.

Now, didn't I work everywhere in my time? Cobb's house, Jack Kelly's, I thatched that in spare time, in the evenings and Saturdays out of the job.

JH You were able to thatch!

MJT Oh, I was a great thatcher in my day. I done all Kylemore in my time. I served my time at that before I got into the Forestry. I thatched all Slattery's house, all the back of it, where there was a parlour. I done all that. I made bobs for the hayshed. When you make what they call a scallop to it, twist the straw like that, it ties the thatch down. I built this house here myself, in spare time.

JH I used to come over from England, and Michael-Joe'd be on it, and I'd come over the next year and Michael-Joe'd be on it again – further up.

MJT I was three years on it. I had nothing when I started it. I had only the week's pay for the job. Thirty-nine shillings when I started. At the time I built the house, I got £2/2/4d. for the week – a forty-eight-hour week. I'd my house paid for, except £20, when I'd finished. And it passed for a grant. I got two grants for it – my own leaving out – I never got anyone draw a plan, d'you know it?

JH It's a credit to you.

MJT I did every bit of this house, now. I plastered it and done all the carpentry work on it. I was working till one o'clock in the night, with a tilley lamp. A tilley lamp. Watson's house below. I sealed every bit of that road with a tilley lamp at night and went to the job the next day. I worked a lot in my time.

JH You had to cycle up to the forest.

MJT I started out and I had to cycle up as far as Derrygoolin, and I had to cycle back near the wasteland cross – go into Abbey, go down to Slattery's cross and go up to Marble Hill and then go up to Marble Hill Wood. And I planted the grove that's outside Marble Hill Wood. It doesn't belong to Marble Hill Wood. It's adjoining the wasteland cross. Oh my God, I used cycle there and leave here at half six in the morning.

That's where I found the stone axe. Marble Hill was all divided, but the ruins of the big house is there. The Burkes of Marble Hill owned it, and they'd their own chapel and all, in it. And in the troubled times, they set it on fire and they burnt it. That little chapel was left – the windows is broke in it, but it wasn't burned at all. I don't know who owns the ould ruins.

JH A fine building. A pity to burn it.

MJT Sure. Pallas, the big house below in Tynagh – that was a mighty building, too. There's nothing there now but a green field. There's some of the cut stones gone out on the Clonmoylan road. They drew them up from that big house and that was a mighty place. They knocked the big house and the land was all divided and farmers got farms in it, like. The Lord, as we'll call him, he used to keep th'ould tax, and he built a room to it. He'd every man for his own trade, the stonecutter was there working, and at that time that room, a simple room, cost, I never forgot it, £18,000. 'Twas the talk of the country that he had spent the £18,000.

JH God, that was big money!

MJT He had twenty-two men working on it. I was in it – 'twas a full mansion. 'Twas a fierce place. There were cellars and everything in it, like – you could look down – a fierce place. And there's nothing only a little track of where the house was. But th'ould castle and all is there. That's a bit of a scenery now, the castle in Pallas, and a big scenery. There's a big wall all around about it, and I think there's a balcony on the wall that's outside it, and Pallas castle is inside it the whole time.

JH Who owns that now?

MJT Well, there were families living all round it, you see, when the land was divided. I don't know who owns the castle. There's no roof on it or anything like that, you know. It's a big ould ruin.

JH It's got history to it, though.

MJT And the best of everything that was ever in a house was in Pallas. The best of furniture, now. What you'd call antique furniture. And that auction, Pallas House, is over about sixty years now. Since 'twas divided. I had a mantelpiece out of Pallas. That mantelpiece, I don't have it any more, now. But that's where that was bought – at th'auction. You seen that mantelpiece, didn't you?

JH I did. God, that was worth a lot, now.

MJT Oh, you'd pay big money for that, now.

JH But the man promised it to you, didn't he?

MJT I'll tell you how it happened. I was working for this man, I often worked for him, and I was working away and he just said to me, 'Would you know of anyone that would buy a nice mirror?' He had it surely about fifty years in the house. I had it about sixteen years only.

'You would never know,' says I. And he brought me into his shed and 'twas in the shed since that time. It was covered with – oh, a great cover. And I saw all the glass perfect and everything. 'Oh, Christ, that's worth money,' I says in my own mind. Says I, 'I'll be on the look-out for a buyer for you' like that.

I done nothing, but I went down and I measured my own mantelpiece there, to see what it would be from the bottom to the top. 'Twas a fraction – it grazed the ceiling. I'd a metal mantelpiece in it. Betty, the Lord have mercy on her, didn't want me to have anything to do with it. She said, 'All that's rubbish.' But I paid no heed to her and I went down on a bicycle and I went down to the house and I measured it and it was a bloody fit, you know.

'I have a buyer,' says I, 'for that mantelpiece if it's not too dear for it.' 'Who's the buyer?' he says. 'Well, it's myself. I'll give you a certain thing for it.' Which I would. 'If it's you that wants that mirror,' he said, 'come here next Tuesday night and you'll get it for nothing.' And I got it for nothing. And I'll never forget the bringing up of it. He got his motor car and trailer, and I'd to get into the trailer to hold it – I couldn't let go of it. And that's how we came up all the time.

JH He must have liked you. You done all the work for him, of course.

MJT I done a lot of work for him. He'd do anything for me all the time. But do you know what happened with him and the mirror? He went to the auction and he said he'd buy a mirror for the new house and when the house was made, there was all those small fireplaces in it and there was no mantel wanted over. He didn't put it in at all – left it in the shed.

JH All them houses belonged to the gentry. And they had the best of stuff in them.

MJT The best of stuff. That mirror was mahogany and all the back was panelled. The glass was in famous condition, perfect.

JH The antique fellows would go to them auctions. They must have got some great bargains.

MJT I'll tell you what wood is good for furniture. They use oak, but they make bowls of that wood called monkey puzzle. You never see wood from it, but you hear about it. That 'tis the world's best. You could make a stairs out of it, 'twould be lovely for a stairs. But there's a lot of knots. They'd be seen. If you see the prongs going out.

MJT The good old days, Jimmy.

JH Hard old days.

MJT You eating your lunch one side of the drain and I the other side. D'you think of that?

JH We'd left school and we got taken on.

MJT We got taken on by Tommy Coen and we were under age, too. I was cutting my pay in it. Me and himself were in it, making that drain in about five yards off of the road. Me and himself were inside shovelling – they were digging up the drain further up and we were behind shovelling it back farther. D'you remember? That was the first time I put on long breeches. I was told I'd get a job if I put on long breeches. The pay was fierce small and I was cutting my pay in it. You went to England, after. You were fairly young.

JH I was only – what? – eighteen.

MJT We were about sixteen then, I suppose. That was my first job, anyway, and very hard to get a job.

JH Very hard! Very hard to get a job! Very, very hard.

MJT Had we Saturday off? I don't think we had.

JH I don't think we had. A six-day week.

MJT We'd lunch with us, and you'd put your hand in your pocket and you'd have it ate before twelve o'clock. And you'd to go till six o'clock in th'evening. Hah?

JH Cuts of bread. Aye, cuts of bread and butter.

MJT You don't feel a lifetime going, and when you get older, time goes quicker. I think.

JH It does. Oh God, it does.

MJT When we were at school, we thought we'd never be at home.

JH That's right. We thought the holidays would never come. Especially, now I've travelled round, different places and that. But yourself and Robbie Watson and most of the farmers who all grew up in the same parish and carried on. Well, do you think that makes it seem longer? Than if you was moving around?

MJT I don't know. 'Tis all a puzzle. The time has gone.

JH The time has gone, aye.

JH Things was rough during the Emergency, as they called it, during the war, things was bad, wasn't they?

MJT Oh! What bad!

JH There was no building.

MJT There was no building and everything was rationed. Oh, leave it, so! No light, no paraffin oil, no tyres for your bike. You'd get a bit of bog deal and – there wouldn't be a range hardly, that time, in the house – put it in the fire and put a match to it and 'twould show you light, all right. 'Twould show you light for a long time. You'd get it in the bog. I often brought it up. You'd get a nice little log in it, but it was fierce dirty. 'Twas like paraffin oil, you know. You'd see it bubbling away. 'Twas full of oil.

JH Tom Slattery was telling us, he got bog oak – it was thirty foot long. He got it up with the digger, but as soon as it came up to the top, it rotted away. It cracked and fell in pieces.

MJT I remember John Slattery. I saw him going to school, but he was a bit older than me. He was a little before me. He could be a good scholar, though, because he could think of anything. He'd be able to tell you anything.

JH I can't remember Jack, my brother, all that well at school. He didn't play hurling, did he? He wasn't rough or anything.

MJT I remember him well and you should, too. And Joey and Davy. He wasn't the teacher's pet, though. There was no pets that time. Master Canning, we went to. He used to go on the booze now and again. Oh, he used.

JH Why wouldn't he?

MJT He used to fall asleep in the school, and he'd have his hat on him. He'd be sitting by the fire – that's the new school, now. This day didn't he fall asleep. You knew the twin Morans, didn't you?

JH Yes.

MJT Well, one of them, she went up and – I don't know where she got them – she put ten or twelve nuts around and about the brink of his hat. And there was a candle put lighting on his hat, as well, a small bit of a candle. And he was still asleep. And she came back to the desk. And there was a big duster, do you know, that you'd wipe the board with, and she stood up her full length and she let fly at the board and she knocked it down and it made a fierce noise – the noise of it was all over the school. Well, we all paid for it. He got up and he murdered everyone that was in the school. Were you there, Jimmy?

JH No. I wasn't at the new school. I can't remember being in the new school. I seen it built but I wasn't in it, or if I was it wasn't long. I think that was 1924.

MJT He stood up and the candle quenched and he got a big rod and he murdered every one of us. He murdered the whole school.

JH Well, why wouldn't he? You all knew who done it, sure.

MJT It was one of the Morans, they were twins.

[*The clocks start to chime. There are five clocks in Michael-Joe's little kitchen.*]

JH You're not short of clocks, Michael-Joe.

MJT I have clocks in every room. I have clocks up in th'other room, too. I was always interested in clocks. I used to repair alarm clocks in my time.

JH What don't you do! You make bodhráns and cut hair and play the fiddle and play the whistle and thatch and build and cut turf and sing and do fencing and go gardens.

MJT I'm what they call a *goban*. What they call them sort of lads, that knows everything and don't know it at all.

I'll tell you about the best wedding I was ever at. Myself and Tom and Bridgie Goonan went down. That same Bridgie lived to be 104. I brought a fiddle under me arm, and it was held all night, abroad in the big store. I was never at a wedding in my life as good. I came up in the morning around four o'clock – it was going all night. There was a fierce crowd in it. That's a nice start ago now. A real country wedding.

As the lass says, 'hapes of drink'. Everything you wanted. I'm telling the truth, now, you see. I never was at anything as good. I was at country weddings everywhere – that was the best I was ever at: John Slattery's wedding. Drink! Anything you want – whiskey, stout, beer. If I'm not mistaken a half barrel or a quarter barrel. Mugs of stout. 'Twas a famous night. And a turkey supper, as far as I think. Every type of cake that was ever made was there. There was two tables in it. One batch would go in and they'd come out to the dancing again, d'you understand?

Music? Me and H. in Tiernascragh. He was a great fiddler. And me and an accordion player. I was playing the fiddle at that time, not the whistle. Oh, 'twas a famous night. What were they wearing? Dare I say that John Slattery was in a navy blue suit, and Mary, the wife, wore a big, long dress down to the ground.

Now, I'm going to sing you a song about the Four Youths of Clare. This song, they don't even have down in Clare, the half of them. I got two-thirds of it, the ballad of it. I was about three year looking for the rest of it. D'you know where I had to go? I heard of an old man had it, back to Ballinakill. Harry Nevills. He had the whole song. I had two-thirds of it and I had it right, too! 'Twas no good when you hadn't it all. Sure, every bit of it is true, and sure they're buried above in Scarriff in the chapel yard, and there's a monument in Killaloe. If you're crossing the bridge, you'll see the big square on the bridge, halfways down, as far as I think. 'Tis a big thing, like and 'tis all Irish written on it. In memory of them. On the bridge where they were shot.

About Egan, now. You'll hear me mentioning him in the song. I'll tell you about Egan, now. He was minding that house in Williamstown and the three that was there on the run – two of them from Scarriff and I think one from Loughrea, like. They passed up here. It was Sunday evening, and they bought jam and a loaf – a pot of jam – at the cross, Power's Cross, passing up. They were on the run – on the run, you know, from the Tans. They arranged with him to stop with him for the night at Williamstown. So they went on up and they went to him, of course. But they were surrounded off of the Shannon at four o'clock in the morning. They were spied on. And the Tans came in (the Black and Tans they were called), they came round about and surrounded the house.

Egan, you can hear him mentioned in the song, now, they quizzed him up as well, d'you see, and he would give them no information, and they brought him along with them and shot him as well. That made the four youths, you see. The three of them were on the run, but Egan was minding the house and they brought him as well, and shot him as well.

[Michael-Joe composes himself and sings the entire song without stumble or pause. It will help to know that 'Killaloe' rhymes with 'billet-doux', and that 'Ogonelloe' rhymes with 'They've gone below'.]

The deadly news through Ireland spread and it ran from shore to shore
Oh, such a deed no living man has ever heard before.
Coarse Cromwell in his day no worse than it would do
Than the Black and Tans that murdered those four youths in Killaloe.

Three of the four were on the run and searched for all around,
'Tis with that hero Egan that morning they were found.
When asked if they were in his house, to the rebels he did prove true
And because he would not sell the past, he was shot in Killaloe.

The sixteenth of November, boys, in history will go down.
They were tracked that day through Galway to that house in Williamstown.
They got no time to make a fight, they were captured in their sleep,
And the way they were ill-treated would cause your blood to creep.

They handcuffed them, both hands and feet, with ties you could not break,
And brought them on to Killaloe in a boat upon the lake.
Without clergyman, judge or jury, on the bridge they were shot down,
And their blood flows with the Shannon, adjacent to the town.

Alfie Rodgers

Michael Egan

Brud Mc Mahon

Martin Gildea

The four youths killed on the bridge at Killaloe.

They threw them in a lorry like timber in a heap,
And brought them back to the barrack-yard, there two nights they did keep,
They kept them closely guarded and let no one in to see,
Not even those who reared them from their infancy.

By faith and perseverance, the third day they let them go.
Their funerals at 10 p.m. passed through Ogonelloe.
If you were at their funerals, it was a lovely sight
For to see one hundred clergy, and they all robed out in white.

It was on to Scarriff chapel for two nights and a day
And in the graves where they do lie, good Christians, for them pray.
The day is fast approaching when we will clear the Saxon crew
And have revenge for those who murdered the four youths in Killaloe.

'Tis a bit of history, now. Going back, because it really happened. Who betrayed them? 'Twas a girl that spied on them, 'twasn't a man. They say 'twas a girl from Whitegate. That's what they said, anyway. I don't know. You wouldn't be sure.... But how did they come on the lake! [*How sly they were!*]

There's a quay fornent it. There's two quays in Williamstown. It's a real old house, now. A big, two-storey old house.

Was I too young to know the Tans? Sure, I think of the Tans! What age was I in 1918? Five! They used to go up and down the road there in the lorries, sure. They used to fire shots there in the woods, for fear they'd be ambushed. I think of it well. I'm the only one that thinks of the Tans around here, now.

You see, English laws was running Ireland at that time. We had th'ould peelers there then, as we called them. And the Tans were sent over then. They done brutal things, the Tans. They tied some lads, tied them to a lorry and dragged them to death behind in Gort. As you go into Gort, they shot a mother and she had a baby in her arms, outside the door, and they shot her son dead outside the door. What are you talking about! They were fierce. All that happened. 'Twas terrible. You wouldn't be sure of your life. You couldn't go out on the road, sure.

Eamon Kelly

born 30th March 1914

Eamon Kelly has had a long and distinguished career as an actor, despite coming to the profession relatively late, and his resonant Kerry voice is instantly recognizable. One of the highlights of his career was being invited to create the role of the father in Brian Friel's early play, Philadelphia Here I Come!, *which won him international acclaim. He lives in Dublin with his wife Maura, an actress, whom he met when they were both members of the Listowel Drama Group.*

WHAT DOES an actor have to do? One time a director said, 'Be on time and know your lines.' Yeah. So that's what I did. I could learn my lines very quickly – I was what they call a 'good study'.

My name is Eamon Kelly, one 'n', as in Eamon de Valera, the President, one of the first leaders of our country after the revolution. Eamonn Andrews had two 'n's – he could afford it – I couldn't.

I began acting in my thirties – in amateur dramatics. Before that, when I was a young man, I went to night school and trained as a teacher of woodwork and I spent ten years teaching.

My father was in the building business in a general way – he was a building contractor in a small way. He could lay blocks – he was part mason, he was a slater, he was a plasterer – he'd plaster the walls and ceilings, he was a painter – he was capable of painting the house as well. When you were living in the country there weren't people specializing in those things. He was a Jack-of-all-trades. And so I did all those things.

Woodwork is a very creative sort of thing. A carpenter sometimes has a drawing for whatever piece of work he's doing, and he has to think it out in his head. If he's making a table, he'll be wondering where the mortices should go, and the crosspieces. When he'd finished and he'd look at a thing he'd made, my father had an obvious relish in what he'd done.

And I worked at it, too. There are houses in Kerry – a very few – that I made myself, from the very foundations up to the roof.

I had left national school, primary school, when I was about 14. I had a lot to learn. I went to night school and I did a scholarship and came to Dublin and trained for two years as a teacher of woodwork.

J. J. O'Connor was in charge of us. He was large, with a pock-marked face and a bulbous nose, a goo-goo eye, and he was bald, with a wisp of hair that never stayed down on his head, but stood up like a cockscomb, and he had a bristly moustache.

I remember when we had an eclipse of the moon, and he filled the blackboard with the stars and their courses. A very interesting man. He was widely read and often talked about Frank O'Connor and Seán Ó'Faoláin, whom he knew. He was stone mad on Shakespeare. When one of us students mutilated a piece of work, J. J. would take the piece and intone:

> *O, pardon me, thou bleeding piece of earth,*
> *That I am meek and gentle with these butchers!*
> *Thou art the ruins of the noblest man*
> *That ever lived in the tide of times.*

He was a born actor, of course, and when he was reciting, his voice would often rise to such a terrifying climax that passing professors would look in at the door to see what was wrong.

One day he made a collection and put in some money himself, and I was despatched down to Fred Hanna's bookshop to get twenty-one copies of *The Merchant of Venice*, which cost 6d. each in the Penguin series. Then in the middle of the woodshavings, sawdust and chips, we sat down to read it. I remember reading the part of the elder Gobbo, while two refined Corkmen were cast as Portia and Nerissa. When the mood moved him, whatever work we were engaged in, J. J. got us to read Shakespeare. He fancied himself as an actor, and often used to give us a blast of Falstaff.

Of course, reciting Shakespeare was a useful exercise for young men who would have to stand before a class, and to improve our voices further, he would herd us along once a week to the storeroom, where we kept the timber. He installed a piano there, and he would get us to sing sea shanties. He sang shantyman himself in a deep, salty voice, while we joined in the chorus.

J. J.	*King Louis was the King of France*
	Before the Revolution
Students	*Away! Haul away! Haul away, Joe!*
J. J.	*King Louis had his head cut off*
	Which spoiled his constitution!
Students	*Away! Haul away! Haul away, Joe!*

J. J. claimed that Dublin was awash with philistines, and so to rescue us from that sad state he would guide our reading and send us to good films and to the theatre. I have a lot to thank him for.

After two years I went back to the country, where I spent ten years teaching in a technical school. A teacher is not so far from what I do now. A teacher, to be a good teacher, has to be an actor. He has to be able to bring what he is saying, bring it alive to the students. Otherwise the students will simply go to sleep.

It was the greatest piece of luck that I was sent teaching in Listowel, County Kerry, for there was an amateur society there, run by Bryan MacMahon, very famous although now he is dead, and he was a great influence on me. He ran a small library called the Argosy Library, and when I went in to put my name down, he said, 'Didn't I hear that name called out on the radio the other night?' He did. Austin Clarke had held a poetry competition and I sent a poem in. I didn't win. Like the mongrel at the dog show, I was highly commended.

Anyway, Bryan MacMahon wrote plays for the Abbey [*Theatre, Dublin*] and even directed plays for them. And he taught me a great deal. He wanted to spend more time with his writing, so I had the experience, you see, not just of acting in plays but of directing them. At that time there were various drama festivals and we got a prize for the best play – in fact we won at various festivals. I remember one was called *The Troubled Bachelor*, and I was a bachelor myself at the time.

It happened that RTE took an interest in us, and some of the plays we did were broadcast. Through that, I had made some money, and around that time I married Maura O'Sullivan. She was one of the Listowel Drama Group, and we both got places in the RTE Players, a repertory company, where I stayed for twelve years. I recall we were in a play called *Michaelmas Eve*, by T. C. Murray. I played the servant boy and Maura was the servant girl, and there was a line in it: 'I could strangle and choke you!' We were rehearsing the play on the top floor of a house where we were staying, and the old couple who owned the house were in the hallway below. When they heard this line they came up the stairs and as we opened the door there they were, wondering whether there would be murder in the house.

Yes, I was twelve years behind a microphone, which was ironic, if you look back on it, after a whole lifetime almost on the stage, to be twelve years hidden from the audience.

While I was engaged in that, I became very widely known as a storyteller. One night on Radio 1, Tyrone Guthrie did a production of *Peer Gynt*, and afterwards we had a party. Someone in the company asked me for a party piece, and I told a story. Micheál Ó'Heithir heard it and he put me into *Take The Floor* with Din-Joe, a very popular programme at the time. From there I got letters from all over the country and I got material by the post that I was able to use.

Then I had my own programme on the radio – it was called *The Rambling House*, set in a country house at night, after the ones I knew in Kerry, with people coming in looking for news, songs and stories. My father's house was a rambling house. Men would go to the fair or a wake and they'd make a story out of it. I remember my mother hunting me off to bed, but I'd listen to what I could.

My earliest memory is of my father putting new shoes on me and I sitting on his knee. Well, my head fell on his waistcoat and I smelled the tobacco. He used to keep a pipe in a pocket of the waistcoat.

Another early memory was of the Black and Tans. It was at night-time and my father was away; my mother was alone with us children, and you'd hear the lorries coming. She'd raise her hand to the light so the place would be dark and we'd go under the table. We'd hear the lorry go chug, chug, chug, and we'd hold our breath until we heard it going away.

I remember, too, my first day at school. I was seven when I went to school. I was a delicate child and my mother wondered if she'd ever rear me. The teacher asked me why I hadn't gone to school before. I said I was waiting until the war would be over. And it was a war. Around that time, two Republican soldiers marched along outside the school and the boys would be putting their hands through the railings to touch the rifles. Some time later, we heard shots. Those soldiers fired on the Free State Army and one of them was shot. He went into a house and he hid under the stairs, but the Free State Army came and found him and pulled him out and put him against a wall and shot him. His name was Mick Sullivan, and one of the teachers knew him. She was crying and was terribly upset. The whole country was very divided between the Free Staters and the Republicans. We used to fight along the road home from school.

Well, back we go to *The Rambling House*. This was back in the 1950s. It used to be broadcast in the evening time, maybe on a Saturday evening and repeated on Sunday after lunch. Here's one of the stories, called *The Tayman*.

I'm bringing you back now to the time when tea was introduced into Ireland, and the Irish people took to it like ducks to water. Well, it was not available in the shops when it came out first, but men used to go around from house to house in a pony and trap, selling the tea, and they were called 'taymen'.

Now, it so happened that a tayman put up with a husband and wife in a single-roomed house in which there was only one bed, and he wouldn't have put up in that house at all that night, the tayman, only it was so wet and stormy he couldn't get to his own lodgings. Now, he put the pony into a makeshift shed that was at the gable of the house outside, and when he went in, the young woman of the house, she had taken up a cake of bread out of the oven and she brought the cake of bread across the floor and she put it up over a shelf of the dresser. Oh, there it was – a beautiful wheel of bread, with a cross on it like the four spokes that you see on a wheel. And the lovely aroma that was from that cake! Oh, the tayman's nostrils...you could see him...[*sniffs*]...and you know that his teeth were swimming inside in his mouth for a taste of it. And she, seeing the hungry look on his face, she was going to break a piece off the cake and give it to him, but the husband said, 'No!' He said, 'You'll only ruin the cake, now, if you break it while 'tis hot, so can't you wait until morning like the rest of us?'

Well, that was that. There's no good going to argue with a cranky husband. They all knelt down and they said their prayers and they all got into bed, the one bed. The wife got into near the wall, the husband got in next to her and then the tayman got in on th'outside. God knows, and that was a narrow enough bed, too, and when one of them would turn, they'd *all* have to turn.

In the course of the night, you know, when the husband had to go out (he suffered from a little frequency – that runs in families) and when he'd go out in the yard, he'd bring the wife out with him because he was jealous to let the wife in the bed with the tayman. And she kicked up going out into the cold, stormy night. Moreover, as she said herself, when she didn't have occasion to go out. And finally, she kicked up altogether and wouldn't go out any more. And then, what the husband did, he'd lift up the heavy cradle with the child inside in it and put the cradle down in the bed between the wife and the tayman, then he'd go off out in the yard. And when he'd come back in again, after shedding the tear for Parnell, he'd lift up the cradle and put it back down on the floor and then get into the middle of the bed. Well, the busy night he had!

About four o'clock in the morning, the storm began to rise and he heard it blowing off the roof of the shed outside the gable of the house and he forgot all about it (like, one danger will make you forget the first danger, you know, when you cut your finger, you'll forget your toothache), he forgot all about the tayman, and hopped out of the bed and went out to tie down the shed.

And when he was gone, the wife turned to the tayman and she said, 'Now's your chance!' So he got up and he ate the cake.

And here's another.

A man went into the town to buy a bucket and the horse he had was very giddy. Well, he went inside, anyway, but the horse broke loose and went away up the street, and he ran out after it, with the bucket still in his hand, and they thought he was stealing it. He was up in court and it was in the papers and everybody read about it. The whole family was shamed. The wife's sister, home from Massachusetts, was ashamed, and after that the wife kept an eye on him. She banned him from going into town. But then it was getting near Christmas and he was let go to get some things, but he was late coming home. 'What kept you?' 'I was at confession.' 'I hope you told him about the bucket.' 'Oh, don't you know well,' he said, 'he saw that in the paper!'

Those were great times, but then opportunity came to go out on the stage, and I took that. I took a part in a play by a very famous writer, Brian Friel – *Philadelphia Here I Come!* One of the great satisfactions in working on the stage, one of the few times in your life when you get the opportunity to *create* a character – you're the first to play a part. I was the first to do the father in that play. The play was so successful here in Ireland that it went to Broadway, and I was twelve months on Broadway playing in it. I was fifty years of age and never been outside of Ireland before. I was sitting in the 'plane with Brian Friel on the way out and he gave me an idea of New York, the avenues going one way and the streets the other, on the grid system.

Many of the Irish in New York came to see me because I was a neighbour's child – they'd never been to a play before in their lives. One of my aunts was married to a cop of Italian extraction and with him was a cop of Irish extraction. American cops are festooned with flashlights and parking tickets and revolvers and batons, and these cops came backstage to see me in the afternoon. I had a little drop of Paddy in my locker and after we'd had a drop, I suggested they put the handcuffs on me and march me out of the theatre. So they did, with the sirens screeching and all the company standing there watching me. How were they going to put the play on tonight with one of the actors in jail? Were they relieved when I rang them to say I'd be there all right!

After Broadway, *Philadelphia Here I Come!* toured in the USA for six weeks, we went to the West End: the Lyric Theatre in Shaftesbury Avenue. That was a great start for my first venture on the stage. That was 1966, and I was nominated for the Tony Awards – four actors only were nominated in the entire season, so it was a great honour.

Philadelphia Here I Come! was first put on at the Gate Theatre in Dublin. Hilton Edwards was the director. He'd ask you to come and read a part, and when he asked me to take it, I said to myself, 'Such a small part.' The thing about Friel, though, is that it's what is between the lines – not so much what is said.

We rehearsed *Philadelphia Here I Come!* in the bar space in the Gaiety Theatre for three weeks, which was considered adequate time for the preparation of a show in those days. I was playing with Donal Donnelly and Patrick Bedford as the private and public sides of Gar O'Donnell. Maureen O'Sullivan was the housekeeper, and I was S. B. O'Donnell (known as 'Screwballs' to the private Gar), owner of the shop, county councillor and father of Gar. I was able to play the part of the father because I could draw from experience. That lack of communication in families – it's an Irish characteristic. Particularly among people who are

Eamon Kelly early in his acting career.

closely related. When there is a third or fourth person in the company, people often speak to their relation *through* the company.

Old S. B. O'Donnell – his love for his son is so apparent through the play. But he was so tied up he couldn't speak it. Several people came to me afterwards and said, 'My father and I were so much like that.' That man was not close to my own father, but close to a man who lived beside me. This man was very silent. His son was going to America, and he never spoke to him about it. The day he was going, the son crossed the room, and he never looked at him. The father didn't want him to go, you see. The son stopped and looked back at him and the father just said, 'You'll be sorry yet.' He shut the door and went away.

The central thing in the play is that the son wanted him to remember a day they spent in a boat together. The father remembers another incident entirely. Brian Friel – it meant a lot to have him in at the rehearsals. I think it's a very good thing to have the author sit in at a play.

The play was presented at the Gaiety Theatre as part of the Dublin Theatre Festival. The previous play ended its run on the Saturday and even though it contained a full-size threshing machine, they struck the set and the next morning the split-level scene of room and kitchen was erected. Hilton Edwards lit it during the day and by the Monday morning we had the technical run-through. That afternoon, we had our dress rehearsal and we went on stage that night – Monday 28th September 1964. All I can remember now is the curtain call. We received thunderous applause and we held the line and bowed until the audience's hands were sore.

My role did go well. I was surprised myself that it worked so well. When you create an atmosphere in a tragic or a moving part by means of your voice, by means of the way things are directed, there is a sense of silence coming from the audience. You bring the audience to that position. *You mustn't give way* – the actor mustn't let his emotion overwhelm him, in his voice, his body language. He must reach a certain pitch and sustain it. You also get great satisfaction from hearing people laugh. There's true satisfaction when someone in the audience gasps or someone is crying because of what you said. Soul to soul.

I was in Shakespeare at the Gate recently. I'm on stage not as frequently as the old days, but I had some comedy lines and they worked brilliantly for me – they worked as well as at any time in my career.

Audiences are very individual. When all the people are seated together it feels to the actors as if they are one unit. The Abbey has been bringing back matinees for the last three or four years, and the matinee audience is usually smaller and better than the night audience. They are dedicated people who attend it, usually, not what we call a paper audience, where the management has invited people to attend, giving them free tickets.

My family were never involved in the theatre. My mother could never understand why I wanted to give up the woodwork teaching. A good position with a pension. But I gave it up and worked for half the salary I'd been getting. I wanted to see if any part of the family had run away with the circus. The only time I would have ever seen the theatre was when it was on tour. I remember I was teaching at the time and I went to see O'Casey's *Juno and the Paycock* in Caherciveen. I left the theatre alone. I was so affected by the tragedy of the family, I walked out on the road for a long time, to be by myself and think it over. That was the power of the theatre. It was a travelling company working on unsuitable stages in very unsuitable halls. And it had an everlasting effect on me. I wrote to O'Casey. He didn't write back to me.

I grew up in Kerry, in the country, and that had a deep effect on the way I speak – not just the accent. Some phrases I would hear my mother say. Some of the language was that way familiar. My mother was very poetic. She had only national school, but she remembered poems she learned in school and she'd use them. If the wind banged a door, she'd say,

> *Tonight will be a stormy night*
> *And you to the town must go.*
> *And take a lantern, child,*
> *To guide your father through the snow.*

Three or four of us used to meet in Dublin for coffee some ten or twenty years ago. In the course of conversation we'd recite a verse of poetry – it stayed with us. My mother used to sing, too.

A lot of us in the Abbey had that background of poetry, and it was with the Abbey that I went to do a play with the Moscow Arts Theatre group – in Leningrad and Moscow. It was directed by Ben Barnes, the present director of the Abbey. It was John B. Keane's *The Field*, and my wife Maura and I were to play Mr and Mrs Dandy McCabe. We set off for Russia in February 1988 and while we were at Shannon Airport, I was interviewed by the media. 'And how do you feel now, Eamon, going to play in the Moscow Arts Theatre?' 'I feel,' said I, 'like an old Kerry priest going to say Mass in the Vatican.' It was a tremendous experience to play there, where the great actors played. I had a little song to sing, I recall. It is called 'The Poor Blind Boy' and it wasn't in the first script at all. I got it from the Cork production. It's sung to the air of *Teddy O'Neill*. The first verse is:

She's left the old field where he played as a baby
The little white cottage that lies by the sea,
The cradle that rocked him is lonesome and shady
As she thinks of those days that were never to be.

And later on,

Far from each other, she cries for her loved one,
By night and by morning since ever he died,
She walks through the field where the cold moon shines down
As she thinks of the fate of the poor blind boy.

The Russian audiences were absolutely wonderful – you could feel the tension from across the footlights. We met Natasha, a brilliant young woman who was our interpreter. The script was translated into Russian and by the seats the audiences had earphones, so that they saw and heard what we were doing as well as hearing the translation. We were there during 1988, when they hadn't yet thrown off the Communist robe.

Leningrad struck me because it had so little traffic. It was like a Western city. We saw cities and buildings built in relation to human beings, not to cars. The Russians were very warm and good – human. To think what they suffered. Hitler bombed them so terribly. Moscow is very different from Leningrad. It's more of an Eastern city. The dome of Saint Basil's Cathedral in Red Square has been likened to an angel holding onions in the sky. I was fortunate to see it without the neon signs, without the McDonalds and other things. It was a view of what Dublin would have looked like in the 1920s and early '30s. No light except the Red Star above the Kremlin.

I don't remember an actual *seanchaí*. But when people came visiting the house, the men would come and sit down and talk. They would tell it as a story, whatever it was, if they'd been to market, a wedding, a wake, whatever it was. When we went to learn Irish in south Kerry we heard the old storytellers, and they impressed me very much.

The first storytellers arose when men were living in caves. One man would sit around at night and tell his adventures of the day. The Red Indians would tell stories. I believe the Arabs and the Irish are the best storytellers. The Jews are good storytellers, too – look at the two Testaments.

Kerry has produced a good lot of writers, both in Irish and English. I learned a lot by being there. There's a feeling for tradition. And you get a ready audience. Storytelling in Ireland is different from in England. In Ireland, the storytellers were addressing the adults.

I have a distinctive voice, it's true. It's a great advantage in many character parts on stage. I could relate to people I knew, nearly always. I was able to pull out of my own experience and life. I was strong at that, but I was not good as a mimic.

One of my early loves was *The Well of the Saints*, by Synge. He is one of the authors I find most interesting, most valuable. I played Christy in *The Playboy of the Western World* when I was very young. In *The Well of the Saints* there are two blind beggars who believed themselves to be beautiful people. Country people had fun with them, but then their sight is restored and they are absolutely appalled at their appearance. He had seen her with golden hair and blue eyes and she the same – saw him as beautiful. And when the sight is restored she sees this little old fellow. I used very much my own voice in that play.

I have always been able to draw on the language I heard around me when I was growing up. There was the gramophone, where I heard mostly Irish songs. But I was hearing the language of a closed community, with all its richness. The language spoken since then has had many more influences on it. But if it didn't change, that would be strange. It is a natural thing for fashions to change. Change is life.

I love living in Ireland. It has a wonderful climate. We don't have extremes. I was in Canada – up in Newfoundland – where the cold is terrible. The following week I was in Texas and the heat was melting. In Ireland, I like to go to the pub. The actor is very much like the performer in the circus. When the monkey or the elephant does his trick, the circus-master has a little titbit in his fist to reward him. When the actor has finished, he looks forward to go across the street to the pub and have a pint. That's like the little titbit the circus-master gives the performer. I am an actor, and I'm retired until the next phone call.

Tommy Hanley

born 9th April 1917

At first glance, it is easy to miss the fact that Tommy Hanley, with his striking head of snow-white hair, is now blind. He carries a stick, but only in the way many countrymen do. The jut of his chin and his eager cross-examination of all comers bear witness to his delight in company and his pleasure in challenging others, just to elicit a reaction. While he talks away indefatigably, his wife looks on with quiet dignity and calm. His old friend Jim Hickey joins in the conversation from time to time.

TAKE OFF YOUR COAT, now. Don't worry, I'm not going to fight you – I'm too warm. Sit there, now. I'm the chairman and [*pointing to his wife, whom he usually calls 'Mam'*] she's the vice-chairman.

I'll tell you about the time Slattery and me went up to the funeral. [*The funeral of Sean MacBride, son of Maude Gonne MacBride, for whom Yeats nursed an unrequited love.*]

On 1st May 1890, our people were evicted and they come on here to Dillon's field to the huts. Maude Gonne MacBride was a maiden at this time. The following Christmas Eve, there was a Doctor Tully, up here, at Bugler's; he served for the local politician, as such. And Maude Gonne MacBride took an awful interest in the evictions, same as you'd go to Bosnia or Kosovo now, or that. And Christmas Eve she came and she had a train – d'ye know what a train is? – and Doctor Tully was holding it up in the puddle, and there was half doors in all the huts, the same as the one out there, and she gave them a ten-shilling note each. The Kennys, the Burkes and the Hanleys and Hallorans, was four huts. And next day they sent somebody with an ass to Woodford and he brought them a quarter barrel of Guinness among all the other things, because, like, two quid would make a Christmas for a prince, that time.

But, anyway, I had that told so often I began to take notice of Sean MacBride up and down the years. Her son, ye know. She married Major MacBride. And the next thing was, anyway, he tried

The eviction of a family in the 1840s. Note the destruction of the thatched roof and the fixed bayonets.

politics a while and next thing he was old, like us all, and John Slattery come in this night. He says, 'MacBride is dead,' he says. 'I heard that,' says he. And says I, 'Will you come bury him?' 'Ah, Jasus!' He thought I was codding him, you know, and he kicks the shoe.

But anyway, a cup of tea and th'ould pipe and he'd leave around ten, and I'd go out with him and vet the weather. I said, 'John, we'll bury him in the morning, around eight.' 'What do you mean?' he says. 'We'll go up there, we're not too busy,' says I. ('Twas February, and the lads [*Tommy's sons*] were here to fodder, and there was no work as such [*for Tommy, so he could take the day off*].)

And we had a little VW, a Golf, a lovely little handy-sized red car, driving well at this time. My bould Slattery was ready with the pipe, and sat in. Arrived in Ballinasloe – parked behind the back of the station, no bother, locked her. And we both had travel passes, presented them to the railway man, he gave us two tickets.

When was this? More than ten years ago. I'm blind ten, and I was driving well that time. [*To his wife*] Twelve, fifteen years, is it, Mam? Fifteen years ago, now, I'd say.

But anyway, we sat in, and I had on th'ould hat – like this, ye see – and John had one, and we were sitting. And she was jug-a-jug-a-jug up along the Midlands, not going too fast. This fellow tapped me on the shoulder. He says, 'Are ye brothers?'

'We are,' says I, in a flash. 'We're twins, and I'm the youngest!' [*Laughter*]

(Slattery:) 'Who are you?'

'I'm Joyce,' he says, 'from Oughterard. Where the hell are ye going?'

'I'm going to a funeral.'

'Go back, you,' he says to me. 'Come out here,' says he to Joyce. I was evicted! There wasn't many on the train, anyway, that morning, like, 'twas a crisp morning. But I sent th'lad out to him, anyway, and he was something like ourselves. 'Twas the memories Slattery was after.

Anyway, we got out at Amiens Street Station. And any fellow with a uniform on the railways is helpful, and I popped across. 'What is th'ould bus for Glasnevin Cemetery?' 'Number seventeen,' he says. 'Straight across there.' On my oath, when I had ould Slattery installed in the bus, I didn't give a pin. And next thing, he sat in beside this lassie. I dunno, the devil! He had a chat with her.

Anyway, up to Glasnevin and we were early. They were in the Pro-Cathedral. There was a big ballyhoo there, but we got to the cemetery before that. We by-passed the church. And we went through Glasnevin. All the great ones – de Valera, Cathal Brugha – talk of who you will. There's an eternal flame flickering there – that's a Republican plot. And there's a great big rock, Dublin Mountain rock, de Valera's name on it.

But anyway, next thing, the hearse landed in – there wasn't all that big a crowd in it from the Pro-Cathedral – that was all television, the lot. But the grave was opened and the coffin lowered. Anyway, Tiernan MacBride was a son – he read a poem. 'Twas a Yeats poem. But the next thing, they were finishing up and this fellow comes across.

'I can tell by the cut of your coats and your boots that ye've come up from the country.' He knew well we were culchies, ye know. Tim Pat Coogan. 'Ye're welcome to Glasnevin,' he says. 'Ye came a bit.' 'It's a mild way of saying it,' I says. But anyway, he says 'How are you?' We said, 'We're from Galway. We want to pay a little debt.' 'How?' he says. Says I, 'His mother gave our people a donation, the time of the evictions.' And he was reaching for a book. Says I, 'Leave up that now, because...' He was going to write it. So anyway, we chatted away. He was a nice man, though! He was a nice fellow, but he was mad to make an article out of it.

But anyway, in an ould bus and back, and there was – 'twouldn't be a full hotel – a take-away, a nice, decent place, near Heuston Station. I said if we had our bit of grub got that we'd be independent. But hadn't they the seats and the tables bolted to the floor! And you see, everybody wants to pull in to the table when they're eating. And Slattery started [*mimes trying to shunt the chair forward*] at the chair. 'Jasus!' And that wouldn't give, and he caught th'ould table and that wouldn't give! Well, Jimmy, I laughed! I was afraid to laugh at him, but I laughed in there now, for ages.

JH Well now, that happened to me, as well! The same place! Up near Heuston Station. On the quays. The father was with us, Helen and me, after the war. (He hadn't been to Ireland for years and years, and me and Helen called on him that night, thinking he'd be ready. He had nothing packed at all. 'Are we really going to Ireland?' he says. Couldn't believe it. We got him geared up and we went over on the boat, of course. Overnight.)

And we landed into Westland Row next morning and went to have something to eat, you know. There was an ould hotel there. The father, he wasn't used to any... There was an ould waiter there, looking rough – he'd had a bad night, I suppose. An ould, a greasy ould suit coat on him. And my father was calling him 'Sir'! Anyway, we had to put the day in, because the bus didn't go down till six o'clock in the evening.

Well, when we'd been walking a while, we tried to get somewhere to eat, you know, but everywhere we went it was too posh for my father. 'Tut, tut,' says my dad. 'We can't go in there. Keep going. Oh, Christ! We can't go in there!' Too posh. In the end we finished up along the quays there, up near Heuston Station, and there was fish and chips and pie and chips and sausage and chips. That was alright. We done the same as you, we went in and sat down. And when we went to pick up the knives and forks, they were on chains! They were chained to the table, and the table was bolted to the floor, and the chairs the same, as you said!

Well, that suited my father, that place, because it wasn't too grand, you see. And I said to the man, 'What the hell is all this about?' 'Ah,' he says [*in a thick Dublin accent*], 'Now, the kind of people that comes in here,' he says 'they'd pick the tables and chairs up and throw them in the Liffey across the road!' I remember that!

TH I said to the fellow we'd have tea and cakes. Slattery was running after the lad with the money, afraid he wouldn't get to pay for it in time. 'Come here!' I said 'Will you sit down? We have to take it first.'

We had a grand voyage home, and, believe me, I got him in above at Slattery's around nine that night. Mission accomplished. Got back here and none of the neighbours even missed me.

Jimmy, if you want to do a thing, you can do it. If you believe in it, ye'll do it. You can only bury a person the one day. There's no second chance.

JH You did the right thing.

TH Now, it was unusual at that time to drive, but if you want to know who taught me, well, listen to me. Hunger! I learned to drive a car in 1956. Paddy Kemple had one and I learned in a few days. No lessons. I was driving along and I did something at the point o'th'wood, and didn't she go faster? So I thought I'd do that again. After that I was flying it.

I remember I had a load of cattle, or was it sheep? I was at the fair in Banagher and I had to go to Listowel, ninety-two miles away. It was foggy enough, and I had a heavy old topcoat on me. The load was paid for. And I had a bit of an ould dinner and went out again. Still foggy. Christ, Jimmy, I couldn't see. So I pulled in to the side and the gardai came along. A lad caught me. 'Get out, you. You're drunk!' I looked for his superior officer – three stripes – and I said, 'I want you a second, sergeant.'

'What's the problem?'

'Excuse me, sergeant, I want you to witness a statement. This man here accused me twice of being drunk and I never took a drop in my life. I'm on the Pioneer Council.'

'Apologize to that man.'

'Oh,' he said 'I thought you were drunk.'

You see how it happens so easy?

I remember th'ould police in England. Th'ould country cop in Bridgwater, he was lovely. Loved the people, he did. Ah, they're grand people in that part. Old-fashioned. One old fellow, he said to me, 'I bain't goin' to tell ye no lies.' That's what he said! 'I bain't goin' to tell ye no lies.' In Somerset the girls are nearly all blondies, because they are so close to France.

I was there in England during the war. And summer days there, we were looking out for the big Heinkel bombers. And an incendiary bomb – 'twas like a bottle of gas upside down. Every town of any size bought a Spitfire. A Spitfire cost about £5,000. ARP – that meant Air Raid Precautions. But the defences we had, they were slow to use. Oh, the war. And in France there was poor old Pétain – he was the Prime Minister. He was as weak as water.

I remember looking at farms in France. We forgot more than they ever learned. But they work. Machinery, now. This man is one of five that take shares in it. They bloody share it. Not like Irishmen, going into debt. You have a machine, say, and it's milling rain on Wednesday and you can't use it. Where's the sense in that?

When I was in France, you'd go into a café, a restaurant, and order an Irish stew and you'd want it and be waiting for it, and what'd come but a box of Vaseline and a few old bits of meat. On my oath!

If ye ever wanted physic, put hot milk in tea. I was in France, Jimmy, and I said, 'Du lait cru, du lait cru, you eejit!' Christ! Hot milk in tea! 'Twould physic a greyhound!

See this bucket? [*Indicates a copper coal scuttle.*] I met a man with two girls, and I said, 'Why have you them two lovely girls with you?' He had two lovely girls, like, around seventeen. Two tallish young girls. 'Twas a schoolday. 'Well,' he says, 'their mother died o'cancer three year ago, and I promised her,' he says, 'I'd keep them till they'd be able to mind themselves.' He was making them buckets above by the side of the ditch in Clare. Pure copper! Makes them out of th'old knapsacks where he has th'ould boilers from heating. If you went into an antique man in Dublin, wouldn't he charge you £50 for it? £10, now, I paid for it. Fifteen year ago, Mam? Fifteen years. I knew when he asked me £10 that the man was deadly honest.

Father John Fahy, the great republican, reared in Abbey, told me that England was full of tinkers, the same as Ireland was full of tinsmiths. And they gave them the tools of their trade; they brought them out on the bog or lowlands, and Birmingham today is the steel city of England. They built a city, th'itinerants did, making them things. Birmingham is one of the top steel places in Britain now. Well, y'see, th'ould land was available, I suppose, and they settled them in.

Ach! They settle them here, too, but 'tis slow, too, now. Human nature was never so human as this century. In fact, here was the home of th'tinkers now, in th'ould days, with the piebald horses. There was some spare land out where the mart is and they went the roads by caravans and all. But the young lads jumped from under the canvas into a Hiace van, and to keep that going, they had to steal. They became the robbers and crooks of Limerick city today. One of the worst towns for robbers and crooks in Ireland, Limerick is. Stab City! Stab City! There's no month but there's a shooting or a stabbing in South Hill or around the suburbs of Limerick, now.

I could go up to Findon, take my lunch, pop into th'Franciscan church and say a prayer, go down to Boyd's for some parcel or two, throw it into the cab and go all round the city until six o'clock and come back and get in and come home. Never did I lock a lorry!

JH How long ago would that be since you was doing that, Tommy?

TH Musha, sure, twenty-five, thirty, thirty-five.... The years fly. But they have to lock the churches in th'daytime now in Limerick. If they open them at confession time, they have a student or somebody checking who comes in. Isn't it sad in holy Ireland? Well, they wouldn't sit down and make a bucket, them lads, now, if they could rob a bank or tie up a poor parish priest or some old man. 'Tis quicker money. Money's lost its value, you know.

Between 1921 and 1926 there were three great forces at work in Ireland – the Catholic Church, the GAA and Fianna Fail. All the purest and finest. Wasn't hurling and Mass half feed to you?

All breeds of political parties, they all stand for criticism. I don't care. If people don't want to go to church... you see them – they stand outside the chapel and don't come in at all. If they were men, wouldn't they go out on a Sunday morning with a dog, and declare themselves? Tell the priest they don't believe, instead of...

I'll tell you one, now. Every so often there'd be a visit from th'Archbishop, and he'd stay above in the hotel in Woodford. The night before, the landlord brought in Mick Spain, and he drilled him – what to call him and all that. And he wanted to get it right for th'Archbishop, so he's repeating it to himself. Well, Dr Duggan came and he said he'd have breakfast at eight o'clock. Bacon screeching in the pan, and gravy in a little jug, brown bread – grand as if you fried it. So Spain went in to the Archbishop with the tray, nervous enough, and he points it up. 'The grace, your gravy.'

If an elephant put a shoulder to that door and come in now, and a little mouse ran between us here, which would give you the greatest fright? The little mouse wouldn't touch you!

Well, we had good gas long ago in Bridgwater – there was only one cinema in the place. George Formby was in his heyday. He met his pal anyway at a races and they were broke. And then they saw this fellow go over to the bookie's and they said 'There's one – that fool.' Down here they were, nodding and watching, they couldn't know what the hell they'd do. Next thing, there was another race come up and didn't George spot a black clock crawling in the grass! He got an empty matchbox and took out one end and put the little clock into it. But anyway, the two boys went over to see the fellow and he had more money. So the next race, George just shook the little...down his back and next thing! [*mimes slapping and writhing*] George nipped in and got at the wallet. Well, we cheered him out of th'house! Cheered him out of th'bloody house! 'Tisn't that we were training rogues, but the bloody clock was down his back! He forgot about racing! 'Twas at the local cinema.

You know, anything'd make a laugh for young boys. There was a fellow here in the school in Shragh – he had an ould blackthorn stick and he'd wipe his nose with the stick, Jimmy! Well, that was better to us than... Stop! 'Twas better to us. He'd pull it across! He'd have a fake drop on the nose, and he'd wipe it with th'end of th'stick. The Lord save us! We were trying it next day with the hurls! 'Tis easy make young lads laugh, you know.

JH The ould hurling matches, Tommy, eh? Going to school or coming back.

TH Hurling matches! Stop! Murder matches! Oh, ye'd be killed! If 'twas played according to the rules... But by heck, you know! Cloonoon'd have to fight the other lads and the Rossmore lads'd have to fight the Clonmoylan lads.

JH Yeah! Davy-Gerard and Joe, my brothers, they'd be on th'other side! We used to peg 'em stones.

TH We were pegging stones one evening and I went to rally my forces. Frank Keane was a good sharp one with a stone and Tarpey was. John-Joe Watson was very quiet, and Willie, my brother, God rest him. 'Lads! Come back!' I says. I said to Keane, 'Say, if you fight Frog, I'll fight Flaherty.' (The Frog was Davy-Gerard and Flaherty was Sonny Hickey.) 'Christ!' he says. 'Come on!' Well, he put down th'ould head and... Well, I might as well be hitting the stone. He used to put them up at me. And Dan Lyons with the holy collar [*now Father Dan Lyons*], he was no saint, ye know. Oh, he'd split you with a stone! Oh but, sure, we were uncultivated, but I suppose 'twas th'old-time sports, you know.

I remember when we used to travel th'country. There'd be cots across the Shannon, or we'd cycle to Ennis, Thurles. We'd go past hurling matches, and when you'd see a big one, you'd back-pedal. The clothes were stuck to our backs from the sheer perspiration!

MRS H You didn't happen to see the film there – was it Sunday night or Monday night? 'Twas about the *Titanic*. An exhibition. He has a lot spent on it, but I'd say there'd be a lot of visitors to it.
JH I was born the year the *Titanic* went down.
TH 1912! Ye little divil, ye're five years older than me!
JH I was reading about it. You know why it went down so quick? It's come out since that there was the Cunard Line and the White Star Line and they were competing with each other as to get across the Atlantic first and fastest. So, this White Star Line – this yoke – was built in Belfast and it was built with a lighter steel to make it faster and that's why, when it hit the iceberg, it went down. If it had been made with the proper steel… but that would make it slower, so, really, it was due to competing with each other.

TH Did you hear about Mrs S., the time her son was going to America and he wondered if he'd meet Treacy, from round here, who was also in America? 'Ah, don't stir your foot,' she says. 'America is as big as from here to Scarriff and from there to Portumna, and more, if I tell it.'
JH Yes, and there was this woman in Kelly's shop, telling how she'd had a letter from her son in Australia, telling about how well he was getting on, and all about the hot weather. Mary D. was there, listening, and she said, 'Willie, is it? Sure, he was always the prime boy. Tell me, how could it be hot in the month of February? Would you talk sense!' She wasn't going to be fooled!

TH Now, when I was cattle-dealing, I learned the trade by genes, inuition, judgement. Common sense. Make one mistake, you'd never make another. There was a lot of unwritten laws. A man's word. I went along and I bought a man's cow. The place was all puddle; I put a bit of puddle on a stick and I marked her side and that was my word. I bought her. I paid for that cow as good as if it was written in a lawyer's office. There was a lot of unwritten laws, and another one was never tell the truth!

When I started out dealing in cattle, well, the first beast I bought at Scarriff, it had only one eye. It was standing against the wall. It was a French beast, what you call a Charolais. I thought if I lost courage, a Clare man would buy. I tell you, I could go to college and I wouldn't learn as much.

I did a great trade. I was to sell to a young chap a beast. I had no advice from the bank but I knew his family, so I put my name on the back of his cheque, and when his father knew I was after aiding his son, he came and ordered six head of cattle. Now!

People used to be very honest. One time I was cleaning out the trap and I found a ten-shilling note and I handed it over. You'd think it was a miracle. 'Oh,' they said, 'we've been looking for that for weeks and weeks.' That was a good bit, then. You'd often find it read out at Mass, 'Ten-shilling note found in Woodford.'

But not always. One time women would make the butter at home and they'd take it in – 7lb or 8lb of butter. And this old woman come in this time to the grocer's and she handed over th'butter and she said, 'There was two dead mice in the cream, but I fired them out and what people don't know won't harm them. Would ye ever take them and I'll have 4lb back for myself and you can give me some tea and some sugar to go with it.' 'Oh, no problem,' says the grocer. 'Do you go and get your messages and I'll have it all ready for you when you come back.' And when she'd gone, he went to the back of the shop and he changed the paper on the butter she handed in and when she come back he give it to her. And when she'd gone he said, 'What ye don't know won't harm ye.'

Ah, but they were mostly honest, too. I was at a fair in Killarney one time and I was passing the back of a fellow with a leather coat, a vet. 'Where are ye from?' I said, 'I'm from Galway.' Told him I was going from Killarney to Tuam. 'Oh,' he said, 'when you're passing the sugar factory, hand this in. Give that to Jackeen in Tuam.' Well, I took it, the envelope, never looked at it. And in Tuam I handed it over and when he opened it, out fell a £5 note. He said, 'That's from

my brother. It's for little Mickeen, my little son, it's for his birthday.
How well he remembered it.' That was a lot of money that time. Now,
wasn't that trust?

JH It's like the woman in Dublin, she was showing the fellow round
the place, he wanted a room. So she was showing him rooms and she
said 'How's this one?' 'Oh,' he said, 'the window's a bit small.' he
said, 'It'd be hard to get out in case of emergencies.' 'There'll be no
emergencies,' she said. 'You pay in advance!'

TH You know, we'll all see a rogue going. How many of us see him
coming? The hawker long ago'd say, 'You may be honest, but you've
the eye of a rogue,' he'd tell you.

*[In the following conversation, Tommy refers to Charles Haughey, a former
Taoiseach, who became embroiled in a scandal concerning alleged bribes and
undeclared monies paid to him by Ben Dunne, who, with his sister Margaret
Heffernan, comes from a family that set up a chain of department stores in
Ireland. Sean Lemass was himself Taoiseach and Charles Haughey married
his daughter Maureen.]*

I said since we got the wealth, we're not the best at managing it.
We've bred a lot of rogues, mind you. A lot of good rogues. Now, long
ago when you were in the bank, you had a halo. Now, they're a bunch
of rogues. If I asked you tomorrow to write the biography of Charlie
Haughey's life, what would you write? I wouldn't ask you to defend
it. But what caused it? I've a notion he was trying to out-Lemass the
Lemasses.

He got Maureen Lemass and she was top of the pile. Her uncle
was shot in the Featherbed Mountains and his character was
impeccable. Her father was a genius, a truthful genius. Charlie
charmed her and he wanted to prove he was as good as her, maybe
better. An island, an estate, helicopters, racehorses. Economic conference centre, you name it. You say he had to keep up with them, but
he was keeping before them!

And, Jimmy, he made one mistake I wouldn't make. He was going
and he was going, ould Dunne, he left Cork or Tipperary a poor man,
and he made Dunne's Stores and he died. A rich man. Millions. And
Margaret Heffernan was his oldest and she found herself having a
heavy load to carry. And Ben, whenever he'd finished school, he was
sent out to buy th'orange groves abroad in Tasmania and that.

He discovered the natives had stuff growing by the bloody orange trees was worth a lot more – the bloody cannabis! And when he got up to his neck in it, Charlie took him out of it! So far, so good. He was very beholden to Charlie and Charlie started milking it, no bother. And Margaret Heffernan saw the thing going wrong and she drove her car out one evening, to Charlie's place. He told her that her brother was unstable. She went down th'avenue at Kinseely and she swore to her Maker she'd get him and she got him big – she had the means of doing it. If Charlie had said to her, 'Listen, Margaret, I was short of cash, and got some from Ben, and I'll pay it back,' she'd pull the bloody pencil through it! Would I be right? He told her that her brother was an eejit – he rubbed her the wrong way. 'Twas the one mistake he made, now. Margaret Heffernan, now, knocked a lot of bricks off of his high wall.

Will I tell you – Portumna railway was stolen one night. As you go into Lorrha, you see where the railway bridge was – it went on into Birr. But it wasn't economic. It was feeding a boat that was plying on the Shannon. Ballantine Flour Mills, he sent flour by boat up the Shannon.
JH It's true. There's a restaurant just opened called 'The Stolen Sleepers'!
TH History, Jimmy, history. They lifted the tracks and took it instead of their money. If you had a £5 share in it and it was closing, you brought a horseload of planks. You thought you were entitled to it.
JH A lot of the railway line is haysheds! They are!
TH There's an ould trailer here and the drawbar is a bit of Portumna railway. But when we went to school, we were taught that one-fifth of Ireland is under roads, and when this roadbuilding is over, it'll be one-fourth! You'll be getting road rage. But wait, now, Lady Hickey, you've the roads and the railways, that's grand. But the finest waterway in Europe is there abroad. In Europe!

Ould Dinny Rafferty, from Cappagh, made his living in Canada. They'd lash ten cedar trees together with steel ropes and Rafferty'd get up on them with a towpole and he'd land them at their destination, by water. He rode a bundle of trees through the river. If I bring timber up along the Shannon, there'll be no potholes in th'evening, will there? In th'ould days everything came into the jetty at Rossmore.
JH The water could be used, of course. The canals could be used.

TH You could sail from Ringsend [*Dublin*] down there below if you wanted to. You could definitely call that a permanent way, couldn't you?

JH It would work. Combined with the railways. I look at the bloody Liffey and both sides of it jammed with cars, and the Liffey, there's nothing on it.

TH Well, now, there's a new form of landlordism. When I was working in the council we were passing CPOs, Compulsory Purchase Orders, for a corner of your garden. Now, they're sticking these CPOs on the values of about twenty years ago. And land has quadrupled in value since. So you have to fight the CPO or take your medicine.

God rest Slattery, we were talking about putting a new road somewhere and they wouldn't have it. He said, 'God blast it, sure, they'll have to get sky-hooks on it.' Hanging out of the bloody sky. They wouldn't enter his field, so they'd have to get sky-hooks. 'Twas the only solution he could see, to stop the embarrassment.

Tell me, *asthore*, have you ever yet been to Glengariff? Did you go out to Garnish? You didn't! Ah, stop! For a solitary pound, now, myself and Mam went out from Glengariff to Garnish Island, and 'tis definitely a Continental island. Well, God Almighty, the plants that are in it! They're not even in any other part of Ireland – South of France stuff. And then he takes you out for a spin to see the seals, Bantry Bay, all for the quid. He's a motorboat abroad. I suppose it's more now, than the quid. But you'd get a lovely half-hour there that you'd never forget!

Did I ever go to Holy Island? Inishcealtra! Madam, I have a headstone inscribed abroad in it. My grandfather's people were buried there, pre-eviction times. Slattery, God rest him – all the Hanleys and John Slattery went down there one day and we gathered *cipíns* and put down a fire and made tea abroad in it. Had a picnic. Don't miss it. Christ, 'tis the best half-hour you'll ever spend, now. Geographic, healthwise, whatever way you look at it, well worth it, that little trip. You'll see the pathways worn, you can't miss it. Goes through a green field. You'll see red mares and foals grazing there. Peaceful and grand.

And did you ever go to the Rock of Dunamase? It's a mile beyond Portlaoise, on the road to Stradbally. Micheál, our second son,

Tommy Hanley and Mary Kemple on their wedding day, 26th September 1949.

thought he'd have a vocation, and he went to the Patricians in Tullow, Carlow, and Mam and I'd often fly down to see him and we brought John Slattery, of course. And this Sunday we seen it and John Slattery said, 'Jasus, what's that?' I said, 'We'll soon know.' Not a heavy climb – the land is high behind it. But you'd see seven counties, no problem. Big rock, platform and footprints in it. Seven counties! The devil's footprints, they say.

Rose Dugdale landed a 'plane in the field beyond it. Didn't she take a prisoner out of the exercise yard. From the jail, Portlaoise jail. She married Eddie Gallagher.

And what happened to Bernardette Devlin [*in the late 1960s, the youngest MP in the House of Commons*]? She's gone very quiet now.
JH Not so quiet, no. She's not known as Bernardette Devlin now. She's Mrs McAliskey.
TH She took some ould MP by the throat one day.
JH She took poor ould Maudling by the throat. Reggie Maudling, his name was. He was Home Secretary and he was in charge of Northern Ireland, Minister for Northern Ireland at the time. And I'll tell you something about old Reggie Maudling. He was up in Northern Ireland one time, he was a minister, and things was very bad at the time, some time in the 'seventies. There was fighting. He was all politeness and the newsmen were all there seeing him off at the airport there. And he

went up the gangway into the 'plane and when he thought he was out of earshot, he said, 'Give us a double brandy, quick. What an effin' awful bloody country,' he says. He didn't know there was a reporter listening.

TH I doubt if Bernardette Devlin would have been good at the finish. Not like John Hume and Seamus Mallon and them.

JH No, she wouldn't. You have to be diplomatic and you have to give and take a bit and be flexible. Bernie, that wouldn't be her style, no.

TH When you give the schoolbooks out to little kids in twenty years time, tell them to write a composition on Ian Paisley, what could you say about him?

JH Well, the only thing I could write is this: you knew where you stood with him.

TH Yes, but what achievements has he?

JH Nothing.

TH He's driving in reverse as long as I've known him now. A rabble-rouser.

JH They stand to lose so much.

TH Upon my oath, Paisley's a troublemaker.

JH But when it comes to election time, he gets a million votes. The same as John Hume gets a million votes also. And the son is as bitter as he is.

TH Sometimes you imagine you'd give that crowd the charity of your silence. They're losing the horsepower day by day, too.

TH Did you ever go up Croagh Patrick? Myself and Larry Shiels went up at twelve o'clock and we were above about half four in the morning, got Mass at five and Clew Bay and all th'islands were a sight to behold as you came down. They sell you lumps of *cullopans* at the bottom – biggish hazel crooks – a *cullopán* is a straight stick with a crook on it. But there's thirty of forty yards very bad in it. Go on your hands and knees. A girl, now, lost her footing in front of us and she hit Shiel a rap on the shoulder and only the two of them fell, she'd be killed at the bottom. She was careering down. 'Tis dangerous. But, well, we came down in the morning and a nun of seventy-four in bare feet was on her way up. Faith and fatherland.

John Slattery did it often, indeed. Mick Donellan and Francis Fahy. On Pattern Sunday, last Sunday in July.

Now, I can tell you tonight what kind of day we'll have tomorrow. If I can chase out here now, maybe throw off my socks and shoes (maybe not) and there's a good dew, I can guarantee you a fine day. Whereas if the midges have bitten the blazes out of me and th'ould grass is dry, 'twill rain during the night. No surer! No surer than that now. The dew from heaven. And there's nothing as good for tender feet, male or female. Go out before you go to bed, if you have any bit of grass on the lawn, swab around in it, let them dry naturally, into bed. Same before you put on your shoes in the morning and you won't want many foot baths. The natural dew. And if you have racehorses in a stable and the feet start cracking, you've got to let them out at night in the dew as well. Close up the cracks.

TH Young lads are always gabbing, and your ears'd be open but there was a fair few of a certain family in Tynagh. This family, they were called horse jobbers, they were horse dealers. And a boy of them, Laurence, decided to go to America. Dad didn't want it. No dad wanted it, if he could avoid it that time. 'You'll come back, Laurence!' 'Dead or alive, I'll come back.' Well, we used to hear it from so high now, at school. Well, on the night the *Titanic* went down, ould S., I think he was Dan, went out to the stable – there was a mare maybe due to foal or something – and when he opened the stable door, young Laurence stepped out from behind it and went out into the dark.

I heard that told, now and we believed it for God's gospel truth. I suppose it was pishroguery, was it?
MRS H I thought it was the mother that heard him – he knocked on the window, or something.
TH Well, like every story, it gets embellished in the telling. But anyway, he appeared. He was lost in it, Jimmy, the *Titanic*. He was lost in it.

I suppose inuition or foresight or…. Sure, the dog in th'yard, he has a high degree of intelligence.
JH I've heard it said that pigs can see the wind.
TH Cattle – they'd know their owner. Bob Cooney, now, used to go droving – he'd go to Scarriff fair and if you bought twenty bullocks from towards Tipperary, he'd bring them home, and when they'd be rested he'd see them snuff, snuff, snuffing. And if they came from Tulla or that country, they'd be there in the morning. They'd get the direction to go back. They'd break back.

Had ye ever had a big argument about why all those things were put in the world? Well, I used to be going to Ennis for cattle for Micheál Page, principally Saturday morning, now, and this side of Tulla there was a bit of a blind laneway and I'd pull in there and have a flask of tea, and just as I pulled up this morning, coming back with my cattle, this nice little girl, about twenty, twenty-one, was coming walking, and she says, 'Mountshannon?' 'Actually,' I said, 'I'm going through it, so sit in.' So I had my flask and I said, 'Will you care for a drop of tea?' 'Oh, lovely,' she said. Then we got on the road, no worries. But anyway, I blessed myself as I was passing a church, and I saw her looking. I says, 'What church have you?' 'I haven't any,' she says. And I said, 'Sure, being a librarian, you must have it read up, to make a difference between them.' 'Well,' she said, 'I just don't believe.' 'Well, you believe in God, anyway?' I said. 'I'm not convinced,' she said. So now, Jimmy, what do you say?

I said, 'Are you convinced there's a hell and heaven?' 'Well,' she says, 'If there's a heaven the Russian astronauts that went up last week didn't get to it!' 'And tell me,' I says, 'how did we arrive here?' 'Oh' she says, 'organic evolution.' Just came like an apple on the tree and ripened up and rotted down again. And I says to her, 'Organic evolution.' But how d'ye contradict it? 'And you don't see any wonders?' 'No,' she said. 'Well, wait now,' I says. ' That's a field of grass inside there.' (We were driving along in the lorry.) 'I put out a young calf there, a young lamb, a young pig and a young horse. And them four will survive on that grass. But,' I said, 'the lamb'll grow wool, the pig'll grow bristle, the horse'll grow horse and the cow cow hair. D'ye call that organic evolution?' 'Well,' she says ''twould be a quirk of nature.' Well, then, where do you go? So I says, 'Sure, who formed nature?' She was a lovely person, now, and I asked her was she married. 'No,' she says. 'I don't believe in marriage.' 'Well,' I says, 'If you trust a person, go and live with them. A few lines in writing shouldn't make any difference.'

God, well, I pitied her – a lovely little one of twenty-one with a great future. What had she to get out of the world? Sure, her life was no better than the sheep in the field, like.

But, by the buck, you know, she'd put you on...you couldn't answer her. The only example I could think of was the four animals in the field. How well they all come different.

JH Mind you, I would ask her about fingerprints. If they ever find two the same, they'd scrap the whole system.

TH How?

JH Everybody's fingerprints is different.

TH Mother of God!

JH The lads in the Scotland Yard, that was invented there.

TH Well, where would they get all the patterns?

JH How there can be so many patterns on the ends of your.... And if they ever find two alike, they'd scrap the whole system. But they've never found any. There's always some difference in them.

TH Now, you heard about Jack Hanlon's father, didn't you? They'd sell cattle long ago in early March in Ballinasloe, and if the fair was good, they'd try and get to Scarriff up here to replace them, ye see. Cattle came from the south to the midlands or to Dublin, ye know. But anyway, ould Hanlon sold his cattle and got paid nearly enough, and got a train down to Limerick. But he wasn't a drinking man anyway. He digged in somewhere and went out for a walk. But there was some ould preacher – down an ould side laneway, there was this ould preacher, would he be Jehovah Witness or what? Anyway, Hanlon went in – 'twas a quiet place, cost him nothing for an hour or two. And the fellow began about 'We'll suppose that God made the world, and we'll suppose Adam and Eve was the first man, and we'll suppose,' he says, 'God got two lumps of clay,' he says, 'and he left them up on the ditch and they dried into Adam and Eve. And all this kind of thing. 'If anyone has any queries,' he says, 'we'll have a codeword.' They agreed the codeword would be 'Clean'. But he was going on about this thing. If God was in it, he left them up on the ditch to dry. 'Clean!' says ould Hanlon. 'Oh! What's the question?' he says. 'If God didn't make the world,' he says, 'if Adam and Eve was the first man,' he says, 'who made the ditch?'

There was pandemonium! They ran to choke him, but he got out anyway, with his life. Hah? 'Twas a valid question, too. He was only killing the night, you know, but he shouldn't have upset the floor.

Well, that was that lassie's defence, now, about no God. By Janey, she'd corner you up! What she said about the Russian astronauts. I suppose they are conquering space.

JH I remember the day the Russians went up into space. We had an electrician working with us, and he was Irish descent, you know. His parents was Catholics and he wasn't, and he was delighted that day. He says, 'I'm going back now to get at them,' he said. 'The Russian astronauts went up there and there was no heaven and no God.' He was fully delighted with it. That was proof to him.

TH You can have a mighty interesting chat with passengers you'd carry. 'Tis a very lonely life in a lorry. One time I was coming out of Maynooth around ten in the morning, a really soggy, hot day now, in June, and there was this fellow in Maynooth, he had a gardai shirt on him. 'God,' I thought, 'this is great now.' So I says, 'Where are you going?' 'Roscommon,' he said. 'Oh God,' I says, 'that's great. I'll bring you most of the way. Where do you work?' 'Store Street,' he says. 'Do ye know Michael Quinn?' And [*he snores*] he was dead asleep.

Now, in respect to ye, there was a smell of stale beer off his clothes, a heavy, rancid ould unwashed... But anyway, I could drop him in Kilbeggan and let him off to hell, find Athlone himself, or I could drop him in Athlone. So I pulled in in Kilbeggan. 'Get out to hell,' says I. 'Ye're not great company.' 'We had a bit of an ould do last night,' he says. 'Well, that wouldn't prevent you from washing your clothing.' Well, he sickened me, he was like a pig lying beside me. And I should have a bit of a chat, you know. In them days, they'd all go for stopping a truck. 'Twould be coming somewhat easier and there'd be liberty, d'ye see?

I drove the lorry for slag one time, to Limerick, and I paid my cash, got my docket and I says to the man in the yard, 'Go down with me to the docks.' Small, little lad he was, all coal, little black eyes. Anyway, I slipped him a half crown and, sure, he nearly brought the hand off me. Half crown was currency that time. 'Have you a great time, now?' says I. 'Middling, only middling.' 'How's the wages?' 'Ah, a tenner,' he says. 'Tenner. Tenner.' Like, it was a good many years back. Hard old work he was at, unloading from the dock, you know. 'Sure, it doesn't go far,' I says. 'Oh, Jasus, what?' he says. 'Have you a family?' 'I have eight,' he says. Says I, 'Sure, 'tis hard enough to rear...' 'Arragh, Jasus,' he says, 'when I give th'ould wife a fiver,' he says, 'what the hell if I fag me and beer me with th'other fiver?' He give the wife a fiver to rear eight kids and he had th'other fiver for fags and beer! Well Christ, I looked across at him and I thought, 'Mother of God! Ireland is rearing them yet!' You know, the division he was making!

Th'only time I miss money now, I can't do with money for the last twelve years, since I lost my sight. I miss it if I happen to be at a funeral and I happen to get stuck in the bar. You want to keep your corner.

JH My eyesight is going now.

TH Ah, but you're an ould lad.

If I could have an operation, I'd take a gamble on it. You have to make the best of it. The lassie that Liam's married to, Edel, she's great gas, you know. She loves an argument. You know how you can be a donor – eyes and hearts. 'Well,' I says 'I'm thinking of being a donor and donating my tongue.' 'Oh, God!' says she, 'They'd give it back! They wouldn't keep it!' She's bloody great gas.

Now, I'm going to tell you something. You should work as if you were going to live for ever, and live as if you were going to die tonight. I met a young fellow, he was a Wesley, and there was bitterness painted on his chin. 'What is the matter with you?' I asked him. 'Well,' he says, 'there's not many girls in my religion and I loved a girl from Wicklow, but that man told lies about me and it came to nothing. Any harm I can do for him in my lifetime, I'll do it.' That's what he said to me, now.

Jimmy, did ye hear this one? This parish priest has a parish near ould Paisley. Up in the north, ye know. Belfast, I suppose. And he heard giggling – and he looked, and it was a cat and a couple of kittens. The cat belonging to Mrs Paisley, ye see. Well, the priest knew the cat and th'kittens would be a distraction in the church, so he went to see her, to ask her to take them back. 'Oh,' she says, 'it's not my cat – it's the Reverend's.'

Well, Paisley was inside, so the priest goes in to him and talks to him. 'Reverend, in your spare time, could you come and take them out the church?' And ould Paisley, he says, 'No need,' he says. 'When they're nine days old and their eyes open, they'll see where they are and they'll come out of there of their own accord!'

JH That's a good one, Tommy. I must tell you about this, now, Tommy. The Garden of Eden, you know, and they got fired out, didn't they? They both got kicked out. And a few years after, Adam's out walking with th'eldest lad, you know.

TH Not so bad!

JH They passed this big estate – the Eden Estate – and the young lad said to him, 'Hey, Dad, who owns that place?' 'Now, look,' he says, 'Son,' he says, 'that belonged to us until your mother ate us out of house and home!'

TH Put 'em on the street!

JH There was another one about Noah in the Ark, you know. They were sailing about the world, you know, and he had two of everything, didn't he? And he caught one of the young lads. He says, 'What are you doing?' 'I'm going fishing,' he says. 'Well,' he says, 'You'll have to be careful with the bait. I've only got two!'

TH Not so bad!

JH He put the blocks on it straight away!

TH Did you ever hear the one about Saint Patrick coming to Woodford? He was up in heaven, Saint Patrick was, and there's three fairs in Woodford, after three saints – Saint Stephen's Day, Saint Patrick's Day and Saint John's Day. Saint Patrick got a longing to come to Woodford, anyway, and he said to Saint Peter, 'There are three priests down there called after me,' he says 'and a fair there in my honour an'all.' 'Well,' says Peter, 'There's a chopper abroad there,' he says. ''Tis full of fuel. And be back here,' he says, 'sharp at ten o'clock.' Patrick hopped into it and he landed above in O'Reilly's field in no time, and he legged it up to Bark Hill and there was Father Pat Naughton, Father Pat Conroy and Father Pat-Joe Kelly. They were dining above in the church. '*Céad míle fáilte*' and whatnot.

But he mentioned that he had to be back at ten, and Father Naughton, he was edging to get him out, but he stuck to the young lads, Kelly and Father Conroy, to leave him to the thing, 'twas above in O'Reilly's field. And coming down by Moran's, 'twas a fair night – before the fair – there was mighty music, dancing. Kelly was mad for th'accordion, and Conroy was mad to dance. And every second lad inside in the pub was called Pat-Joe or Patrick or Paddy or Pakky – 'twas all of them. Wonderful *craic*, anyway, until Moran's shut, about eleven o'clock, and the two boys left him back in O'Reilly's about eleven o'clock.

'Oh, begod,' says Saint Peter. 'You're coming out no more,' he says. 'I could lose my job. You should be back at ten,' he said, 'and the chopper could be wanting, and it's a quarter past eleven now.' Well, old Patrick never looked at him or never answered him.

But th'year after, he was planning – didn't he come at Saint Joseph, the most sensible man in heaven. He says, 'There's a place over in Roscrea,' he says 'called after you, the Saint Joseph Monastery – penny dinners. There's a road out of it from Portumna here to Woodford, the Saint Joseph Road.' On my oath, anyway, they put their case to Saint Peter. 'Well,' Saint Peter says, 'on my oath, Joseph, that fellow now, got out last year, should have got back here at ten – it was ten past eleven. I could lose my job. You watch it now! And as a concession,' he says ' be back at eleven.'

Well, the lads in Roscrea, sure, were celebrating and on to Woodford and Bark Hill and the three Pats was in it, and Father Naughton opened the little bottle there in the press, and down to Moran's and every lad in it was called Pat-Joe or Joey or Joe or Joseph. They got back, anyway. Five past twelve. Peter came out ranting and raving away. Poor old Patrick daren't answer him. 'I could lose my job,' he says, and he gave out. 'Have you it all said, now?' says Joseph. 'I have,' he says. 'Well,' says Joseph 'I was here before ever you arrived.'(Which he was.) 'Bring me out my wife and child and shut down the joint,' he says, 'and you'll have no job to mind then!' That took the gab of Saint Peter! 'Bring out my wife and child,' he says. Close the joint – shut it to hell! 'Deed, but Kelly'd laugh at that now! He's bloody prime, Kelly is!

There was word came here that Joe, God rest him, was buried in New Zealand, and this Saturday night, now, around half eight or nine, I heard one of the young ones inside say, 'Would you ever give Dalgan Park a ring?' (I can't ring.) But anyway, they got the number and a nice, quiet voice came on and I says, 'Can I speak to Father P-J Kelly?'

'Well,' he says, ' he's gone out for a short while. And I don't know when he'll be back.' And I says, 'How far is the local?' He didn't laugh. He didn't laugh, but I heard him give a little chuckle. But the next thing, anyway, half an hour went by and the phone rang. I says, 'Hello.' 'Listen, Hanley,' he says, 'I'm back from the local!' Your man told Kelly!

They had a great game in th'ould days. These lads, they wouldn't recognize the court, d'ye know? [*For political reasons.*] There was an ould judge, anyway, up in Ennis, and he was a bit of a lady's man as well, and whiskey. And there was a line of ould barristers, d'ye see, much the same type. This poor woman, she was charged with soliciting money in the street or something, and he took up th'ould book and he says, 'Do you recognize the court?' he says. And she gave a look. 'Every bloody one of them!' Hah! They were all customers! And, faith, sure maybe she was telling the truth!

Danny Cummins in Loughrea had a tramp in for... he was doing a lot of thefting. Ould Cahill says, 'What sort of evidence have you,' he says, 'to support this man's case?' 'Oh, the finest, Your Honour,' he says, 'if it could be believed.' Hah?

JH Football's gone to hell.

TH They're beginning to cock up their ears here, too, Jimmy, some of the good hurlers. To have an association. The GAA doesn't like it.

JH I read the President of the GAA, he says there's about thirty county managers that's getting paid, quietly, under the counter.

TH We do know, from the grandchildren, it costs a bloody fortune bring a family to Croke Park. A bloody fortune, Jimmy! Now, Micheál, because of his work, he gets a free seat in Croke Park – a bloody corporate box. But, Christ, he says, you'd go quare above in it. Sitting above in it waiting for an operation and looking through a glass. Liam still plays – he loves it. Well, I suppose the little team is great for the young lads. Keeps them together. When we were playing 'twas unofficial. 'Twas unofficial. Didn't have a proper ball or nothing.

Now, in th'ould days there was only the paraffin oil lamp, ye see. Summertime you sometimes didn't light it – you washed your feet, when you were in the bare feet, and you said the rosary and you [*claps hands*] bed. But Frank Keane, God rest him, came down, anyway, and he had an ould thread ball. And we went up there (we had a bit of a field of ours) with Willie, God rest him, my brother, and we hurled until the light failed and we come in, sure, hardly a candle – straight to bed.

But Master Canning, that time, he'd give you a line of words to make sentences. Pick out six or eight words of the dictionary, you know. But he'd stand us all round in a ring and, of course, I hadn't gone near the lessons and neither had... But Bridie Kelly (she died a nun, after) Cloonoon, she read her bit. 'Next!' He was sitting above in his little chair, ye see. I went up. 'I couldn't find the dictionary, sir.' 'Next!' Keane again. [*In a sing-song voice*] 'I couldn't find the dictionary, sir.' 'Oh, Jesus!' he says. Well, he grabbed the black rod and he beat the two of us. If the common ape had to say anything, you know! I had my certificate got! No bother! And mine was a grand little excuse. But the ape, you know! Of all things! Will you stop! And, of course, unless th'ould teacher was made of wood, he'd know 'twas a gimmick when the second lad give it! It was! Oh, good God. But was it a good education, Jimmy? Was it a good education? It was!

They used to tell a yarn – sometime the teacher'd give them – he'd pick words, ye see. Defence, defeat and detail. This little lad, he had no brains. He wrote 'When the cat goes over defence, defeat go in front of detail.' He got away with it! He got away with it!

We were talking and gabbing one day in the class, and Mikey Canning was reading. (Mikey was Master Canning.) He was reading – who the hell? Was it Cuchullain or somebody? But he said that 'he carried a scimitar'. S-c-i-m-i-t-a-r. A short sword, isn't it? But he saw us talking, and he grabbed me. 'What's a scimitar?' [*Makes the sound of the rod whipping*] Next one, 'What's a scimitar?' [*Makes whipping sounds again*]. By Christ, I tell you! When that went in, it stayed in. He beat about twelve, Jimmy. Not one could answer him! He didn't just pick it so fast then – he knew we wasn't paying attention. By Christ, if I met a scimitar since, I'd rise my hat to it! Oh, Christ, stop! He'd give you a clatter there now, and it'd shake the teeth in your head – with the back of the hand!

Mikey was from Derrygoolin above Woodford, you know. But he gave a commentary about Woodford, a few words about the population – 'twas at the foot of the Slieve Aughty Mountains. But didn't he slap Lyons, Larry Lyons, for talking – himself and Ralph Kelly. 'Woodford is a struggling little village at the foot of the Slieve Aughty Mountains, and the inhabitants are on the verge of starvation.' Lyons! Called it off at that. Well, he beat the cold out of him, Mikey did.

JH Well, that was.... He used to do that every year. The way he used to say it, Master Canning, 'Woodford is a small but prosperous town situated at the foot of the Slieve Aughty Mountains.' And Larry Lyons, ''Tis a mean little village at the butt of a hill,' he says. Oh, God!

TH He started at £30 a year in Eyrecourt, Mikey did.

JH Is that what he was on?

TH Under the British government, yes. An assistant teacher in Eyrecourt. He came on then to Shragh.

JH Well, you see, Tommy, I found out since, them national schools were set up by the British government to break the people off from speaking Irish. Because everything had to be taught through English, you know, and they were kind of colonizing.

TH Listen to me, Jimmy. There was four thousand hedge schools operating in Ireland at that time, now, before they went to build the schools. Below in Cloonoon there, there was a Ned Kelly, hedge schoolmaster. My grandfather went to school to him. Under the ditch! Great men, they were. But they kept the whole thing – English and Irish – going.

JH Oh, yes, the history and the Irish language, and the songs and everything like that. Kept it going. Some of them could teach Latin and that, too.

TH Well, sure, listen to me, Jimmy, the best or the worst of languages – necessity would really teach them to you. When you're stuck in a country, you have to get on, haven't you? To make do some way.

Awareness is very scarce in the world. I was here in the house on my own a start ago. A few mental prayers, and next thing there was a man in front of me. I could see th'shadow. I put up my stick and I said, 'Thus far and further!' I was feared of my life. Who'd know who it could be? 'Oh,' says he, ''tis only the priest.' 'Well, Father,' I says, 'What are ye trying to prove?' To come to a blind man, ye know!

Ah, sure, anything that happens a day at a time won't hurt you. ''Tis not to those who can inflict the most, but to those who can suffer the most will victory be assured.' That was said by Thomas Ashe before he died on hunger strike. Octoberish, 'twas.

Now, would you like to hear a little poem? 'Tis called 'The Confession'. The seal of the confession has never been broken. Whoever heard of it? But in this case, 'tis imaginary. A man facing death the next day.

The Confession

With the sign of the cross on my forehead, as I kneel on the cold dungeon floor,
As I kneel at your feet, reverend father, and none but my God to the fore,
But my heart opened out for your reading, and no hope or thought of release,
From the death that at daybreak tomorrow is staring me straight in the face.

I've told you the faults of my childhood, the follies and sins of my youth,
But now to a crime of my manhood, I confess with the God's naked truth.

You see, sir, the land was our people's. For ninety good years of their toil,
What first was a bare bit of mountain brought into good fruit-bearing soil.

'Twas their hands raised the walls of the cabin where our children were born
  and bred,
Where our weddings and christenings were merry, where we waked and
  keened over the dead.

We were honest and fair to the landlord, and paid him the price of the day
And it wasn't our fault if our hard sweat he wasted and squandered away
On the cards and the dice and the racecourse, aye, and often in deeper
  disgrace
That no tongue could relate without bringing a blush to a decent man's face.

But the day came at last that he worked for, when the castles, the mansions,
  the lands,
He should hold but in trust for his people, to his shame passed away from
  his hands.
And our place sold, too, into auction. By many the acres were sought
And what cared the stranger who purchased who made him the good soil he
  bought?

The old folks were gone, thank God for it, where troubles and cares
  can't pursue.
But the wife and the childer, oh Father in Heaven, what was I to do?
So I thought I'd go speak to the new man. I'd tell him of me and of mine
And the trifle I'd gathered together I'd place in his hand for a fine.
The old whore was worth six times the money, and maybe his heart wasn't cold.
But the scoundrel who bought the thief's parts was worse than the pauper
  who sold.

But I chased him to house and to office, wherever I thought he'd be met
I offered all he'd put on it, but, no, 'twas the land he should get.
I prayed as men only to God pray, but that prayer was spurned and
  denied,
And what matter how just my poor right was, for he had the law on his side.

I am young but a good few years married, to one with a voice like a bird
As she sang the old songs of our country, every feeling within me was stirred.
Oh, I see her before me this minute, and her foot wouldn't bend a
  thrauneen,
Her laughing lips lifted to kiss me, my darling, my bright-eyed Eileen.
How often with pride have I watched her, her soft arm fondling our boy,
Until he chased the smile from her red lips, and silenced the song of her joy.

Tommy Hanley

Whist, father, have patience a minute. Let me wipe the big drops from my brow.
And, father, I'll try not to curse him, but I ask you, don't preach to me now.
Exciting myself? Sure, I know it. But my story is now nearly done.
And, father, your own breast is heaving. I can see the tears down from you run.

Well, he threatened, he coaxed, then evicted, though we tried to think of the place
That was mine, aye, far more than 'twas his, sir. I told him right up to his face.
But the little I had melted from me in making a fight for my own
And a beggar with three helpless children all out in the world I was thrown.
And Eileen would soon have another, another that never drew breath.
The neighbours were good to us always, but what could I do against death?
For my wife and my infant before me lay dead, and by him they were killed
As true as I'm kneeling before you to own to my share of the guilt.

I laughed all consoling to scorn, I didn't mind much what I said
With Eileen a corpse in a barn, with a bundle of straw for a bed.
But the blood in my veins boiled to madness. Do they think that a man is a log?
I tracked him once more for the last time, and I shot him that night like a dog.

Yes, I did it, I shot him. But, father, let them who make laws for the land
Look, too, when they come to judgement for the blood that lies red on my hand.
If I used the gun, 'twas they caused it, and left him stone cold in the sod
And from their bar where I got my sentence I appeal to the high bar of God.

For bare justice I never got from them – even right from their hands was
*   unknown,*
Still – I'll say it at last, sure, I'm sorry I took the law into my own.
That I stole out that night in the darkness, while mad at my grief and
*   despair,*
And I blew the black soul from his body without leaving him time for a prayer.

Well, 'tis told, sir. You have the whole story. God forgive me now, for my own sins.
My life is now ending, but, father, the young ones – for them life begins.
You'll look to poor Eileen's young orphans? God bless you, and now I'm at peace
And resigned to the death that tomorrow is staring me straight in the face.

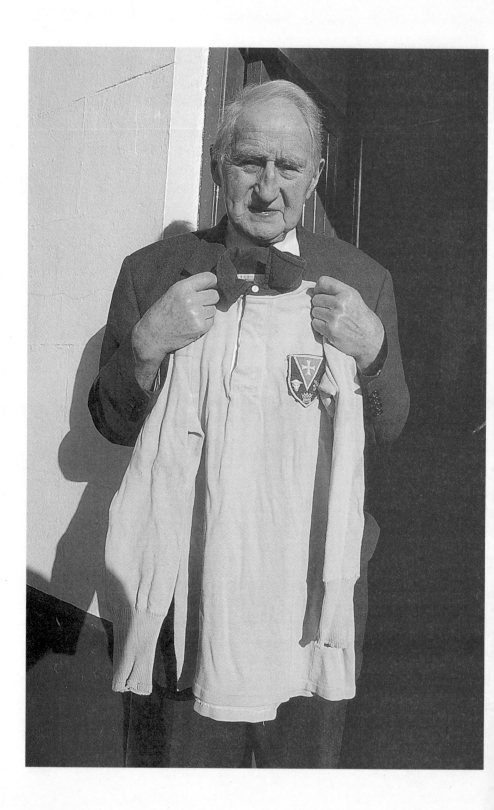

Jimmy Murray

born 5th May 1917

Jimmy Murray lives, and always has lived, beside the grocery and bar in Knockcroghery that bears his name. Walk into the back room of the bar and it is instantly clear, from all the framed photographs and sporting memorabilia, that this is a shrine to Gaelic football and hurling. Still trim and youthful in his manner, Jimmy continues to be 'stone cracked on football'.

I WAS BORN IN THIS HOUSE on 5th May 1917. My father came here in 1915, so we've been nearly a hundred years in this town. I can go back a fair bit in my memories – my mind is very clear, still. This place was a pub, a small grocery, and my father improved it, and I came along and I added my expertise to it and my son has enlarged it considerably, so it's the third generation – a country business. A country business – it's different to a town business – you stock nearly everything. As my father said, from a needle to an anchor. We stocked paraffin oil before the ESB came in. The ESB made a big change to the country – it changed life completely for country people, really. The older generation, older people, were a bit sceptic about it though, all right.

Knockcroghery was famous for making clay pipes – the dudeens. You heard of a dudeen – a chalk or clay pipe. It was smoked by all the people – all the men, the old people in Ireland – prior to the cigarettes. My father often said the cigarettes didn't come rightly in here until the First World War, the 1914–18 war. The fellows came back from the Front and they had cigarettes with them. They were just coming into fashion, but before that it was clay pipes that were smoked in the country places and Knockcroghery was the home of the clay-pipe industry. Actually, it was well known all over Ireland, I believe. There were about four or five families engaged in the clay-pipe factories, as they were called, manufacturing clay pipes, sending them round the country on horses and carts. As you know, there was no motor transport back in the 1950s and earlier. They went on a horse and cart down to Tipperary and up to Donegal and up to County Down and all over. They'd go off on Monday morning with a load of pipes and might not be back till Saturday night, you know. Knockcroghery was famous for clay pipes.

People tell me that in the 1900s the village was very much bigger. There were more houses and a lot of people employed. There was a furnace – the clay pipes had to be baked in furnaces and there were three or four of those. Turf had to be used. The umbrella spread out a bit, because turf had to be bought, so it gave a lot of employment.

At first the clay was quarried somewhere convenient to the village, but eventually it came from England, from Cornwall, an old man told me. It came in blocks, came here to the railway station. It was in square blocks that had to be steeped. It was very hard, so it had to be steeped for a night or two in order to make it pliable, to make into the clay-pipe shapes. A lot of women were employed in the industry because it was not hard manual work. The clay went into cast iron moulds and they were put into the furnace. It was a big process, I believe, but I never saw it; I heard about it. That made Knockcroghery. Brendan Shine, he sings a song about the dudeens and he brings Knockcroghery into it. And there's a song called 'Knockcroghery'. Peadar Kearney wrote it. He was Brendan Behan's uncle, and he wrote our national anthem. And he wrote 'Knockcroghery'. It's a kind of ould ditty. We do sing it now and again here. It's not that great a song.

Knockcroghery – the name itself means 'Hangman's Hill'. People say, 'How did it get that name?', you know. Well, there's a hill just behind the village, a small hill, and they say in Cromwell's time, people were hanged there. There was a platform for hanging people during Cromwell's time, that's how the name came.

Then again, this village of Knockcroghery, as you know, it's a fairly modern-looking village, but back in 1921 it was a large village of whitewashed, thatched cottages, during the Black and Tans wars. This whole village was burned by the Black and Tans in 1921 as a reprisal against some army officer who'd been shot, up in Athlone. They came to the conclusion that it was people from this area that committed the crime. As a result, they came here and burnt the whole village to the ground. It wasn't hard to burn it, now, with the thatched houses. It was a very warm summer, middle of June, 21st June 1921. The truce came after. There were two slated houses, this one and another one, and they came safe. Well, they set fire to the door, but it didn't do much damage. The thatched roof went immediately, of course. They'd put a bit of petrol on the thatched roof and put a match to it and off it went. Knockcroghery was famous for that reason as well. The people got compensation after, but the pipe industry finished that night, that finished it. One family tried to revive it afterwards, but, as I said, cigarettes were coming in and it was dying anyway. It may have been a blessing in disguise that they burnt it – they were well compensated.

The Black and Tans, by all accounts, terrorized people. It was a terrible time. What they did was, you see... [*The Black and Tans targeted the shop*]. My father said to me, he had two lads working in the shop and they were members of the IRA, as they called it that time. Of course, it was a different IRA from the one we have now. But that's beside the point. They could hear the lorries coming – 'tisn't like it is now. That time you knew it was coming, and they ran up the yard. They took to their heels, but my father had to stand his ground and bear the brunt of the attack, as it were. But it was tough times, all right.

I was the eldest of a large family. Ten – eight boys and two girls. I went off to serve my time in the trade – first I went off to Roscommon to a bigger business there, learned a bit of the trade there, and then took over with my father. My brothers and sisters, he educated them fairly well. I had two brothers doctors, two brothers engineers, a brother a priest and a brother a shopkeeper and a farmer, so we were well spread around. My two sisters, one got married and one didn't get married at all. They all stayed in Ireland. Well, one brother actually was a doctor in Nottingham for years but he's here now, retired. That was an achievement, for them all to stay in Ireland that time, long ago.

In the pub, the beer was all in barrels, and then, of course, the barrels were tapped by hand, wooden barrels. It was a bit of an art to tap that barrel. If you hit it too hard, 'twould all fly around the place. But it was quite different, the shop was completely different from what it is at the moment. I often said if my father came back here and looked at that shop, he'd think we'd all gone crazy. There's a big stack of milk in the corner and a heap of potatoes and carrots and parsnips and cabbages. All those were produced by the farmers themselves in his time. And the chickens there in the fridge – they were all produced locally. They were very self-sufficient, the old people were. The only thing they bought that time was flour and tea and sugar. They had their own eggs – we'd our own hens. All this is sold in shops at the moment. Even people today who have cows of their own buy the milk, the pasteurized. Especially with a young family. The doctors more or less frightened the people to get pasteurized milk for the youngsters, I think, instead of straight from the cow.

Then Knockcroghery, of course, would have fairs, here in the street. Cattle and sheep are all sold now in the marts. They regulate them with the marts, which came into Ireland in about the 1960s. Prior to that, it was fairs in every town and village in the country. A certain day of the month was fair day, on the calendar, it was well known. People brought their stock into the street. You'd stand there on the street and you sold your stock by hand, you see. They made their bargains, as they called it. You'd the cattle and I'd go up and bid you, and you told me what you wanted, and I'd bid you. Not what *you* wanted. I'd want them as cheap as I could and you'd want as much as you could, so a lot of bargaining went on – for twenty minutes or maybe *hours*. But eventually, they were sold. That's how the stock were sold prior to the marts coming in.

But that was a hard time, too, for the farmers, who'd have to get up at two or three o'clock in the morning to drive the cattle, maybe nine, ten miles into the town to get a good place to stand. If you weren't in early, you could be crushed out, you see. You'd try to get a good place for your stock.

But a fair day in Knockcroghery would be a huge day for the village there, the place'd be – here – the bar'd be packed out. They'd all be drinking. We had big glass windows, but they'd be protected on fair day from the stock.

In the pub, the hours are longer at the moment, I think. That time, we used to always close at ten o'clock – there wouldn't be a light anywhere much – very, very little. There was a bona fide law at operation that you couldn't sell drink after ten o'clock, except it was a traveller – he'd have to come three or four mile, anyway. Now, sure, the hours are much longer. I often say it's harder on my son. A lot longer. When I was a child, the shop was closed at ten.

Fair day was a big day in Knockcroghery. It is a country area, farming area; there's no industry of any other sort around here. 'Tis good country – great land, great sheep country. Roscommon is famous for its sheep. Roscommon Sheep Stealers, they call Roscommon people. They've the Galway Blazers and the Clare, I don't know what they call them, but Roscommon Sheep Stealers are referred to because, simply, the sheep were so plentiful in Roscommon and fellows'd be maybe stealing them. That went on in a big way, one time, stealing sheep.

Then the railway station that time was a very important place in Knockcroghery. It's over there still. It's the Westport–Dublin line. There's a junction in Athlone and another junction in Claremorris. No buses at that time, and only four trains up and down every day. I went to school to Roscommon as a youngster every day in the train; it was exciting. But the station then was big. Everything came by rail that time, to the shops. Everything came by rail – there were no lorries and everything was delivered to the door, because there were two or three shops in the village. The stout and the flour and the meal, all the groceries all came by rail. There was a horse and cart continually on the go, back and forth, bringing stuff over and bringing things back. Empties had to be returned. Everything had to go back to the station again. It's hard to imagine. The young people can hardly imagine how different it is now. That time, in the shop, everything had to be weighed up; they had to weigh up the sugar and the tea and the flour and the bread soda, wrap it. Oh, it was all a completely different show of pictures, altogether.

People would bring in eggs. Eggs were a big thing. You bought the eggs and you'd give them tea and sugar. You'd have change going back with them, probably, and sometimes they mightn't have it. The eggs were a great means of getting a few pounds – the women especially. That was their egg money.

At Christmas time, they'd rear the big bunch of turkeys and they were sold for the big turkey market. They sold them live – there'd be a big turkey market here and a buyer'd come in from some of the big towns and he'd buy all the turkeys here. Geese, turkeys and hens, but turkeys were the big one.

I went to serve my time at fourteen, fifteen, I suppose, but I was helping out earlier than that in the shop. Of course, the children are mad for that kind of work, anxious for it, it's a great thing to be serving people in the shop. You get a kind of thrill from it. I'd say the youngsters still get a thrill – they think 'Oh, it's great to be in a shop. 'Twould be lovely living in a shop.'

Sport was part of my life, indeed. At school, in primary school, there's a green opposite the school and I'd kick a football there as a youngster, and I got very, very fond of it. And then I started at secondary school in Roscommon and I played football there. There was a local team – my earliest recollection – they had a football team in the village here, called Knockcroghery, you see, so I looked at those. I was brought there by my father or somebody to watch the games and got a liking for it.

I was fairly useful at it, or good at it, you see, and I got put on the team very young, I used to follow them round the county in the minor team, under-eighteens, you see, and follow up from that. You were looked after pretty well and kept playing if they found you useful.

I was always very fond of it – nothing could keep me away from it – and to be fair to them, my father and mother knew I was good and they wanted to see me getting on. They knew I enjoyed it and, as my father often said, 'You could be at something a lot worse than playing football in the field.'

Well, it got me a bit of fame. *Not* fortune, but fame, all right. Because Roscommon did very well during my time playing with them. It's a small county, as you know, and it wasn't very well known for football. 'Twas too small for either hurling or football. The population is too small. But something happened during my time – a bunch of lads came along, very good fellows. CBS Roscommon, the Christian Brothers School, had a great team at the time and that's where it started from. But just a good bunch came up. And we'd got a chairman called Dan O'Rourke from Castlerea; he was a TD and a teacher. I always give him credit for starting the thing. He got a man down from Galway to train us – brought us to his own house and kept us there and trained us there. That was how the success started. We went on and won a Junior All-Ireland and a Minor All-Ireland and two Senior All-Irelands. And they haven't won it since, the County Roscommon, I'm sorry to say.

But we won the Senior in 1943 and 1944 and I had the honour of being captain on both occasions. So, captain of an All-Ireland football team, you're kind of a celebrity. You see that photograph – that's the greatest moment of my life, being carried across Croke Park. There were 80,000 people at the match. You can see the crowds around. That's the Sam Maguire Cup, the famous Sam Maguire Cup, a huge cup. The photographer took it in 1944. Oh, it was a great moment, indeed. It's a huge cup and the same cup is still around. But that was a great day for Roscommon. I was a hero, that time, all right. Well, they were all heroes, the whole fifteen, but the captain – you were at the head of the table at the receptions. It was a great honour. I doubt if I'll forget it.

I'd a brother on the team as well – Phelim. I'd two other brothers played football. Four of us won All-Irelands for the county, now. Phelim and I won Senior All-Irelands, my brother Tommy won a Minor and my brother Ollie won a Minor. Minor is Under-Eighteen and, of course, Under-Twenty-One speaks for itself: under twenty-one on 1st January of that year. Junior doesn't really matter. You're not on the Senior team. The second pick would be called the Junior Team, the next selection. Seniors are over twenty-one, but you can be younger if you're good enough. I played in the Seniors at twenty. You could play Senior and Under Twenty-One in the one year for your county. You could be a Minor and play Senior, if you're good enough. It did happen a few times, that fellows played Minor and Senior in the one year. It happened here in Roscommon, two or three fellows. Dermot Earley, the famous Dermot Earley, played Minors and Senior in the one year. So did Micheál Finneran. Dermot Earley, he's a high-ranking army man at the moment. Several fellows played Minor and Senior. I did that myself, now, played at twenty. A bit unusual, yeah.

Jimmy Murray in 1946.

I was a forward, a centre-half. Number eleven. You'd know by the number of the jerseys. Number eleven was my number always. Always in the one position. I always regarded it as my lucky number for doing the Lotto or anything. Number eleven is always put down, my football number, and five is my birthday, so those two are always included.

A lot of that team, of course, have passed away, indeed, to their eternal reward. The whole eighteen of us played in the two years. Eighteen of us took part – fifteen on the team and the second year, a few fellows got injured. One man retired and two other fellows were injured, which meant that we had to get three new players on to the team, so that's eighteen.

But of that eighteen, there's just six remaining. Even recently one of them died in London and there was a Mass for him, actually last night. I was down at Castlerea at Mass for him last night. But they're disappearing, so I'm beginning to worry a bit. Who's going to be next? No, thank God, I'm in great form at the moment.

But the football was a great part and parcel of my life, and still is. I'm still very keen on it. I go to matches every Sunday, indeed I do. Well, during the summertime, if the weather's right I go to the games.

I think camogie and hurling should both be summer games. The ball is very small. The football should be in summer, too, by right, but the ball is much larger and you have some hope. But the hurling ball is so small that if the ground is wet and sticky, well, it gets stuck in the mud. It's nearly impossible to play hurling and camogie in the wintertime. But some fellows, when they'd stop playing football, some fellows in my team would hardly go to a game. But I had the bug, all right, and still have the bug.

Then I played golf a good bit, too, when I stopped playing football. I love the game of golf. It's lovely to get hold of a golf club on a nice, fine evening and you'd forget all your troubles. It's competitive, too. A lovely pastime. I enjoy it.

But in football, I always played in the eleven spot. I don't know how. Going to school, I suppose, the teacher'd spot you and say, 'This fellow can score', probably, and put you up there, and from then on, if you were scoring, they kept you up there. We were all very enthusiastic, all right.

Of course, that time there was nothing else to do much, anyway. I often say the money wasn't as plentiful as it is now. If I was a young fellow… Like my son, he has a car at his disposal (there were no motor cars that time) and I probably wouldn't bother as much either. We're inclined to give out and say, 'Why don't they bother?' But probably we'd do the very same as they. If I had a motor car, too, I wouldn't be at home. I wouldn't have been playing so much football in the evenings, either. So you have to live with the times. But that time was completely different. Nothing else to do except football and hurling. There are too many other counter-attractions these days.

When you were young, you didn't get fifteen together always. One day you might be five-a-side, one day it could be six, might be ten the next day and could be back to three the day after. You made an ould game. The whole point was you were playing football and you were getting practice and you were getting good the whole time. They say to me, that people are fitter now, but the simple fact is that we played every evening of the week during the summertime, now. There was a football spot out there, opposite the shop, now, that green spot, and you played there every evening, kicking a football there for hours. You didn't tog up or anything – just pulled your socks up outside your shoes, your normal shoes, and you were kicking and smashing around there. But you got the feel of the blooming thing into your hand and you got so good at playing it on your toe or catching it and kicking it. Now, they don't play as much football at all, so I don't think they're as good at the basic skills as we were. It stands to reason – they don't practise as much with the football. Probably they're faster, because that time it took us five and a half minutes to run the mile and they're running it in four minutes at the moment, you know.

But then, the people were fitter, of course, at that time. We cycled everywhere. Cycling, to me, is great exercise. I cycled to the dances, and I cycled to the football matches as well, and you cycled to the pictures as well. Wherever you went within a range of fifteen miles, you cycled, anyway. You never thought about it. There was no one passing you out in a car, because there were no cars around, you know. Then the farmers were working far harder. Now, every farmer has a tractor. He's sitting up on the tractor and that does all the work for him. That time, he had a shovel in his hand and he had a rake and he had a slane for cutting turf down the bogs. It was very hard manual labour indeed. And then he didn't need much training, you know. Our lads had no need of that kind of work at all.

The club matches and county matches used to get huge crowds. Roscommon used to host the Connaught Final for years and there were always twenty-five to thirty thousand people at the games. That time it cost (I have a ticket there) sixpence to get to a game. I've a programme of an All-Ireland Final: twopence for the programme, you know. I think it's £2 now for a programme, but it was twopence in 1943 or '44. But money was awful scarce at that time. 'Twas as hard to get the pennies as to get the pounds now, nearly.

We'd a local band here in Knockcroghery at that time, too. And all the important matches, they always played. The County Final, now, is a big event in every county. The County Football Final, my local team here, we won six when I was playing football. Six County Finals. We played in ten, which meant that we won nearly every year, but our local band, now, was carrying that day, playing the teams around the field. We'd an affinity with them, you know. They were part and parcel of the whole set-up. But there was always a band behind the teams, now, apart from the Knockcroghery Band. There was always a band there to march them on. Marches like 'O'Donnell Abu' and those kind of ones. Before the game started and at half time they'd give a recital, probably.

Our strip, Roscommon's, blue and gold, was the same colours as Clare, but a different combination of colours. There are several counties with blue and gold, but you combine them differently. Roscommon is completely yellow or gold, with the blue cuffs and blue collar, a yellow jersey and white shorts. Clare is blue with a yellow band around it. Tipperary is yellow with a blue band. They ring the changes. Roscommon was blue when we started playing first. We were completely blue with a yellow band, the very same as Tipperary at the moment. But we met Cavan in 1943 in the final, and Cavan were all blue, so there was a kind of clash of colours, and they sent for someone who said, 'You'll toss, now, to see who'll have to change the colours.' So we tossed and we lost the toss, so we had to change our strip. They gave us a completely yellow jersey with a blue cuff so it was easy to distinguish us from Cavan, blue. And we won the All-Ireland, so we never changed back. I would never change. We said, 'We'll stick with this colour now.' That's how the present Roscommon colour came into being.

There was a *bit* of sponsorship at that time, not like at the present time, but. Churchgate collections, and there'd be an odd ad in the paper. You got a few private subscriptions and some of the firms might give a fiver, a £5 note, maybe, and that time that was a lot of money. But nothing like at the moment. Even the team that won the All-Ireland, we didn't get the jerseys to keep – just shows you. Now, they're swapping jerseys every game they play. We had to hand them back. Eventually you'd get new jerseys, now and again. I managed to keep the number eleven, I did. I have it somewhere upstairs, it's probably all moth-eaten by now, but it's there.

There used to be a bit of dissension with the referee now and then, naturally enough. Sure, it goes on. It's all part and parcel of every game. No big trouble. Always a bit of argy-bargy goes on, but not too much, now.

When I was a boy, I never thought that I'd get up to Croke Park. It was my boyhood dream. I dreamt about it, all right. I was stone cracked on football always, and it was my ambition. I was longing to be there and I was praying at night as a young fellow. I even said a prayer that I'd get to Croke Park. It might not be the right thing to admit it, but I think I did, though. I'm sure, I was so blooming keen on it that I'd do anything to get there. But I got there all right. I always said it was my dream come true. Somebody up there likes me…

It was lovely September weather in '43, and '44. That was a wet day. It came wet, 'twas a bit wet there, all right. Damp. Fairly good weather – September's not so bad. It was 23rd September 1943, the third Sunday in September and it was September again in 1944, I think it was the 24th.

There's a ball, the 1944 ball which we won the All-Ireland with, I had it down the other night, now. We had a Mass for this man that died in London, so they made me bring down the ball, to show it to his relations there. It's the actual ball that we played with. We had a fire here in the pub and it was burned here but it came safe, you know. It is a memento. We all get together, the lads that played, get together for a dinner. About three years ago, the last one we had, and two of them have passed away since that, now. So there's only six of us left now to gather up again some time. But we used to get together every couple of years for a meal in some hotel, now, and have a chat – it was grand.

We played Cavan in '43, a very famous team at that time. They've gone down a lot since. At that time they were winning the Ulster every year. They won five or six All-Irelands at that time. And, of course, we beat Kerry in '44. That was a feather in our cap and we got to the Final again in '46 and Kerry beat us. I was captain that day, too. Kerry beat us on a replay. It was a draw the first day and, believe it or not, in the first game Roscommon was leading by six points, and the time was almost up. Then Kerry scored two goals to draw with us, and they beat us on the replay. It was a heartbreak. I still think of it. About two minutes away from winning a third All-Ireland – well, five minutes. The people were leaving Croke Park, thinking it was over. On the first day, two goals were scored. Paddy Burke scored one goal for Kerry and Gagga O'Connor scored the other one. They scored two goals in the last five minutes. Then Gus Cremins was the name of the Kerry player that scored the winning point the second day. He'd come in as a sub, actually. He wasn't in the team to start off. They brought him in so he could make a long point from the middle of the field.

But those were great memories – good ones and bad ones. I often say that '46 is the one five minutes I'd love to forget. If I had to go over it again, I'd make sure they wouldn't get those two goals, anyway. It looked one-sided. We were completely on top. 'Twas hard to imagine, you know. Even the Kerry players... Some of the Kerry players, I'm very friendly with them, and I'd go there and meet them on holidays, and they often said, 'We thought you had us beaten.' They were sure that they were going to lose. Wee bit of luck attached to those two goals, now. One of them was a very lucky kind of a goal, now. The other one was good enough.

You'd keep the cup for the twelve months. 'I had it inside in the sitting room,' I often say to my sons, now (of course, they were very keen on football, naturally enough) and to my grandchildren. The Sam Maguire Cup was brought here about two years ago. Somebody brought it into the shop here. Galway won it, and brought it here to show it to us. They knew I wanted to see it, anyway. But I said to my grandson, 'That was for two years sitting on top of our piano.' Oh, it was, you know. For two whole years. I gave it back for the week before the game, brighten it up, get it fixed up. But 'twas there for two whole years in the house. Just amazing to think of it. It was sitting there and it could have been stolen and there wouldn't be a bit remarks passed on it.

Sam Maguire was a Corkman; he was Church of Ireland, now, which sounds a bit fantastic. He wasn't a Catholic, but he was a great friend of Michael Collins's. He was in the IRB [*Irish Republican Brotherhood*] as far as I know. They said he was a great man for getting information for Collins – he worked in the post office. Anyway, he wasn't killed in the Rising, but when he died, they called the cup after him. 1928 was the first year the Sam Maguire Cup came into being, 1928. Before that, it was just called the Championship. And the Sam Maguire became famous. The Sam, they call it. 'We'll get the ould Sam next year', you know.

Now, I think players in the GAA are not well looked after. They should be better looked after. They should get their expenses definitely. They're beginning to get things now, though. It's a lot better than it was. They get so much a mile for bringing their cars.

Our time, now, there were very few married men played in the teams. They're getting married younger now, let's put it that way. In our time nobody got married till they were thirty years of age, very, very few fellows married. Well, you wouldn't, you see. I wasn't married till I was over thirty. We won in 1943 with no married man on the team at all. Fifteen bachelors. One fellow married the second year, but that first year the whole team, they were all bachelors. Those lads weren't too pushed over getting money or anything. But if you had a wife and a couple of children at home, it would be a different story, you know. That's the way at the moment now. Half the team is married now, Roscommon team. They've a wife at home on a Sunday. Galloping off to a football game – I'm sure she gets a bit annoyed, naturally enough. A football widow can be a very lonesome person. If she's annoyed you couldn't blame her. But going back, if you could fire out a few pounds for your evening, well, that's some excuse, but if you came home and just said, 'Well, we got well beat' or 'We won well', that's not much good to her.

They're covered for injury pretty well, with insurance, but rugby has gone professional – it was supposed to be the best of amateurism until five or six years ago and they had to change it. It was changed in spite of them, you see and now they're getting huge money, a lot of international players. I couldn't afford to go professional. Ireland couldn't afford it, a small country like this. But I wouldn't like to see it go professional. It'd mean a few good fellows would be getting it all, too, and th'other poor ould devil farther down the line, he would get nothing much because 'twouldn't be there for him to get. The same thing for the rugby. I go to the rugby matches in Athlone, the Buccaneers play there – a couple of evenings I've seen them playing. But I know quite a few fellows who're involved, and they tell me that they're a bit annoyed. They said two or three good players in the team, they're playing for the county and they're getting huge money, and th'other fellows get nothing. So there's for and against it, but, as I say, I couldn't see the GAA going professional. They couldn't afford it, anyway.

Gaelic football is closer to rugby than to soccer because you can catch the ball and it is often said that Gaelic players would make better rugby players than soccer players. If you had to convert, 'twould be easier to make him a rugby player, but there are some great Gaelic players who became great soccer players, too, and vice versa. But for my own sake, I'd say if I was playing tomorrow, I'd say I could switch to rugby fairly fast, you know. Kevin Moran of Dublin, he went over to Manchester United. He won an All-Ireland Gaelic and he became an international Manchester United soccer player.

Now, some counties are football and some counties are hurling, and one or two counties are both. It's traditional, anyway. Traditional hurling counties – the south of Ireland – hurling – always was. I go back seventy years. They're doing their bit to promote it, they're gradually promoting it, now. A very few of the strong counties are good at both games. Cork, now, is such a huge county. Galway's a huge county, again. They are good at both games. Tipperary used to be good at both games, but they've failed a bit at the football. When I was young, Tipperary was quite a good football team. But the one small county I admire at the moment is Offaly. Offaly is a very small county, smaller than Roscommon. And in both hurling and football they have won All-Irelands in both in the last twenty years. They're great for a small county. They have only nine or ten clubs playing football and hurling and still they can hold their own with the best and always have done. They've some great tradition there in Offaly, great spirit. You have to admire them.

Hurling is a great game, a lovely game, hurling is. I hurled, too, for Roscommon. It was my first game going to school, hurling in Roscommon. CBS, the Christian Brothers, De La Salle Brothers, were very keen on hurling. My first medal was for hurling. The first medal I ever had was for hurling, but you'd have nearly to be born with a hurley in your hand. I often say you could take a good athlete, now, at twenty years of age, a fellow who never played football or hurling, and you'd make a footballer out of him. You'd have an awful job to make a hurler out of him, because it's too scientific and skilful – you'd make a footballer of him easy enough but you'd have a job to make him a hurler.

There's some kind of relation between hurling and golf. I had one advantage – I always played hurling with the wrong grip, with the golf grip. I hadn't to change at all. But it helped me with the golf, definitely, because you'd an eye for the ball. Hurlers make very good golfers often, they do indeed. Some of the top hurlers in the county are very low handicap golfers. A lot of the Clare team and the Kilkenny team. Golf used to have a kind of snobby status to it but the last twenty, thirty years golf has come down to... everybody is playing golf now. Everybody. The Roscommon Golf Club there, now, I was President a couple of years ago. There's a huge membership in there now. I joined a long, long time ago, when it was very few who played there, you know. A bit snobby at the time. But I was kind of famous with the football and one of the golf fellows, he was always raising funds and giving us a hand, and he said to me, 'Oh, come on. Give us a few quid and join the golf club.' So I joined it that way, with no intention of playing much, but I kept at it afterwards.

Football and hurling, it was an all-man's world, it definitely was. Ladies were kind of outsiders, all right. She'd be asked to go to the dances or you'd bring them to the pictures with you, but it was a man's world – ladies didn't take part. My mother never watched. My sisters went to the games, now, they were dead keen. The girls were keen enough that time, going to the matches all right – they were probably doing lines with fellows or had brothers on the team, or cousins. My cousins all came to see me. I remember we'd a big follow-on; there were plenty of girls following us, all right, but the girls didn't take any part, they didn't play any sport. My sisters didn't play any sport. One of them played camogie, eventually, but very little. I don't know what year camogie started to rise its head. Of course, now, the girls, they're playing Gaelic football and playing soccer, and golf is a great outlet for the girls. They're playing golf as long as I can remember, all right.

When we played at Croke Park we stayed in Dublin in a hotel the night before. I'd stay on Sunday night and come back on Monday. Sometimes you'd come back on Sunday. We played a lot of games in Dublin, now. They wouldn't all be All-Irelands, there'd be some other tournament matches. For the big games, you went up on Saturday, and there would usually be some reception for you on the Sunday night, a banquet or a big meal. So you stayed over and came home on Monday. You'd have a light breakfast before the match, maybe a cup of tea around twelve or one o'clock. No big meal before a game. No athlete takes anything. An empty stomach is the best way to be.

Some fellows would be very nervous, some fellows would be very cool – there's a big difference in people. I was nervous, not too bad, you know. The papers used to say I was very cool. 'Cool in all emergencies', some fellow wrote one time about me. I don't know. But I wouldn't be so cool inside. I'd be very nervous the night before or the morning of the game, but when you got on the field you'd forget your nerves. They say butterflies in the stomach are a good thing. They claim if you've butterflies in the stomach you're on good form. But to be a captain, well, you were a bit of a boss, I suppose. Cheeky, a bit cheeky.

Micheál Ó'Heithir was the commentator at all those matches. There was no television – 'twas radio. Micheál Ó'Heithir brought it to everybody. I was very friendly with him indeed. He used to call in to see me here. A lovely man. He was from Dublin, but his father was a Clare man and his mother was Dublin.

He did the racing as well, horse racing. He'd be in Roscommon Races and he'd come in to me here on the way down and on the way back in the evening. For a chat, here in the shop. He never took a drink – he was a Pioneer. I had a good snap of him and it was burnt – we'd a fire in the pub. I lost the snap of himself and myself there, 'twas a great snap. A lovely photograph. It was burnt now, and I'm very sorry to lose it.

But he often said to me that Roscommon and Cavan, those teams of that era, were his own age group, you see. He was just the very same age as me – a couple of years younger than me. He was at college with my brother Phelim and with Donal Keenan, who also played in the All-Ireland with us – three or four of our team were in UCD [*University College, Dublin*]. He was there with them, doing some science degree. He was a young fellow going to college and four or five of the Cavan team were there – students in the teams, all going to UCD. He was friendly with all those lads. So when he started broadcasting on Sundays, he knew their background, and they'd be telling him things about one another. He often said to me he had more in common with our team than with any other teams. Those ten or fifteen years when he was mixing with all those fellows, he said, they were the golden years for him, too.

The horse racing, he was terrific. He could name the horses as they'd fly over the fences, now. He got a stroke, poor fellow, and the last part of his life he was in a wheelchair, and they had a big dinner for him, in honour of him, up in Dublin. They invited us all up, all the footballers and hurlers that he had met, and horse-racing people. We all passed by and he shook hands with us all. He remembered us all, and he was dead two weeks after. Amazing. He died two weeks after. I was up at his funeral as well. But he was a great character. He was on great form on the night. 'Twas perfect. One of the greatest commentators in Ireland.

He was a Pioneer and there were a lot of Pioneers at that time in the country. The organization was huge at that time. It's gone now completely. In our team I suppose there were about nine or ten Pioneers. A lot of them took a drink afterwards. But drink, it hadn't the scene the way it is at the moment. It's the hub of everything now. I admire Dr Michael Loftus. He's very much against the GAA having anything to do with the drink advertising, because they shouldn't take sponsorship from drink firms. You can enjoy yourself without having a drink.

Going back to the early days when we were kicking a ball about. 'Twas hard enough to get a ball. We'd have a collection at school, put in your twopence each. Probably the teacher would put in a shilling. You'd get a ball for five shillings. We were never without a ball, I know that much. The teacher, I suppose, thought it was an easy way to keep fellows out of devilment. Kicking the ball out there, he knew where they were.

Running a pub was hard. My parents let me go off as best they could. They suffered more than I did. I enjoyed the football and they had to carry that extra load. It got busy at nighttime from seven o'clock on and I was gone to Castlerea or Roscommon to train for the football. Sometimes I'd stay and say, 'I won't go this evening' and they said, 'You will go. Go on, go on.' They were great.

The life of a football player – twenty years is a long period, now. Ten, fifteen years is the usual span. You could keep going to your mid-thirties. Thirty-six, thirty-seven would be the finish of it, definitely. You just fade away. They start taking you off the team and you know it's time to get up. I was finished early enough. I hurt my knee badly out on my last county match. I was thirty years of age – that was young, you know. I was very, very fit, but I hurt my knee badly. I'd have had three or four years more, I'd say, only for that. That was a disappointment, of course.

The ball in my days was a leather ball. On a wet day 'twould be very, very weighty. 'Twould be about half a stone in weight, like a lump of lead. The result was when it hopped on your fingers....I'll show you on my own fingers there. A few of them are bent and broken from the ball hopping on them. It knocked your joints out of place, you see. Not too badly. They'd come back eventually. Not too seriously, but they're a bit crooked. You see that one's well bent, and you'd get a fat thumb – that thumb was put back up to the wrist. But those things happen. That was a wet, heavy ball did that. Was a bit of a change.

Signatures on the 1944 All-Ireland Final football

O. Hoare	L. Gilmartin
W. Jackson	F. Kinlough
J. P. O'Callaghan	J. Murray (captain)
J Casserley	D. Keenan
B. Lynch	H. Gibbons
L. Carlos	J. McQuillan
P. Murray	J. J. Nurney

Sister Carmel Walsh

born 24th January 1918

Sister Carmel, whose vigorous manner belies her age, lives in the grounds of an old house, Moore Abbey, once the home of Count John McCormack. These days it is a complex of buildings given over to the care of mentally handicapped people and run by the Sisters of Charity. Much of Sister Carmel's working life was spent here as an extremely effective Chief Executive Officer, using her skills as nurse, administrator and negotiator. On the sculpted stone crest over the door in the portico is a pertinent motto, 'Fortes Cadere Cedere Non Potest' – 'The strong cannot fall nor yield'.

I'D LIKE TO WELCOME YOU to Moore Abbey. I hope that you'll find your first visit very fruitful. We have a lot of visitors, some of them very interested in the work we do, and more just come to see where McCormack lived. But other than that, we're kept busy.

I was born on 24th January 1918 (the war was just over) and there I naturally grew up and went to school – the Sisters of Mercy – and I always wanted to be a nurse. Funnily enough (how the Lord works, you know) I got a letter from an aunt of mine in Australia, in Brisbane, and she enclosed a small picture of Christ on His crucifix and a little girl at His feet, and underneath it she wrote, 'Could this be you?' Now, that's the very first time that I ever thought of being a nun. She planted the idea in my mind and I could not get rid of it. *No way!*

I come from Kerry, a place called Moyvan, near Listowel; both my parents were Kerry. We were quite a religious family, used to say the family rosary and all that. We had a great upbringing – my parents were strict, but not too strict. I was the youngest, so I got least of all, but I'm afraid I was out sometimes when I shouldn't be out! I was the youngest, but I didn't need to wear hand-me-downs, she didn't do that, now, to me, my mother.

I was inclined to be delicate. I had my tonsils out years ago in Cork and I had a very bad haemorrhage and I got glands in my neck because of it. So because of that I was always taken to Ballybunnion. I was always kept a month, for the fresh air and all that kind of thing.

Anyway, this letter came and I thought to myself, 'Gosh!' (Amazing, isn't it?) So sat down and I wrote to her, all right, but I never said whether I would or I wouldn't be a nun. I had to give myself time. I was about eighteen, I suppose, at the time.

Then, I knew a nun who was in this Order, so I got to know the Order. My sister had entered this Order before me, and through that, I thought to myself, 'I'd like to nurse,' and at that time, Jervis Street in Dublin was the place to go nursing. So I had my papers and all for Jervis Street, but Mother John Walsh came the way and she was the one that changed my mind for me. She said, 'Think about this, now,' she said, and she'd a twinkle in her eye, you know. 'I think you should enter first, and then,' she said, 'I'll make sure that you get trained in London.' And I thought, 'That's strange, now, why doesn't she let me go and train?' But, however, she was so nice, I took her at her word and I said, 'Mother, give me time to think about it.' And she did, she gave me quite a while to think about it, and then I wrote to her and I said, yes, I'd been thinking about it and I'd accept her advice, which I did.

I had talked it over with my parents, of course. And with some of the priests. One priest thought it was a crazy idea; he thought I would have been a very good mother. He was more or less trying to put me off. But I pressed on; I didn't take much notice of him, although he was a very nice man and you could talk to him. He didn't say, 'Oh, you should, you should, you *should* go.' He did the opposite. When I came to say goodbye to him he was quite annoyed with me, that I *was* going.

We were shopkeepers and we had a farm as well, and I had no interest in either of them. I was quite good at school but I hated it. There's one thing I regret in life and that's that I never played the piano. I began to play with a Mercy nun, but she hit me so much across the knuckles that I pitched her to – I wouldn't like to tell you where! I can sing, though. My sister, now, she's great at the organ and that kind of thing and she's a very good teacher. She went out to India, we were separated for a long time. A very different temperament to me. A great teacher, beautiful dancer, loves music, but more retiring, not outgoing like me.

When I was starting out in religious life, we had to cut our hair and my sister cut it. She cut it right to the bone, but it grew all the nicer. But I was very upset about that, because I'd nice hair. She always wore an Eton crop at home, but I'd nice hair. We used wear Panama hats and so on. But I was terribly upset. In those days, though, everything was different. We weren't allowed out, not to go down as far as the post office, even. Why, I don't know. That was the rule. We had to accept it, take it or leave it. But that was crazy. When you think back on it, they're all man-made rules. The Lord never meant that, not at all. Not at all.

You have to have a team spirit. Right throughout the house, there are various departments and they're all trusted to get on with things. And that's where the team spirit comes in. As a nun, you take a vow of obedience to your major superiors. You don't take a vow of obedience to the people you're working with. That's the advantage to it there.

There's poverty, chastity and obedience, you know. They were all difficult at times, if you want to be honest about it, now. They were. Poverty, now, we were all well fed, well clothed, we'd nothing to worry about that. Obedience, well, not a problem until I got my walking paper to come to Moore Abbey. That was tough, because I didn't know where I was coming, I didn't know what I was doing and I

Hannah Walsh, before she became Sister Carmel.

wanted to go to Belgium for the year. Chastity. Well, I got away with that, mind you, but a lot of them don't. I suppose you'd think, before you made your profession, 'Am I doing the right thing? Should I have stayed at home, should I have got married and had a family of my own?' But then, if that were true, it would last with you and you wouldn't be able to get away with it.

Like the picture that my aunt sent me. I couldn't get that out of my head. I could do nothing else but enter a convent. It's a remarkable thing, now.

I wrote to my aunt – she wrote back reams of letters – she was very elderly but she was well able to handle the pen. She wrote a whole diary on her way to Australia, and we all got a copy of it. She was delighted, of course. Delighted. Matilda was her name. In those days they had religious names. My religious name was Carmel, but my sister's name was Liam – she took it after my brother. Her own name is Sheila. I was known by Carmel and no other name, *including* Mary.

Anyway, I went in August and we were met at the boat by two sisters who were over from the house I was going to in Hollymount, Bury, Lancashire, and that was where I was going to be the postulant. And Mother John met us (there were three or four more with me) and we started there and we were there for a year. And I loved it. We had to work, you know! We had to clean and this and that, as novices would, as postulants, you know. All the trials, isn't it? To become a religious, first you're a postulant, then a novice, then you're professed, then there's final profession. In my time, you were three years to do that.

Then at Hollymount, Mother John called us one evening, and she said, 'You're going to Ghent, to the mother house.' So we arrived in Ghent via Ostend, and a lovely coach, a carriage, was waiting for us and we were met by the Assistant General and there was great excitement – the Irish had come! *Les Irlandaises*! I thoroughly enjoyed the novitiate in Ghent. We'd done some French in school, but I was very good in Irish and when I found myself in Ghent I just learned the French quite quickly. There was nothing but French and we just had to get on with it, and we *did* get on with it. 'Twas tough going, but we regarded it as part of the novitiate. There was cleaning and scrubbing and all the domestic chores.

And then I was put in a ward with the elderly. I said, 'This is great.' We did night duty and there was nothing there but Dutch and French people. But you know, it is amazing how the language would come to you, because your common sense would tell you what they wanted. But it was a privilege that way, you see, because I was being prepared for nursing, if you like.

I loved the Sunday mass in Belgium. Every mass was important, but I loved the Sunday mass, with the rows of novices. And you'd pick out the black veils and the white veils and the postulants and it was something tremendous. I'll never forget that to this day. And the spiritual formation was very important. We'd a Mistress of Novices and she was very strict, but she had to be. She tested our obedience and explained our vows and she did everything.

The profession was beautiful, now. We'd a lovely chapel in Ghent and we were there and we got our name. I asked for Carmel for my religious name and they said they'd give it to me if I put Mary in front of it. So I took Mary, but, sure I never got Mary in my life, once

I came back to England. I'm Carmel since the day I got professed. I was born Hannah. My other sister, Sister Liam, she was Sheila. We made final vows in St Francis College, because of the war. We couldn't go back to Belgium for that because it was occupied.

There were six of us. I knew the culture was going to be very different – the language, *everything* was going to be very different. But yet I felt 'twas a challenge and I thought, 'Why not? Why not take it? It isn't going to be the end of the world, you know.' And I was young and ready for anything. I must say I was very happy. I was – *very* happy there.

We started off the novitiate the next morning; we got our working clothes, as it were, we were in a habit then. We were Cistercians you see, the Cistercian habit. And they were all very helpful with the language and very nice and we got used to the food, quite quickly. Anybody that came over from England on St Patrick's Day, they brought a cake or something that would be different – a brack, maybe. Although the bracks in Belgium were beautiful. Beautiful!

And then we were two years there, and the day we were professed, first profession, Mother John, we went to her and she said, 'Now, you're going to go to St John's and St Elizabeth's Hospital in London for training.'

And you know, I arrived in London in the middle of all the war. World War II was on.'Twas an experience. A very good experience in one way and a very horrible one in another way. But we were young, and when you have youth on your side, you can cope with a lot of things. This was 1944, the thick of it. The war only stopped in '45, didn't it? There was still bombing, still doodlebugs and all the rest of it. And when we were on night duty, then, we got great experience in the sense of the bombs would fall and we would hear the siren go and say, 'What time will the next siren go?' Five o'clock time and we were going on night duty at eight. And the bombs would fall and you'd go flat on the floor, just in case.

And the hospital didn't escape, either. There were Sisters of Mercy in the hospital, and they were marvellous nurses. They were great help and great support to us. A great support altogether, now, I will say that for them. But they were tough times, you know. Every night, our main worry was 'When is the siren going to go and who's going to get the bombing tonight?' And during the night, two or three o'clock in the morning we'd be in the throes of it, and we'd go up to the balcony off the wards, and you could go out and see the smoke and we knew it was either from Oxford Street or Baker Street. And next morning, because we'd been on night duty we could go for a walk, and we'd go down to see where the bombs had dropped and, oh, it was devastating! Oh, 'twas desperate to see. And yet there weren't that many casualties. 'Twas mostly buildings that were hit. Our hospital was in St John's Wood, with one entrance on Circus Road, not far from Regent's Park.

One day we went down, another sister and myself, went down to Regent's Park to study. We were heading for our final. And this bobby came along and he said, 'I'm very sorry, now, sisters,' he said (he knew we were from the hospital), 'but I must ask you to leave because the people in the flats are unhappy about you being here.' This was the time people came down dressed as nuns. Just makeshift kind of thing, they were dropped from the 'plane dressed up as nuns. D'you remember that? Germans disguised as nuns. The people in the flats were naturally very frightened. They saw us and they thought, 'Here's more of it. Here's two more', you see. And he came up and he was very nice. And I had my textbook open and I was studying the heart and the other nun had the kidneys, and I said, 'Gracious! We're only studying.' But he said, 'Sister, I know exactly what you're doing, but the people in the flats, they don't understand. So I'd be very grateful if you'd move.' So we did move – out of their way, anyway; we went for a walk. Our habit at that time, we were all in white, with a headcovering and a white veil. So we moved on, then we came home and we went to bed. We had to creep into the convent because we wouldn't be allowed up beyond twelve midday, as we were on night duty that night.

But that night there was an incendiary bomb fell at the hospital gate and – this was very funny! (Well, it wasn't very funny for *him*, but we got a great bang out of it.) I was in the male surgical ward and the bomb hit the nurses' home, just at the gate and *he* was on duty, and he got a broken ankle. And he was admitted to my ward! We were all in white, then, but when we were in Regent's Park we had a black cloak. Anyway, I went up to Sister Camillus and I said, 'Come to see what I have,' I said, and she shone the torch and I said, 'That's the man we had in the park today.' And she said, 'God, it is!' she said. So he had to get morphine and he was given an X-ray and all the rest of it.

Morning came anyway, and we had to get the breakfast – 'tis great look after a lot of men, you know, they're up and around in the morning helping with breakfast and setting trays and tables. And I looked at him, and I said 'D'you remember me?' 'God,' he said, 'I do and I don't.' 'Well,' I said, 'you were the man that sent us out of the park yesterday!' Well! 'Well,' he said, 'Sister, I hope you won't take that out on me.' He was in for about a fortnight, and we had the best fortnight of eating I've ever had in my life. His wife, she was a very nice woman and she was so grateful for being nice to him, she'd bring us rashers and eggs every night. 'Twas great fun and we talked over it and we said, 'We'll give him a time of it now!' and she knew we wouldn't, you know. He was a real Londoner.

The war lasted a long time, far too long, but you got used to it. Ireland wasn't involved in it, but in some ways it was. But to forget about our policeman, life went on and we were on night duty and then day duty. Day duty was even worse, because when the siren went at night, we couldn't get to sleep – we were so frightened.

Anyway, that went on for a long time. With all that, I enjoyed it. I wanted the challenge and I got it. One time we were on night duty, Sister Camillus and myself (Lord have mercy on Camillus, she's dead since), we were full of pranks, I suppose, and we wanted something to take our minds off the bombs, and I said, 'Cam, the doctors are going out tonight, we'll put up a coat and a stethoscope on Lord Brampton.' There was a bust of Lord Brampton on my corridor. 'I'll dress him up,' I said, and we put a white coat and a stethoscope around his neck and we forgot about him and the doctors came in around half two, half three and we didn't think about him any more, never thought to remove all the regalia. Anyway, next morning, Night Sister came up and she said, 'Sister Carmel, do you know anything about Lord Brampton?' 'Oh, God, sister, I do,' said I. 'I put a white coat on him last night. Why?' 'Oh,' she said, 'you must go to the Matron's office.' So down I had to go to the Matron's office and she saw *me* coming. 'Don't tell me', she said, 'that *you* dressed up Lord Brampton?' 'I did, Matron, and I'm very sorry about it.' We meant to frighten the doctors and what did we do but frighten Reverend Mother! She was coming up in the lift with the Blessed Sacrament, with the priest, going up to the priest's floor and what did the lift do but stop dead in front of Lord Brampton!

And I had to go from that to the convent, and *she* said, 'Sister Carmel, don't tell me that *you* dressed up Lord Brampton!' (We hardly ever had to go to the convent, unless we'd get into trouble.)

'Mother, I did,' I said, 'I suppose it was a bit of diversion from the bombs. I'm not making any excuses, now, about it,' I said. 'We did it and that was it. We got busy, you know, and I forgot all about him.' But it was funny, you know.

Then another time, I was taken off night duty, and I was put on day duty, on Ward Two. Mr Mulvaney, who was one of the examiners, he used to go to the North of England. (During the war, of course, the doctors and nurses naturally couldn't come down to London.) He came in to me one morning and he said to me, 'Will you come down to me tomorrow morning now, very early?' (I was sleeping out in the corridor.) 'I'm going to Ireland in the morning and I want you to strap my chest,' he said. 'I want to take money with me.' You weren't allowed – you could only take so much, you see. Now, he was a very good man. Never got married, funnily enough. But a great lecturer. So, anyway, I said to myself, 'My God! Having to strap Mulvaney's chest! That's going to be something. That'll go in the *Telegraph*!' So I went in and I said, 'Will you let me know every time you want to breathe?' 'Oh, I'll let you know when I'm going to breathe. So, then, you get on with it,' he said. So I gave my cup of tea to him, sat him up on the bed and I strapped the chest. He'd four envelopes, two in the front and two in his back. 'And,' I said, 'what'll happen if they ask you what happened to you?' 'Oh, sure,' he said, 'I'll tell them I've cracked ribs or something.' He wasn't undressed at all. In those times, they were undressing them, coming over to Ireland! They were!

Back comes Mulvaney, now, with two half sides of bacon. And we had loads of eggs at the convent – plenty of them. We were *living* on eggs. So we had rashers and eggs for I don't know how long. In thanksgiving for strapping his chest. Those kind of things are what makes life easy, you know. We had a great laugh about it. A bit of fun. A bit of fun. I was full of it, full of devilment on top of it, I suppose.

Anyway, I finished at St John and Elizabeth's and I came home to Rocksley Court and our Superior General came from Ghent and he asked me, he said, 'They want an English-speaking nurse in Louvain. Would you be willing to go?' I said, 'I'd love to go!' Again, a challenge. I jumped at it. This was in about 1945, just after the war.

This place, Moore Abbey, had been bought, you see, before the war. We heard that as novices, back in Belgium. Monseigneur van Rechem had said, 'I was in Eerland and I deed buy an abbey in Monasterevan. I wass entertained by the parish priest Fazer Gorrey, and 'e put a bottle of Vat 69 in one 'and, 'e put a candle in the other and 'e said, "I'll see you in the morning,"' And that's how Moore Abbey was bought!

What was the home of Count John McCormack, the famous Irish tenor, and he had leased it from the Earl of Drogheda in 1925. I had no interest in it. I didn't know where Monasterevin was, even. And I came out and I said to a couple of them, 'I'm going to Belgium.' I said. 'I'm going to Louvain. They want an English-speaking nurse, so I've offered to go.' But the Mother Superior stopped it. She knew she was coming here to Moore Abbey and she wanted a nurse and she had me in mind. So, of course, she threw her hands up and she said no, she wasn't to go to Belgium. (And it wasn't fair, either, even though I'm very happy here.) And I cried! I cried. (But I didn't know anything about Moore Abbey or that they planned to bring me here.) And I cried!

Some time later, I was upstairs in one of the rooms at Rocksley and I came out with a bowl of roses in my hand and Mother Superior said, 'Well, are you ready?' ' Ready for what, Mother?' I said. 'You're one of the four for Moore Abbey.' And *down* went the bowl of roses. And it was a posh house, you know, and a lovely drawing room and a big hall under the stairs as well. And all the water went down, flowers and all. And I went into the chapel and I cried and cried and cried. She got upset, because she wanted me for here, you see, and yet she didn't want to see me upset. So after about half an hour, she came upstairs to see how was the land lying. 'Could you tell me,' she said, 'where could we stay the night in Dublin?' I had no more interest in Dublin than I had in the man in the moon. And I said, 'Oh, I can only remember where the Kerry team stayed.' I said. So she booked us into Vaughan's Hotel, as it was in those days.

Anyway, that put me in good form, and I rang home and I said, 'What'll I do? Where's Monasterevin, anyway?' And they told me it was forty miles from Dublin. It was an amazing thing, you know, but we didn't know our own history. We didn't know Ireland. You know, where would we be going? Where we went was Ballybunnion, for the sea, and we went to Dublin an odd time. And we knew Tralee, Killarney, Dingle. We knew all our own southern parts, but as for

Monasterevin, I didn't know in the name of God where it was. It was all fixed up and there was no more to it than we had to come and the date was given. McCormack had moved out some ten years before.

The four sisters who first came here were Redempta McNamee, Mother Finbarr Broderick, May Rose Gleeson and me, Carmel Walsh. I was the only nurse among them. We were met with a big car but it was pretty full and I travelled down with a big statue of Our Lady on my lap and I was sitting in a butter box. I thought we'd never get there.

So we arrived on 15th April 1946 at the Kildare Gate, big double gates. John McCormack never used the town gate because he was a bit of an intellectual snob. Well, coming down the drive, we saw this big abbey. It was sort of austere-looking. I saw it and I thought, 'My God! Isn't that desperate?' It was grey, dull, bare, cold-looking. Not a bit inviting, the Abbey. 'Is it here we're going to be living?' (I didn't realize I'd be here for the rest of my life.) And I wondered, 'What'll it be like inside?' We came up and it was desperate, altogether.

There wasn't a stick of furniture anywhere (except for one thing – Count John McCormack's grand piano). And it was dusty and dirty and unfurnished. We came in and unpacked and, oh God, we were upset.

When we first came here, the place was so big and rambling nobody would go on their own anywhere, so if one went, all four went. And one day Mother Finbar said we'd go to the courtyard, see what was there. Going up the stairs and into the courtyard, she said, 'Carmel, you're lively,' she said, 'you go first.' And I went along to the third room, and it was just littered with empty champagne bottles. A man came down from Dublin and took them and she got thirty shillings for them. There were 350 of them, empty champagne bottles! He entertained lavishly. He'd all the bishops and archbishops and cardinals entertained here. He was a great singer and he'd sing all his songs outside the door there, the piano was there.

And then, on top of it, in March '47 we had a major fire. You see, McCormack, of course, kept no heating in it and what happened was that the walls got all damp and when we took it over and we put on turf and logs and so on and it dried too much, so much that it went up in fire! We lost everything. All we had was what we stood up in. Half six in the evening and the fire wasn't over until about half three in the morning. We rang the Curragh and Portlaoise and Dublin for the fire brigade. The Superior was in Dublin and she was in an awful state. But we got over it. You have to get over all these things. But the mother house in Belgium was very good and the day after the fire, they sent over a nun with a trousseau for each one of us, the very next day. 'Twas great support.

The fire, it destroyed the west wing as you come up the drive. You could stand up in any of those rooms and look up at the sky. Oh, 'twas desperate, desperate! And we had the blankets and the sheets and the beds and everything ready for to take in the patients. And that meant they didn't come in for another year. They only came in in '48. And Dr Noel Browne, the Health Minister at the time, opened the house and he gave Mother Finbarr, the Superior at the time, £11,000, towards the fire, which was very welcome you know.

We bought the whole place back in 1937, for £8,000, you know, which was for a song. In those days, it was a lot of money. But we got 300 acres with it as well. 'Twas a good buy, but not for a hospital. We have no lift. We can't put any lift in this house, because it's listed. We manage. We've a chair lift, but the girls are getting old, you see.

Knowing what we were up against, being a general trained nurse, you learned very little if anything about epilepsy and I knew I was going to be a nurse here and I was going to be responsible, so I asked to go somewhere, so I went to Chalfont St Giles in Buckinghamshire, for six to eight weeks. And there were 690 men and women, and I can assure you, I learned an awful lot in that time.

I spent ten years at Moore Abbey with the epileptic women and then in 1958 I was sent over to Delvin, County Westmeath, about eleven miles from Mullingar, where we had to build for children who were suffering from epilepsy. (I was building a lot of my time, you know.) I came back in 1964, and 'twas then I got in with the Department of Health and also Education. Now, I didn't know much about education, but there was a school in Delvin and when it came to the nursing side, I knew it all, you see. I finished over there in 1964, and Sean McEntee, the Minister for Health, came over and he opened it, and the Superior General asked him what was going to happen to Moore Abbey. A house was needed for epileptic women of all ages, so we got talking to McEntee and he said, 'I will allocate money for Monasterevin. And when the children grow up, they can go over to Monasterevin as adults.' And that's what's happening to this day.

We've gone a long way since then. You see, we had ninety here in this main house, all adults. Severe epileptics, severe enough. But with treatment we could do a lot. Dr Blake, he was a great psychiatrist, and he kept the same girl going with the tablets until we saw the epilepsy was growing less and less.

What I did with the epileptic cases was this. They found that their day was long, so I did this thing with the workshop. I did *Jack and the Beanstalk* with them, and I did *Sleeping Beauty* and *Cinderella*. And we practised inside here in the room and then we put it on outside in the main hall. Which was great for them. Marvellous for them. And the people came in to see them, and they loved an audience. And then, the families at home were very pleased that they were here.

But I wish, now, I could play the piano. My sister can play and there's pianos all over the place. We've John McCormack's piano. He left it here. His son tried to take it away from us and I said, if you want to take it out of the house, you'll have to write me a letter asking for it and give it to me in your own handwriting, and I'll frame it and put it up in the hall, because all the people of Monasterevin could say we sold the piano. So it stayed. Well, it left the house once to go up to the concert hall in Dublin and Sister Liam and myself went up to see and I said, 'I'm not leaving here until I see McCormack's piano,' and we went down into the basement and it was there, full of dust, and it was covered over with an old blanket, all full of holes. But it came back again. It was intended to be here.

This was John McCormack's last home. He never bothered much with the local people. One time he sang for Benediction up in the chapel and the parish priest charged £20 a head to go to Benediction. Now! More of it! That's not good for religion. John wasn't that liked, but a marvellous singer, of course.

Because it isn't easy to look after someone with epilepsy in their own home. You see, with epilepsy, you get a warning, but they can swallow their tongue and they can fall and have a major attack. And they can sleep it off. But you have to have someone there to watch them. At night it's particularly dangerous because they could turn on the pillow and smother. But that's the way epilepsy goes.

A lot of the girls who came in here to us were engaged, and the fellows didn't know why they were coming here, until they were told. I'd to get a priest to explain it to them and some of them broke it off (and more of them didn't), and then the ones that broke it off didn't get married. It was a huge responsibility. We used to go out for a walk, one nun at the front and one at the back and about forty girls in between, in case one of them would get a seizure.

And I had to meet all the ministers for health. Noel Browne came here and Charlie Haughey was very good to us, very good. They all were very good, give them their due, once they knew you. And of course I *lived* in the Custom House, up and down looking for things. You see, men don't always know what you'd want. Bed linen, that was clear cut. Then they gave us this book, combined purchasing. You were supposed to buy from that. And I looked through this thing and I thought, 'Name of God, what time will I have to go to Galway, looking for things!' So I went up to them and I said, 'Gentlemen, I have no time to be doing all that. Why can't I go to Clery's?' [*A department store in Dublin.*] So I did go to Clery's and there was a great Corkman down there and he gave me the things at the same price and even sixpence cheaper. Much more convenient.

But I invited them down and I must say they got an awful shock, because they did not know what a mentally handicapped child was all about. They didn't. They've done a lot more since my time, but still you can't get beds for adults.

And the families were almost ashamed of them, they didn't want to know. I often heard that they'd say, 'Oh, we have a child up in school in Moore Abbey', and that'd mean nothing to the neighbours down at home. That was so stupid, but that was the way it was at the time. But, thank God, that's getting less.

Anyway, we saw a great necessity to take the children from Delvin with physical disabilities over here, those who were becoming adults. So I came over here in '64 and I brought ten with me, and they weren't that welcome at all with the epileptics. Those epileptic women said, 'We're not handicapped, you know.' But after a time they broke in and settled in and I decided to break all the rules. I decided that the epileptics should help, so we went outside to the tennis court and we had a picnic around the tennis court. I said, 'Now, girls, we'll feed all these children' – that's what we called them, and we sat around the tennis court and we had a meal and we, the staff, had our sandwiches with the girls who suffered from epilepsy. And that's what broke down the barriers. 'Tis all mentally handicapped we have now.

We've opened, I suppose, about eighteen houses, now. And they're out in the parish. They're in Kildare and they're in Laois and they're in Offaly, in houses. Some are supervised, more of them aren't, depending on their disability and that's a great thing, a wonderful thing altogether. And they've great independence. They come to the office and they pay their little bills and they buy their own clothes and they're more independent. 'Tis great for them and 'tis great for me, it gives me great pleasure and satisfaction to see them. You see, I knew what they were and to see what they are today. Beautiful!

And they're going off out to the theatre in Portlaoise and they go up to the Olympia in Dublin, and they want to see *Cinderella*. And they come to me and they say, 'Sister, we want to go out and there's five of us and we're going on our own.' We give them the transport and they have a meal out. And they'd put their own money for the meal, but I'd pay for the tickets. And they've an annual holiday, and they go home for Easter, the summer and Christmas. 'Tis a great work, there's no doubt in the world about that. It's a great charity. But it's unfortunate to see that the people who could come to see them and who are well off enough to come to see them, don't come and the people that aren't well off enough, they make the effort to come.

Eventually, I was getting tired. I bought a few houses for counselling. The psychologist's working in a house up in Mullingar. And one here in Abbey View. And one in Naas. But after that I was getting tired, so the Provincial came over, and I asked her could I retire. At first, she said, 'No, wait for another year.' So I waited for another year, and the next time she came over, I reminded her. So I did. I retired. And they all said, 'What's she going to do? She's going to die!' But I must say I was very happy up to this moment.

I knew that when I left, I was up there, up on top, and when I came back, I'd be down there. But I prepared myself for it. I thought, 'What of it? I've had my day and I did all I could do and I hope I did it well. And I hope the others continue the good work. Keep up the ethos and carry on what we have been doing. I am fully convinced that's going to happen.

Now, it's not all worldly things. We have certain hours for chapel, of course, and we have to be there. We go in for office at ten o'clock in the morning and then we have half an hour's meditation after the dinner and a quarter of an hour's spiritual reading and office again in the evening. The hours are shorter now than when I first joined. Oh, then we were up in the morning at half past five and chapel at half past six. Tough! But we were young and we could do it. I know there are still some Orders and they're in their eighties and they're up at six, anyway, and I think that's too harsh. They won't live that long. 'Tis very stringent, I find that.

And we had fasts. During Lent. And we stood at breakfast. Always. We'd have very little. Bread and butter – there was no such thing as marmalade or jam. No. No. We were well fed, but not the way we are today. You wouldn't see a rasher or a sausage or an egg. Not really. Especially during Lent. Oh, we hated it! But now – we've a Jacuzzi now! The one thing we weren't allowed, which was a stupid thing, if you went for a bath you had to wear your vest. I never did that. The minute I got the others out of the way, I'd remove my vest and wash myself properly. They were man-made rules, should never have been there. I just used my common sense.

The habit is gone years ago. No regrets. They're buying off the rack, now.

Why has religion gone down in Ireland? People aren't even going to Mass. I find that tragic. People have gone very materialist. I think it's the lay people that will bring Ireland back to the way it was. I think the wheel will turn. If it doesn't, God help it.

I want to say, and to be candid with you, I've been in the religious life all these years, fifty-two years, and I've never been unhappy. I might have been anxious now and again, but I've never been really unhappy. And I'd start all over again. It was the right thing for me to do and I've no regrets about that. No regrets whatsoever. None. None.

If I hadn't received that letter, I could have got married and had six children or I could have gone abroad nursing. It's amazing how the Lord works, isn't it?

Charlie Coughlan

born 12th October 1918

*Charlie Coughlan of Sopwell, County Tipperary, was born in his present house
and, since his wife moved in after their marriage, he has lived here all his life.
Inside, in the kitchen, are framed photographs of horses, to which he refers in
turn during the course of the conversation, and on the windowsill is a statue of
a huntsman in the saddle, with a foxhound beside him. The inscription on the
base reads, 'Presentation to Charlie Coughlan to commemorate his sixty-fifth
season hunting with the Ormond. 27th February 1993.'*

I STARTED HUNTING at eight years of age. I was always mad
about horses. My father, too, he used to work and plough with
horses – there was very little tractors then. I'd come from school
when I was little and he'd be out ploughing and about six in
th'evening, he'd be unyoking them and he'd put me on the horse's
back. So I started riding about six years old. I used to ride my pony
to school in Newtown – about three miles. I was mad about horses.

When I was eight years of age my father bought me a pony, up
above at Moneygall, from a man called Armitage. We went up to get
it driving a horse and a back-to-back trap, and we brought it home
with some breaking tackle. Mouldering is what we call it when you
put a bit in his mouth. He'd get used to it, and that'd make a soft
mouth. There's no bother in holding them then.

My first hunt was at the age of eight in 1926. One day I heard the
hounds on Knockshegowna (the Hill of the Fairies). The land around
here is flat, so this small hill is great for the Ormond Hunt. I decided to
go down on my pony and have a look. I put a saddle on the pony and
away with me down the road like hell. I was dying to join in. They put
up a fox and the fox was after barking, and I got in a gate and away
with me after him. Well, he ran right across into the Forestry. It was a
man's land with a ditch and a wall between and another ditch. That
pony, I couldn't hold him! The pony saw the other horses jumping and
he wanted to go! When I did hold him, he turned round on me.

Well, he came to a mighty jump and Des Kenny came up to me and didn't he shout at me, 'Let him into it!' So I turned the pony and, well, he flew it! That man, he came on, and I above on th'avenue, and he says to me, he says, 'That's the best jump I ever seen a pony doing.' Indeed he did. He put his hand in his pocket and he gave me a half crown. I thought I was a millenaire.

When I got home I got an eating! 'You could have been hurted! You could have been killed!' There was a meeting in Cloughjordan the next week and I craved them to let me go. Well, I went and from that day to this I'm hunting. That was my setting off. From that day to this of a Saturday, I've hunted.

In those days we used to hack to the meet and hack back. There was none of this business of using cars or whatever. One evening we were hunting a few miles from Lorrha. It was late and I did not leave the village until 6.30. And I had to hack all the way home, which was a good distance. I often said one should hunt at dawn to about eleven in the morning, then stop for a few hours and hunt again until dusk. The scent is always best at dawn!

Well, I started in and I kept hunting. My father and mother used to go to Birr to sell eggs and butter and they used to drive a cob, fourteen hands high, under this back-to-back trap. That was all right. The first day I had him jumping, he wasn't a great jumper at home at all, but I had to get him to jump. That first pony, he couldn't jump, but he got excited with all the horses galloping, you see.

After that, I had a bay – all you had to do was sit on him. It didn't matter what you met, he'd jump. Dandy, he was called. Twelve-two or thirteen hands. Fourteen-two is cobs, between a pony and a cob. A horse is sixteen hands high or more. Then I had Socks, because he had white socks around his hoofs. And Delilah.

There was this pony I used to ride out. The following year I started, my father said, 'Put him in now, he's stronger. You can hunt him.' I tipped him – that means you clip the hair off him, or he'd be sweating and you'd have a job cleaning him. Well, there was never a day that I took him hunting (I used to hunt him once a fortnight) and the next day he'd be lame. 'What are you doing to that horse?' says my father. I was hunting him too soon. Their bones aren't set. You shouldn't really hunt them till they're five years of age. But I didn't sell him, even if he did keep going lame. The next year I hunted him two days a week. The bones were thicker. You'll see in the races, they don't put thoroughbred horses over the jumps, not until they're five years old.

I have a jacket. Some people say pink, but I call it red. Mine has a yellow collar. There's a collar on them, different colours, and more of them is with a plain collar. And white breeches and the boots. These boots of mine [*Aigle boots, made in France, in rubber, lined at the top with leather*], your feet would never be cold in them. Then there's a waist-coat, but I never wore one. And a white scarf. It's a yellow waistcoat. Masters wear them, but 'deed, be the...[*gesture of disdain*] I didn't.

And the hat? The cap, you mean. [*He brings out a riding cap made by Christy, with its hat-band padded out with strips of newspaper.*] I seen a lad coming up only in his hair, and the Master ordered him home. 'If you fell or was hurted!' There's big insurance on a hunt. No one can claim off a farmer now. It's up to themselves.

I wore pull-ups one day. 'Twas milling rain and I wore them. 'Take them off,' says the Master. 'There's visitors.' 'I will not,' says I. And when the hunt was over, I took them off and I was dry under them. Some hunts, now, you couldn't do that. The hunts around Dublin and Kildare, they'd be stricter. You could get some of it second-hand, but saddles are grown very dear now. You could pay £500 for a good saddle. If you started out hunting it'd cost a big lot of money. To get a decent hunting horse. Horses are making an awful price these days. You wouldn't get anything under two and a half, three thousand for one that has hunted.

Look at that fellow in the photograph there. That fellow went mad on me! Look at the head of him! That's Kelly.

It was the day of a meet and this man came without a horse, and I gave him a horse to ride. I was riding the chestnut and Kelly was the horse I lent him. I christened him Kelly. Anyway, we started for a couple of miles and then I saw him go. That horse, he jumped a ditch with this man and after, the man came up to me and he said, 'I couldn't get a pull out of him.' That means he pulled at the reins but the horse wouldn't behave. Well, I thought the man'd be killed. We were coming to a main road, outside Lorrha. The other horses were pulled up at the gate and Kelly, he came up, anyway and the fact that the other horses were stopped, he didn't jump. But that man says to me, 'Jasus, I wasn't able to get a pull out of him.' Well, I brought him home and I says, 'I won't hunt that fellow any more now.' I had a mare, she was grand and sensible. Ah, he was mad, that horse.

Well, I *did* take him out again. Kearns came down one morning to a cub hunt and he ran a fox into Sopwell, the big house. I went up and I thought, 'I'll take him.' Now, wasn't there a field of turnips and the fox with the hounds after him. There was a six-foot tube gate, with palings on both sides of it. A couple of ones in cars hadn't shut the gate, and didn't the fox turn back? Right opposite the gate. Kearns came on; the hounds had gone into the woods again. Says I, 'You're *not* going. I'll hold you.' He was going stone mad. He gave a sort of rear up and I says, ' I'll make a drive in spite of you.' But what could I do? I had to let him at the gate. Well, he jumped the gate, the hounds and everything. He pulled up when I got to him. Says I, 'That finishes that, now. You won't be hunting with me.' There was not a dry hair on him. I says, 'No one else is going to hunt Kelly. He's going to the factory.' I took him up to Slavin's and got £450. Oh, he'd have killed someone! But I was not frightened. Never.

Charlie Coughlan on Socks.

Another time, I went to Birr. I had a horse, but it was a twenty-two-year-old, going on. There was a horse mart in it. This man had a lovely two-year-old and an oldish mare in it. 'Are you selling the two of them?' says I. 'I am.' 'Is that her mother?' 'No.' 'What will you take?' 'I won't sell till she goes into the ring.' Fair enough. Now, Noel Cosgrave, wasn't he bidding for the two-year-old as well. I bought her for £400. Noel put £380 – the last bid. He didn't know I was bidding. When he seen me, he stopped.

I brought her home and let her off [*put her out in the field*]. A grand mare. I let her off till she was three years old. She was out the whole winter. I gave her a lock of hay outside in the field. The following winter, I started to train her. I said, 'I'll have you.' I mouldered her. I got up on her and rode her.

Now, I had a twisted bit. When I broke her, it was a plain bit. (A twisted bit can be too severe. You'd need it only for a strong horse.) Well, I put on the other bridle and the twisted bit in it. She was always chopping on it, like that. [*Mimics a horse trying to spit out its bit*.] I thought, 'You don't like that.' I tried her a few times – just for the exercise. So I said, 'I'll put a bridle and a bit on you, the one I broke you with.'

Anyway, this day, I was about one and a half miles up the avenue and I was coming back along, about fifty or sixty yards along the ride, and there was a big heap of laurels and a clear place above it. Something gave her a start, she gave an unmerciful leap at the laurels. What happened? She pulled and I tried to turn her, and as I pulled on the reins, didn't the stitching go at the join! So I had no reins on one side.

I patted her on the neck and I held on to her mane, but I only had reins on one side. This was a year, a year and a half ago. 'What will I do? I must keep going round.' And I talking to her all the time. But she wouldn't stop. So the only thing to do, I thought, is to take my feet out of the stirrups and let myself off. I caught the top of the saddle with that hand, and up! she stopped. She thought to herself, 'What was here?' I came down in the grass on the stump of a tree. It was hidden in the grass. Well, the tree met me here, at the side. [*Puts his hand to his back*.] Oh, gee, the pain! 'Twas something desperate. And I lying where I was, I'd never be found. The whole world started to go round, but I put back my hand and I got relief. But not if I got the world could I shout.

Well, *that* was all right. I says to myself, 'What am I going to do? How am I going to get home?' The sweat came rolling down off me. Says I, 'If the mare got home, herself will be wondering am I dead.' So I started to move, and I came to a stile and I got over it. And I got home, and I says to herself, 'Will you for God's sake ring for the doctor?' He came out in a very short time, and he says, 'The only place for him is in the hospital in Nenagh. There could be ribs broke.' Out came the ambulance with a nurse and the only chance I had was lying down. Did you ever go in an ambulance? They're solid. No springs. The nurse had me on a stretcher and I thought I'd never get into Nenagh.

I had three ribs broke and one fractured. Well, that was all right. They plastered me up and after a week I was right as paint. After two days I was up. Your ribs will take in maybe two days, that's all. *That wasn't the whole of it at all!*

For seven, eight, nine, ten days I was good, but stiff in this leg, d'you see. Man, I was travelling around. Well, this morning at four o'clock, I wokened. Now, I put out a disc in my back six or eight year ago and had to go to Cork and the doctor pinned it in. The surgeon told me to keep on hunting as it would actually be good for me, and I was ordered to sleep on a plank bed. The missus was sleeping in one room and I another, and 'Jesus!' says I, 'What's under me?' I switched on the light and there were clots of black blood, nearly half a bucket of it. 'Oh merciful God,' says I. I called her. 'What's wrong with you?' 'Look at the bed!' 'Where did it come from?' 'Will ye ring Nenagh, for God's sake. I'm weak.'

Well, for luck, didn't the blood stop halfways to Nenagh, and when we got to the hospital they were waiting for me, a black doctor and a nurse. He gave me four or five injections. 'Are you weak? You must have a quare lot of blood lost.' Says I, 'Is it stopped?' Well, a doctor came in, the same doctor as with the ribs, and he says, 'Did you lose a lot of blood? Wait till I test you. Well, you've half your blood lost.' He gave me nine banks of blood. They had seven and they needed two more. They'd run out, and the nurse says, 'We'll try.' And a girl in County Clare was after giving two banks of blood. By the hokey, that was it. By the ninth one was up, I could jump up over a wall.

Now, my back was as black as that cap, but after that, I'm as young and frisky. 'It's going to be the crowning of you,' says he. 'You have all that young blood going into you.'

That mare, now, in that photo. I bought her in Birr and never minded what kind of action she had – trotting or not. One evening, I took up a barrel of water and as she came down I saw she was trotting with one foot perfect and the other swinging round. Well, I took her to Ballinasloe [*horse fair*] and I went to Miley Cash – he'd buy every sort of a horse – strong ones, everything. A niece of my own was riding her. 'Is that your mare?' says Miley. 'What do ye want for her?' 'Eight hundred pounds.' 'Trot her up there,' says he. 'Begod,' he says. 'There's one thing. I'll ship her. If I ship her and the ship goes down, she'll swim up!' 'Twas the action, d'ye see? She'd swing her leg like swimming! Three or four men came to look at her and wouldn't take her with the wind on her. Oh, Jesus, they won't buy them with winds on them. No one would buy them for to hunt or anything. Winds – the same as if you were swimming!

I have a mare and foal now. That time I was giving her nuts and she was in foal. Her time wouldn't be up for a month. When I came in view of the field, she'd come on. Up I went one day with the nuts and I going up, I could see this thing coming behind her. 'Jesus! Is the mare foaled?' says I. 'Twas a deer! On he came, a certain distance and stopped. Twenty yards. She came on and I gave her a few nuts. I left him there. I enquired for miles around, and I went to Gurteen Agricultural College. I approached a student. 'Will you tell me, did you ever see a deer in any of the fields?' 'Never.' 'There's a deer up here. Would you like to see him? He's there yet.' If you saw them two playing! He's about that height. [*Indicates three foot or so.*] He's a buck. Maybe something happened the female. I was asking different ones. A deer won't take up with sheep. With horses or cattle. That's all. Extraordinary thing.

Is it cruel to hunt the fox? Not one bit cruel to the fox. Is he cruel to lambs? What about the man lost thirty lambs last summer?

We had a big tiger cat. A tom cat. I got a job done on him the way he wouldn't go rambling. If I walked to Cloughjordan, he'd follow me. I'd say, 'Come on for a walk!' If you'd see that cat killing a rat! I pulled back the plastic on some potatoes, and what jumped out but a big rat. He got him like a lion takes a deer.

A fox will kill cats. They go mad for cats. Three cats disappeared, then two cats disappeared. 'Twas a fox. Them boys wouldn't be sorry for a lamb. Only for the hunt, there'd be more of them. This year there were never more young foxes out. They're everywhere.

Charlie Coughlan out hunting.

It's as quick a death as anything else. Ones could be firing shots at him and 'twould only wound them. Anything that's vermin should be done away with, like that.

Banning hunting? I don't believe it could come here. Look at the employment it's giving – the Laois hounds, the Limerick hounds – employing I don't know how many.

I went to see drag hunting at Scarriff. A hunt! Not at all! They all know where they're going. You'd see more in a car in a drag hunt. You could hear the hounds speaking – giving tongue after them. The hounds roaring it out of it. 'Tis only a cod. They never get blood or anything like that.

Without hunting, the horse industry would be finished. You give a subscription to the hunt. Some give £200, more can give £50. They leave it to yourself. Then there's cap money, £10, when you go out. In the twenties, when I started, it was free. Now, you meet back in the pub. All weathers, except snow or heavy frost. Then you might come out on foot. You couldn't ride horses in snow. The snow would gather under the hoofs.

I remember there was one hunt at an island near Portumna. [*Here, the Shannon opens out into Lough Derg, and little islets and peninsulas jut out into the water.*] The fox can't get away because it's an island. We parked a lorry and the hunt started, and the best of it all was he didn't go into the island first. The fox turned there before it. We lined the main road so no fox could cross it. (There could be quare damage done if you had a hunt out on the road.) He was heading into the island and the hounds after him, and the Master says to me, 'Go on where there's a ride. Stand at the ride and you'll see him crossing.' I galloped on to the next one. Three rounds that fox done. The fourth time, the people standing there let him off. You never heard such sounds. It's grand to hear them – the music that is out of them hounds. Hear them all giving tongue. There's in the region of eighteen or twenty couple. He does have around forty couple of hounds up above – he only takes a certain amount of them.

Foxhounds are pure bred. Beagles – ye'd go on foot with them. They're great gas altogether!

Ye'd never get a cold, no matter how wet it is, riding a horse. Never got a cold, often got a wetting.

I hunted with the Ormond Hunt for seventy-two seasons – until 1998. I whipped in for twelve seasons – until 1994. Whipping in, if you don't know, is like this: the Master is in front – he hunts the hounds. My job was to stay behind and keep them going after him. When he'd go into a cover to draw it, the next thing, they'll start a fox. I'd be at the other side to see will a fox come back. If a fox did happen to back out and go, I'd let out a shout. It was hard work! In the end I said I'd rather take it easy and let someone else take my place.

There are a number of hunts around here: the Galway Blazers, you heard of them, the East Galway Hounds, the North Tipperary Hounds, and the Ormonds. Each hunt has its own country. You have to subscribe to the hounds if you ride, or you can follow in a car.

If you come out on a hunt here, now, you'd find the present Master, Pat Lynch, only around thirty years of age. He was trained by Michael Dempsey in the Galway Blazers; he was whip for six years. Dempsey recommended this young fellow – he was good with hounds, and he has it took up. He resigned and the whip resigned when he did.

Hunting people often have a fox's brush around the place. [*Charlie brings out four foxes' brushes to demonstrate.*] You preserve them with salt. There's a bone running through the tail, now. You pull the bone out. You cut around the top of the brush with a knife and get the lash of the whip, wrap it round, put your foot on the fox to hold it, and you pull, and the tail comes away. You know by the brush if it's a dog fox or a vixen. A dog fox has a white tip at the end of the brush. That's how you know.

At the moment we're cub hunting. That's to scatter the cub foxes. If you meet four cubs, you scatter them. You'll never get a hunt where there's a whole lot of foxes. You let people know – you send out cards to tell of the meets. You'd start off around 11.30. We go from the Gluepot – Donoghue's. We can get big numbers. On Saint Stephen's Day [26th December] 1998 there was a meet in Cloughjordan where 108 came on horseback, and there were 94 out in 1999. On an ordinary day, though, you'd get 30 to 35. Young children on ponies, too.

Does I feel stiff after a day's hunting? No. I was often stiffer when I was a younger man. Nowadays I'm often not stiff at all after a day's hunting. I'll stop when I'm not able to get my leg over a horse's back. [*At which Mrs Coughlan, his wife, pipes up:* 'But someone will always lift you up onto the horse.']

I was seventy-five when I retired from whipping in. Looking back, I think of when there was little wire. Only at an odd place you'd meet wire and also the ditches would be all cut by workmen with billhooks. I'd say the hunting back then wasn't inhibited by the big conifer woods that we have nowadays. Overall, the hunting then was very good.

[*The record of the oldest man hunting is believed to be held by a man hunting with the Duhallow Hunt in County Cork. He was seventy-four years hunting in 1996 and was eighty-four years of age then. Had Charlie any ambitions in that regard?*]

No, I'm not out to beat any records.

Robert Taylor Carson

born 21st February 1919

With his soft voice and rather dreamy, abstracted air, Robert Taylor Carson seems as if he lives in his own – artist's – world. But the portraitist has to be acutely observant, too, and Robert Taylor Carson somehow combines a pragmatic, unsentimental streak and an uncommon frankess with an air of boyish wonder. He has no false modesty about his talent and is proud of his work, but relates tales of success as if they had happened to someone else. He seems astonished to have drawn such a lucky ticket in the lottery of life.

MY LIFE REALLY STARTED about six years of age. I was always drawing and painting, and my father said, 'I think he'll be an artist – we'd best send him to art school.' So that's what happened.

I went on painting and drawing, and my father died when I was twelve. He was a bricklayer, and we hadn't much money, so my mother, she was in a terrible state. I had other brothers and sisters. And when she married again, she had all these step-children to look after. Very difficult for her.

I left school when I was fourteen. I left school, but I always wanted to be an artist and it was always at the back of my mind to go to art school, but we couldn't afford it. I was out cutting the hedge one day and this neighbour passed by and asked me would I like to cut her hedge, so I said, 'Yes', and I went round and we chatted a while. She said her husband was an Englishman, the foreman artist at this place in Belfast, this big bill-poster place called S. C. Allen, where they did these posters.

So anyway, she spoke to him about me (I was about fourteen at the time). And he said, 'Ask him to bring in some drawings.' So I did that, and he was very interested, and after I went in for an interview they agreed I'd work as an apprentice. There were a couple of other apprentices as well as myself, but older, and there were about twenty artists there. And what they did, they got paintings from London in England, advertising Guinness and Boots drug stores and all that.

They'd photograph them first, and blow them up and then we, as apprentices, would go round with black chalk and draw the lines on these big frames. They'd blow them up in a dark room and they had these big sheets of paper and we got on ladders and drew all round. They were then rubbed down on these big aluminium plates. Black chalk, greasy black chalk it was. And they had thirteen colours and thirteen plates done – these were all printed on top of each other.

We were sent to art school in the evening and then I even got them to send us for one afternoon during the week, and that went on until 1939. We had seven years to do in full, and I had done five years or so, but during the September of 1939 the war broke out and the firm abdicated, which meant we went on the dole.

And, of course, I hadn't finished my art course and I was doing very well. So the headmaster of the art school, who was a Scotsman, he went to the Ministry of Education and he asked, 'These two boys [it was me and a chap called Rowell Friers] are the best two students I have. Could you pay to get them to keep in the art school as they haven't finished?'

So this was grand for me as we were getting the dole as well in those days, fourteen shillings a week. (We just had my brother who was working, and there was not much money coming into our house.) So, anyway, every Friday I went to the dole and we were going to art school to finish our courses, when one Friday this chap said, 'You two boys are wanted in the glasshouse.' This was a big room where these men were working – these were the managers. He said, 'I understand you are painting at th'art school.' I said, 'That's it.' 'Oh, we can't have that,' he said. 'You've got to do nothing to get your dole.' 'But,' I said, 'we're finishing our course.' 'Oh, no,' he said. 'But,' he said, 'think about it.'

So next week I happened to see a big poster beside the lifts, asking students to take up work in aircraft. They paid you so much for working from six in the early morning till twelve and then they had th'afternoon, and they changed these every month. I discovered I'd be getting around £4 a week, just as a student, making things for aircraft, from aluminium and all those things, and that meant I could get some money and also work in the art school. So I went in for it, and I was working away at this stuff and I said to this fellow, 'You know, I should be on the top floor of the art school – I'm a student.' So he said, 'Would you like to draw me?' I said I would, and in no time I was doing far better work down there than I was up in th'art school. These men were sitting for me and I was also being paid. Wonderful.

When I finished my course in 1941, my mother took me, my sister and brother up to Portrush by the sea for a couple of weeks and I happened to meet an architect, who used to come up to the class at th'art school to paint. I said, 'Bertie, what are you doing?' 'Oh,' he said, 'I'm a civilian draughtsman in the Royal Engineers. And,' he said 'what are you doing?' 'Oh,' I said 'I suppose I'll join up and I'll be peeling spuds!' But he mentioned this to his colonel, a man called ffrench-Mullen. He mentioned it to him – that I was one of the best students in the art school. 'Is that not terrible to be asked to go to peel spuds?' 'Send him to me.' So I was sent in to him that day and he said, 'I think you could help us. You know nothing about draughtsmanship?' I said, 'No'. But he said, 'Finish these drawings for us.' So that's what I did. I was on £5 a week and there were four or five other draughtsmen. It went very well and I was painting during the evenings.

Then the Americans arrived and we were making camps all round for them. We knew the Americans were arriving – the Air Force – so when they came I was sent round to show them – the officers – where they were to go – they took over hotels and things. And they were telling people that they were going to Iceland, but they weren't. That was to put off the U-boats.

So, anyhow, I was with them and they were sitting round playing guitars and I said, 'Would you like to sit for me and I'll paint you?' 'Oh, yes.' So I did these marvellous paintings of them. And that night they were put around the base to dry, and the officer of the day came in and he wanted to know who did these paintings. 'Oh, it's a civilian draughtsman.' And he mentioned these to his colonel, who was very keen on painting – he was a Jewish man from Ottawa or some place. So he said, 'How would you like to be a war artist?' I said, 'It'd be marvellous.' He said to me, 'The Signal Corps will take a selection of your paintings.' So that's what we did. I went up to Belfast, into the big room where all these officers were sitting – all American – and he said he liked these very much and so forth, and it was arranged that I was to go as a war artist. Suddenly, an English voice popped up. He said, 'You can't. He's a British subject.' If you're a British subject, you can't join the American Air Force, so that was that.

I went back to my draughtsmanship, but about eleven months later – would you believe this? – eleven months later, the phone rang and this fellow said, 'Is that Robert Taylor Carson?' I said, 'Yes.' 'A big portfolio has arrived for you from Washington, so you come up.' They'd taken over a post office in Belfast and it was a big public relations thing. He took out this portfolio and it was full of my pictures. A General Dolittle, who was chief then, he'd seen my work and he'd said, 'Let this man into our four or five Northern Ireland bases and let him paint.'

So I resigned from the Royal Engineers and I did that. I went to these bases and I spent about three months in each of them. They gave me half a Nissen hut, as if I was a Senator or Congressman. I had a batman and they gave me a bicycle to cycle round the base to paint what I wanted. And at night I did paintings of the officers which they sent home, and, of course, I got paid for these, and I was doing very well, and also keeping the paintings I was doing of the American Air Force. And then there were these paintings I was doing living among local Ulster people because it was full of farms all over the place.

A portrait of Robert Taylor Carson as a young artist.

Eventually, when the war was ended, they invited me to America with an exhibition of my work, the end of 1946, I suppose, and I went over on a ship that was full of war brides. I did a portrait of the captain of the ship, so he brought me up to sit at his table, and I was treated just like an officer.

When we arrived in America I had this exhibition, and although I was supposed to be going for two weeks, I stayed for ten months! I got commissions as one thing led to another, and I did very well. There was a big competition on in New York for artists, and I showed them one of my portraits, which I'd done in Ballymena, of a postman. And that got first prize. I was fully surprised. It was in all the papers and so on. Because, really, it's one of those things. I got away with it!

Then the British Consul, Sir Francis Evans, he invited me to paint his portrait. I'd taken a big carton of Irish pictures with me, but none of the galleries in New York would show them because they were booked up years ahead. But then one gallery rang up to say that their artist had taken ill. Would I like to fill in? I said, 'If you get them framed, I will.' So they got a Jewish framer to do them – he worked all night on them. Th'exhibition opened and I did very well because Sir Francis Evans, the British Consul, he opened it for me. After the war, in America, he was top for opening places, you know, because they thought a lot of Britain.

So he bought a few as well, and then a lady came in one wet day and she said to me, 'Are you the artist?' I said, 'Yes.' She said, 'I thought you were Irish.' Anyway, she took away the catalogue. She was married to the people who built some famous aircraft. Very wealthy. They lived up in a big penthouse on Park Avenue, New York. She was an actress away back in the silent days and still very attractive, only about sixty. And she got me to paint her.

The way it came about, she and her two daughters (one was married, and th'other was a ballet dancer), I used to have dinner with them at night. The young one, the ballet dancer, said, 'Mother, why don't you let Irish paint you?' (They called me 'Irish'.) So she said, 'No. When I was in Hollywood I wouldn't let any artist paint me.' I don't know whatever it was about me, but she rang me up a couple of days later and said, 'I'm going to let you do my portrait.'

So I arrived in a taxi at this big place, and the doormen came out in uniforms and they saw what I was carrying and they said, 'Rear entrance, bub.' I said, 'What do you mean?' They thought I was a seller or a buyer or something. 'Oh,' I said, 'No. This is for Mrs S.' Oh, they came out and apologized to me, brought all my stuff up in th'lift.

I painted her, and I said I was going to go round America if I could, possibly. She said, 'If you go to Hollywood, you'll have to meet a friend of mine. Mary Pickford. She'd love to meet my son, Tim.' And she said to me, 'You haven't met him yet.' She told me he was about my age, and he was up at her sister's house away in Massachusetts. In actual fact, he was being dried out from the whiskey, drinking water in this hospital.

But she said for me to come in, and I did this portrait in about a week, and while I was doing it she brought me up and put me into an apartment near her. I couldn't believe it! A lovely place. She paid for all this, for me to stay there and paint. There was plenty of money in these places. To give you an idea of it, Greta Garbo was there and Fred Astaire. I remember seeing him in the corridor and he'd be half dancing along, doing little steps, you know. I chatted to Fred Astaire a few times – I'd seen him with Ginger Rogers in all the movies. And in the lift, there was a beautiful blonde girl, Madeleine Carroll from *The Thirty-nine Steps*.

Mrs S. said to me, 'That's her. I bet you a dollar.' And when we got up close, it was her. But, you see, they're all done up for the films. She wasn't done up in the lift. To meet all these people was fantastic. Ridiculous!

She said, 'My son is just out of the cavalry' (this was in '47), and she said, 'If you took him with you, I'll give you a car to drive.' He was supposed to do half the driving. So I said, 'Well, if he likes me and I like him, why not?' So she brought him down to meet me and I thought he was coming down from his aunt's but he'd been in a hospital being dried out.

His father was a big, handsome man with white hair, and he agreed, so I went down to the National Geographic to get all these big maps, and we went right through America. Just think! Mrs S. gave us an Oldsmobile station wagon with beds in it, because she said we might go to cities where it'd be packed out. It took us three and a half months. We spent three weeks in Hollywood, then right up to Canada, back into parts of America, like Yellowstone Park, and then over to Florida and on up to Toronto before we came back to New York. We only left out Kentucky and some other place that was flat.

Well, on our trip around America I followed up these addresses Sir Francis Evans had given me. He was British Consul in New York, but he had been in Hollywood, and he'd said, 'If you ever go on a trip, I'll give you a lot of addresses – nearly all very good English actors.' I remember they were making a film, *Mourning Becomes Electra*. I think the girl was Vivien Leigh. She had on these big stiff clothes, frocks, whatever period it was, and they had made this big seat for her to rest on. Anyway, I enjoyed meeting all these people and seeing them making films, and I got in because of Sir Francis Evans and also because of Mrs S., or Louise H. as she was when she'd acted with Mary Pickford in the silent films. Louise's son Tim and I, we went to see Mary. She was very attractive, even then, though she must have been over sixty. And she was so glad to meet Tim, she invited us to have a meal. Most amazing how I had to meet all these people. Hollywood was marvellous. Something new. People in masses of different costumes – you didn't know what you'd meet – they had streets – towns – built in Hollywood. The money it must have cost!

We wandered as far north as Canada and saw Yellowstone Park on the way. I wasn't sketching much then, I was driving most of the time. But I did do a little painting, and I remember one time Tim calling to me in Yellowstone Park. 'Don't move! There's a snake behind you.' He went ahead of it with a rope and he pulled it round and the snake got involved with the rope and he said, 'You slip away quick!' Unbelievable, isn't it? These were not vipers but something that, if he had stabbed me with his tongue, I would have been in trouble.

I remember, too, in Quebec, we were having a meal in a restaurant and they were nearly all French, but the girl who served us, she came in and said, 'I have to tell my boss that you speak like her.' And this girl's boss was from Larne! We didn't have to pay anything, she was so glad to meet me. She'd read about me in the papers.

Then we went up to Banff Springs, the hotel, but it was so packed up, a whole three thousand people. Fantastic! So we stayed in the village and I went up to paint the falls there. About lunchtime I went to have something to eat. Of course, there were three lines of people, and when it came to me, I had no jacket on. The waiter, he said, 'Sorry. You need a jacket.' I said, 'Usually you have one to lend.' 'No,' he said, 'there's none left.' The big head waiter, a big portly fellow, he came up and he said, 'What the hell's holding up the line?' So he explained. I said, 'Look, it doesn't matter.' And I walked away. 'Come back,' he said. 'What did you say?' I repeated it and he said, 'Where are you from?' I said, 'Belfast' and he said, 'I'm from Raphoe, Donegal.' Could you believe it? And he brought us down and put us behind the orchestra, behind a screen there, and we had a marvellous lunch, and he said, 'Come up and have a dance tonight.' No charge! Just because I said, 'Ah, it doesn't matter.' The way I was disgusted. It was the voice. Going round, people would pick me up because of my accent.

Before I left Belfast, I went to see the editor of the *Belfast Newsletter*, and he invited me round to his club, the Ulster Club. So the then Prime Minister of Northern Ireland passed down and he introduced me. 'The artist Taylor Carson.' He shook his hands with me and (he was a bit deaf) he said, 'Young man, wherever you go, don't forget you're an Ulsterman.' He didn't mean it politically. He meant, to speak Ulster. It gets you round. It taught me a lesson.

And I did a second year back again in America, in Chicago. Of course, how lucky I was. I had an exhibition there, and a young chap, my age, came in and he was a grandson of the chewing gum people – Wrigley. He said to me, 'Would you like to paint my daughter, only three?' So I painted the daughter and he said, 'Have you ever been to a baseball game?' I said, 'No, never.' So they owned the Chicago Cubs and he took me up and we were way up at the very top. 'Would you like to do some sketches?' I said, 'This game is like what we call in Ireland rounders.' So I did these drawings and I didn't realize that the television camera was on me. He'd arranged this – they shot me working while the teams were out resting. After it was over, I got a big fat cheque from the TV people. I couldn't believe it!

So I went to have dinner with all these big players, six foot four. And I always remember, because you're an artist, they think in America that you're homosexual. At an exhibition I'd had the year before, they all came in to meet me, these homosexual boys. Isn't that interesting? In this case, I was having my meal and this fellow came down, a big brute, and he sits down beside me and he says, 'I'd love to sit on your ass.' I didn't know what he meant and suddenly it hit me and I said, 'No, you've the wrong man.' That's typical American.

And also in Chicago I met this major, and when he'd been in Ireland he was in the Air Force. He invited me out. He said, 'I'm with J. Walter Thompson,' and he said to me, 'I want to take you out for a special dinner. We've brought out a new drink and I want to send it to Ireland. All you have to do...' All he wanted me to do was to take this to Ireland and go into a bottler and they would bottle this stuff and sell it, and they would pay me a penny a bottle as sold. Just you think! I turned it down. I was an artist and I didn't want to get caught up in all this. And, really, you wouldn't have got caught up in a thing. It was a simple thing: bring an envelope and go into them. He said, 'Only people like you would get this chance.' I often think today what I'd be worth when I look around and see all the 7-Up.

But in Chicago this man came into the exhibition and bought some pictures. He was in the steel business, from Pittsburgh. And he said to me, 'We have a summer home on Michigan Lake. You come up this weekend.' I went up and he had all these friends, and he explained that they had a big ship waiting at San Francisco. He'd been in the war, flying 'planes over the Pacific, and he saw these islands. And when the war was over he bought one of them, and they were going out to this island. He said the women were half-naked – you know, the usual – and he said, 'You could paint them. Would you like to come? We're going out for nine months and we're taking all the food with us.' He said, 'You could be like Gauguin.' I said, 'Away for nine months?' 'Yes.' But I thought these boys could be half homosexual, you see, and I could be heartbroken, so I said, 'No.' And I went back to Ireland and married my wife.

It happened this way. With Maurice Wilkes, a famous painter, ten years older than me, we went up in 1946 to paint in Downings, County Donegal. We were there in digs for four weeks, and we met a local man called McNutt who said, 'Have you ever met the nice girl in the hotel?' (A small place, called the Beach Hotel.) I said, 'No.' 'A very attractive girl.' So we were away painting and we met these two Presbyterian clergymen who knew Maurice Wilkes, and they invited us for a drink in the Beach, where they were staying. And as I walked in she was coming down the stairs and this woman staying in the hotel had just done her hair and she looked very attractive. And that's how I met her first. So eventually we married and had Patricia, my daughter, and Michael, my son.

My ability to draw and paint, I never thought about it until my father said, 'You're going to be an artist.' He played the violin a bit, traditional, Irish songs. He was a bricklayer – in those days you didn't get paid for a wet day. There could be maybe a week with no wages, and then when he died I was twelve. Terrible. It meant my life stopped. I couldn't be going to art school in Belfast. We had no money. But working at S. C. Allen helped. When I was there, Winsor and Newton had a competition and I won it, and they sent me a whole big easel and paints. Which I could never have got. Just lucky.

The Americans coming – that was marvellous for me. When I arrived in America, immediately I was on TV and radio. I painted Raymond Massey and all these people. Raymond Massey, I met him through painting Sir Francis Evans, and he invited me out for a meal. I was delighted and when we went out they were all looking at us because he was a very well-known actor. And the Lord Mayor for New York got me. He was from Bohola in Mayo. O'Dwyer was his name. He had me to paint him. It's wonderful how you just can't stop it. One thing just led to another.

I didn't tell the full story of travelling around America. 'Twasn't all easy. Tim S., he was always drinking whiskey, and when we got to Alberta you were allowed to buy whiskey, but you had to show how you got it. Well, we booked into the Banff Springs Hotel, marvellous place, and I noticed Tim away at the entrance and there was a whole row going on. I said, 'Just a minute. Is there something wrong?' And Tim had bought a bottle of whiskey and he was pouring it into a paper cup, and of course the manager said, 'They'll have us closed up.' Tim said, 'My father, he knows the President. He goes to see him once a month.' (His father was a big businessman.) 'And,' he says, 'this man here painted Mayor O'Dwyer.' But the manager says, 'This is Alberta. You're not allowed to drink. You have to have permission to get a bottle.'

But Tim was one of those people who didn't give a damn. At night, I'd be writing home, and he'd be away out with some prostitute. He'd ring his mother up and she'd send him money. She knew what was going on. She thought I'd be a good influence on him because I was different altogether. I just took a beer.

Now, Mrs S., she used to be married to the Governor of one of the southern states. And then she got divorced and married this fellow, he was very wealthy, made aeroplanes, a big white-haired man. And she brought up this black woman with her, a cook. So I used to eat there and the food was very good and there were these marvellous sweets, beautiful, famous ones. And I said to this woman, 'These are marvellous.' And the tears went down her cheeks because they never said a word to her about the food. Isn't that awful? What sort of people...? And she said, 'Oh, that's so nice of you.'

There was this night and Tim wanted to go to this new place just opened in New York, and he wanted $50. 'I'll take Irish,' he said, and his mother said no because she wanted to keep him off the drink. So soon after, his father came in and we'd seen his father that afternoon in a club, the old man sitting with this lovely blonde, and she was getting space for *Time* magazine and *Life* magazine, but you could see there was more to it than that. So anyway, Tim said 'I want to take Irish to this new place.' And the father said, 'Oh, sure, sure.'

I wasn't tempted to stay there in America, though, because I found it was all a rat race, quite honestly. Everyone was trying to push th'other one out, and that was why I was so glad to get back to Ireland, because you just do what you want to do.

When I was little, I might copy something or I saw my mother sitting and I might draw a little sketch of her. When I was at elementary school we had an art class with a fellow called Adams and although I was ten or eleven, in actual fact I was better than he was. It's true. And he asked me to take the class, at that age! And I remember the *Belfast Telegraph* used to have a competition every Christmas. They had drawings in the paper and asked you to do something like that. And I was helping the class and we all got prizes! Rowell Friers, he was doing them, too.

Generally, I was most interested in portraits, figures. When I was about eighteen years of age the art teacher I had, an English chap called Mansfield, he was very good. He was very encouraged with my work and they used to bring these old boys in from Belfast, from the homes, and they used to pay them to sit. I did this fellow and Mansfield said he must send it to the Royal Hibernian. I said, 'Are you sure?' 'Oh, yes.' So he got it sent down and I went to see it at the opening. It was very crowded and I knew nobody in it, but as I was walking out, this voice said, 'Hello, young man.' Here was the President, Dermot Bryant, in his robes. He said, 'Let me tell you, this portrait is very good. Keep at that.' Wasn't it wonderful? I was only eighteen.

I'd like a lot of painters, but Manet was my painter. I liked all the French Impressionists, but I used to copy his pictures. No, I wasn't copying them, but I was painting like him, he impressed me so much.

When I'm doing a portrait, I start with a small brush with raw sienna. I was a very quick painter, that's the truth. I would paint a picture in a sitting. Eventually, I did longer sittings, but they used to say to me, 'You're too quick.' I did a marvellous portrait of my wife when we got married. I didn't finish the hair but I have it still. I did it by tilley lamp. Way back there was no electricity, and the tilley lamp was marvellous. You painted pictures like the Old Masters, like Rembrandt, just light and shade – beautiful.

I can paint with or without a background, it doesn't matter. My wife was very dark, so I'd paint something to complement it. When I'm painting I ask people to sit naturally and I'd just chat away, though I ask them not to answer me. People could never paint children, and that was my big point. I could. People coming up the Beach Hotel, they'd children of five or six and want them painted and I got them up to sit. They watched me mixing the colours and they were completely engrossed in it. All I wanted was one good sitting. For example, I did one very good one of my son Michael, about six years of age, in a *bainin* sweater.

When I do a portrait, I'm quick, as I say. I used to get the likeness at one sitting. And also, if I don't get that, I change it. I know it's coming on but if it's not like the person I just get another canvas and start off again. Because I know myself if it's right. Especially children. I can get them very quickly, their nice little faces. The first sitting with them is great – they can't get over it, but after that I'm fine.

One of the nice things that happened me, my wife and I went caravanning from Donegal to Cork and back – we took about six months. I used to send canvases to different parts of the west – Galway, Kerry and so forth. In Connemara, we stayed beside this little house and my wife was pregnant at the time. I'd be away painting and she used to keep her eye on the caravan, because a lot of tinkers were about and they would walk in and lift things if you didn't watch them.

A portrait of Mrs O'Malley by Robert Taylor Carson

This Mrs O'Malley, she used to go out with a hatchet. Her husband was living in London, working, and he used to come home for two weeks every year and they'd have a child every year, so you may guess how unhappy it was for her. Anyway, she kept this hatchet and she protected my wife from these people. I think it was very kind, so I always kept the painting I did of her just because of that. We had a colourful shawl which we put around her and it made a very good painting.

I used to get people to sit for me as well as doing landscapes; maybe children who'd deliver the milk – I'd ask them to sit for me and that's what my life as a painter was – characters and landscapes. You met people and you'd realize there was something very colourful about them. And I'd pay them. I painted Mrs O'Malley in the early 'fifties (my son Michael wasn't born then), and although I honestly don't remember what I paid her, she was well paid.

I now keep a record of people who buy my paintings – give the title of the picture and the price, although I didn't do that at the start. One time we'd come back from winter in Majorca, and my wife was very dark and she had this marvellous suntan on her face. When we stayed in Connemara, in Roundstone, I'd leave my pictures in the window of Millar's tweed shop in Clifden and they'd sell them for me. When people asked how could they go to see this painter, they'd say, 'Go to Roundstone and if you see a woman and you can't believe she's Irish, that's his wife.' I paid this farmer, Lord Bolton he was called, so much to rent one of the rooms in his house. He gave me a big key, about twelve inches long, and I'd be up there painting, made it a studio. He was a very pleasant man and a very colourful man. I painted him also.

We used to try to spend the winters in Spain. The first time was in 1955 and we went for the winter to Majorca. The children were small and I rang the AA to find us somewhere to stay in all the villages along the way, all the way through France and into Spain. One place we rented a house and the little cooker was so small and only nuts to burn, that when Ruby, my wife, tried to do it she was smothered in smoke. But then this Spanish girl came along and she did everything. She cooked us four-course meals, but she wouldn't eat them – instead, she'd go down to the rocks and pick mussels and have some olive oil in the palm of her hand and some bread, and that was her meal. When we left, she kissed us and ran into the woods and we never saw her again. Aren't they lovely, Spanish people? Not all that different from Irish people in some ways.

I went to Tory Island and got to know the people there and the Blasket Islands, too. So wild. The house we were staying in, there were beams going across the house and the hens'd be roosting there. They'd say, 'Watch when you're having your meal or you might get hit with an egg.' And at night you'd hear the young seals crying, just like babies. The people there didn't have a thatch on the house, as they used in Donegal, just black oiled cloth. In Donegal the thatch is every-where, and I missed that.

None of my brothers and sisters showed much interest in my work. The only one was my mother's second husband's child. He used to go to Queen's University, not as a student – he just used to go and listen to people and chat to them. He encouraged me a lot. The others never bothered. You won't believe it, but in Northern Ireland then, if you were a painter you were a cissy! And when you think of all the good painters in Northern Ireland! But my mother was very interested. When I became quite well known, in the papers, she was delighted. I've painted her a few times.

These days I am an Honorary Academician in Northern Ireland. The Royal Ulster Academy. About two or three years ago they made me an honorary. You don't have to pay anything. I don't show my pictures in galleries, don't bother now, because people come from all over Ireland to buy them.

Early in my career, I painted the VC – McGuinness – and it was in the Royal Academy. Now, that chap, he was a Roman Catholic from the Falls Road and in those days, when I painted him, he got very little publicity. Because he was a Catholic, do you understand? Not that I care about the religious part. And the amazing thing is that just recently they had a big meeting in City Hall, Belfast, to compliment him. To try to make amends, I suppose. Most unusual. But with this thing going on now about the peace, they brought the painting down to the City Hall in Belfast and it's there at the moment, to let people see it. The British Legion bought it.

He's very sad, that boy. Because he was Catholic, when he came back, all the papers just barely mentioned it. He sold his VC to make money. Isn't that awful? He went to live in England, got a job. Died eventually. He was in the Royal Navy, and he and his lieutenant – he was just an Able-Bodied Seaman – they were off Japan and they were sent in a small submarine – just held two people – with this big bomb. They went underneath the security in Japan and they attached it to this big warship and they got out. They got the VC for that, you see.

But, you see, it's a terrible thing in Northern Ireland – just because of religion. The poor boy, they should have given him a job or something. Awful, isn't it? It lets you know how bitter it is. Terrible. But these are things that happened. I couldn't do anything about it. Sure, the whole thing's ridiculous. I mean, what does it matter? There mightn't be a hereafter. The whole thing's crazy.

But I felt so sorry for him, because he had to go abroad. Go to England to work. I don't think he had a family. I mean, they made a big fuss of him in England because he got the VC and they gave him a job. I always remember the way he sat for his portrait. On the chair, back to front, with his legs out.

I can change some things in a portrait if I want to. If whatever they are wearing isn't right for the picture, I might change it to a blue, say. I never do a flattering portrait – I paint people as they are. It's no good making a young woman out of an old woman. A lady wanted me to make her like Greer Garson – *she* was Ulster. She didn't take the picture I painted of her! I sold it eventually. But people often buy pictures of someone they don't know. This family wanted their boy's picture done for – at thirteen in the Jewish religion – a bar mitzvah. I painted him, a very nice dark boy. Whatever it was, the mother really wasn't very interested. So what I did was, I put an Aran sweater on him and a background, a seascape. The next big exhibition it was there, it was sold. She was so annoyed that her boy's portrait had been bought. I said, 'Blast it, you didn't want it! I could have forced you to take it.' But I didn't want to force people. She was very annoyed at that. That's the sort of thing you get in life. To me it was one of those things.

The amazing thing is that most of the good painters in Ireland are from the North of Ireland. Paul Henry was from Belfast, and Frank McKelvey, another Belfast man. Sir John Lavery – he was from Lurgan. Derek Hill, another from the North.

Jewish people seem to like my work. They know it's good. Sure, they had a rabbi called Rabbi Schachter. As he got older, they commissioned me to paint his portrait. Now, he had a wee beard. What amused me, the beard was thin – you could see his clothes through it. He asked me, 'Would you not make my beard a little stronger?' I mean – lets you see even a rabbi… Marvellous!

I saw my name in a book, *Best Artists from a Thousand Years*. Taylor Carson. It was a painting of a donkey standing waiting for two women to stop talking. It was done in Clifden and I called it *The Patient Donkey*. A very good picture, done with a palette knife. I did it way back in Connemara in the 1950s. I was quite surprised to see my name there. But that's just one of those things.

Patrick Mackenzie

born 16th March 1919

*A tall figure, with an altogether gentler and more humorous air than is generally
expected in a judge, Patrick Mackenzie is most courteous, engagingly outspoken
and entertaining. He reminisces about colourful characters he knew during his
long years practising law, and he relishes the drama of the courtroom.*

I WAS BORN in Blackrock, County Dublin, and law was in the
family – my maternal grandfather was a prominent Dublin solicitor.
I had an inkling I'd go into law – I studied in UCD and the King's
Inns. There were sixteen students in my year – that was regarded as an
enormous amount. Sixteen students called to the bar. They said,
'There's going to be no living in here for them,' but four or five of us
became judges and the others all made a living, too. There were very
few judges in those days – six judges in the High Court, five in the
Supreme Court. Now there are twenty in the High Court and seven in
the Supreme Court. There's more litigation today, and more crime, too.

I was a barrister for thirty years and a senior barrister at fifty-two.
I became a judge at sixty-seven and practised as such for five years. I
chose to begin my career on the Eastern Circuit, which consisted of
Wicklow, Wexford, Kildare, Meath, Louth and Dublin.

I had my first venture on the Circuit in February 1942. I was living
in Dublin and I got on a tram at the bottom of Ailesbury Road to
catch the quarter-to-seven train from Westland Row. I had with me my
black cloth bag, initials stitched in red, containing a tin box with a wig
and gown, but no briefs. I had less than £3 in my pocket – enough for
the train fare and some lunch for several days. I could cover my
expenses if I got the most meagre brief, which of course I did not.

It was a foggy, freezing morning and the train was to take one
hour and three quarters to do the thirty-mile run. It was powered by
a furnace of damp turf and a few sticks. Clouds of steam filled the
carriage, coming from a pipe which was supposed to heat the passengers. Sitting there in the compartment, I can't say I felt cheerful. I

had the prospect of a lonely journey to an unknown place without even a newspaper to read. Then the door opened and in came The O'Rathaille, a barrister who later became a very good friend, then Sean MacBride, and finally Vivian de Valera. All were established at the Bar, recognized me as a newcomer, and in a most friendly way introduced themselves. As a huge red sun emerged from the sea over Killiney Bay, I felt things were looking up.

Wicklow courthouse stands at the southern end of the town, with a former prison behind it. Below the courtrooms is a series of gloomy cells, and in the prison yard many people were led from the place of condemnation to the gallows and executed. This happened particularly after the battles and uprising of 1798.

Two rooms in the Wicklow courthouse are set aside for the legal profession, one for solicitors, the other for barristers, both equally dismal. Heating at that time came from a fireplace upon which two damp sods of turf would smoulder. The courtrooms, however, were beautiful, if somewhat decayed, and have since been restored.

Judge Michael Comyn, who presided over the Eastern Circuit at that time, was the most popular and humane of judges. He was a stout old man with a battered wig and across his large corporation was a gleaming gold watch chain. From time to time he took snuff with a loud sniff and a blow of his nose. All cases had a great fascination for him. He frequently made remarks after hearing the opening statement, such as 'Oh, I'll hear this case. I'll try this case. I'll get to the bottom of it if I have to stay here all night.' Then he'd instruct counsel. 'Put up your witnesses now.' One of the leaders on the Circuit at that time was Art O'Connor, and I remember him introducing a case. 'My client, m'Lord, is a widow.'

'You don't say. That's all right, Mr O'Connor,' said Judge Comyn. 'She's a widow, is she? We'll do right by the widow.'

This particular morning, the first case to go on was an appeal against a sentence of imprisonment on a young girl who was working as a maid in a big house in the neighbourhood of Arklow. Not being able to produce a guinea for counsel, she was represented by a local solicitor, Mr Louth, a good country practitioner. The girl had stolen her employer's jewellery and some silver spoons. A great case was put up by Mr Louth, explaining how the young lady was under the influence of a man who had falsely promised marriage, and that was why she had committed the crime. Mr Louth even quoted from James Joyce's short story, 'Two Gallants', much to the judge's interest. The jewellery had been returned, but the man-friend had apparently absconded with the spoons and the girl would not betray his whereabouts.

'Now,' said Michael Comyn, 'that's a great plea you have made, Mr Louth, great eloquence you have displayed, and I'm inclined to be lenient with her. But what about those spoons? The lady will have to get them back, they are valuable spoons, Cork eighteenth-century silver. Marvellous craftsmen they were in those days.'

'Yes, m'Lord, I'll do my best if you'll allow me to speak to my client once more again. I'll try her.' He went and whispered with her, then returned.

'Well now, Mr Louth?' said Michael. 'Ah,' said Louth, 'this is not the first time I've spoken to her, m'Lord. I'll tell you what. No man could have pressed her more. I've pressed her and I've pressed her upside down and inside out and I can't get a spoon out of her.' Naturally, we all roared with laughter, including the judge, and the girl was merely bound to the peace to be of good behaviour.

It was a pleasant start to my first day out of the Law Library and as we adjourned for lunch, I had a good appetite. I asked the young lady what there was on the menu. 'Eggs,' she replied. Thinking of fluffy scrambled eggs, omelettes, or even eggs Florentine, I asked her what way they were done. 'Hard boiled, medium boiled or soft boiled,' she said. And that was the fare. We all sat around one big table. Gus Cullen, the State Solicitor, presided, slopping out cups of tea from a huge tin teapot. We waited and waited until the girl came in with thick rounds of toast and a pot of marmalade. Eventually the eggs arrived in a bowl. 'Which are these?' asked Gus. 'These are the hard boiled,' said she. Five minutes later the medium arrived and the soft boiled last of all. I could never get to the bottom of why they invariably arrived in this order.

I repeated that train journey every day for two weeks, the duration of the sessions. No one ever considered that I had any existence, though some were kind enough to talk to me occasionally, particularly some solicitors who, outside the courtroom would smoke a cigarette, commencing their conversation with, 'Now, I've a funny old case in the office. Now, what would you make of this? I never had the situation before – what do you think of it?' Some query would then be put to me that would baffle even the Chief Justice. Putting on a knowing look, I would always reply, 'You'll have to go back to basics and find what the real contract is' or some such rubbish. I would produce some sort of garbage to ease their problem. A year later, they began to remember my name.

When a barrister is not out on circuit, his home is the Four Courts in Dublin, on the north side of the Liffey. It is a tremendous building. Entering it and passing through the lobby, one cannot but be impressed by the marvellous rotunda beneath a magnificent dome. Four imposing chambers have their entrances here and, as in good Georgian architecture, the length, breadth and height of the rooms bear certain recognized proportions to each other, giving them their graceful appearances. The ceilings have been well restored. The building is not, however, called after these four courtrooms, as you might suppose, but after the old divisions of the Courts of Chancery, Exchequer, Common Pleas and King's Bench. A barrister is said to be 'in the Round Hall' if he specializes in personal injury, defamation actions or similar common law suits which are usually tried in these chambers. Nowadays Round Hall people are supposed to have very high incomes, sometimes receiving several thousand pounds for a brief. In the 1940s, however, the recognized senior fee for a common law action with a jury was twelve guineas, or, at the very most, fifteen. My first fee, I remember, was three guineas. Three guineas.

I worked in the Law Library for forty-five years and I have to say that whoever rebuilt it at the rear of the Four Courts must have specialized in hay sheds. This is a chamber without any beauty and without the excuse of even being functional. In those forty-five years I had an air space of about 19 cubic feet. I sat at a desk about 3 foot long and 18 inches in breadth.

Now, before he took his call, the aspiring barrister usually purchased a wig and gown. In charge of the senior dressing room was a man whose name was Geraghty. His job was to measure the paraphernalia of the profession. He had a very alcoholic face, spectacles which must have been fitted with incorrect lenses and, especially, a very shaky hand. Consequently, it was impossible to obtain a wig of proper fit. As he passed the tape around the victim's skull and wrote the measurements down, the great tremor in his hand was obvious. Collecting my wig from him, in a shiny black box with my name engraved on it, followed by the words 'Esquire' and 'Barrister at Law' in bold gold letters, I found inside a horse-hair object suitable for the head of a midget. It perched on the top of my head and remained perched there for many years. The wig of one of my colleagues came down over his ears, making him look like Dr Samuel Johnson. Nothing could be done about it, though. Geraghty was in the impregnable position of security and, if criticized, would probably have said that your head had either shrunk or swollen.

The most important job for the Library staff was the Door. A man called Campion held that position in my time. He sat on a high desk at the entrance, preventing anyone from entering the chamber beyond the threshold, which was an imaginary line 6 feet inwards. He was also required to bellow out names of barristers when asked for by solicitors, and, lastly, to take note of the whereabouts of each member. To perform this last function, he had a large sheet of paper on which was printed in alphabetical order the name of every practitioner. A fresh sheet was used each day. If a solicitor ever requested someone by name and there was no answer, the Door would look at the sheet and shout, 'Two,' 'Six' or 'The Soup.' This was understood to mean that he who was sought was to be found in either Court Two, Court Six or the Supreme Court.

When Campion retired, a Dubliner called Paddy took over. The Door confused him. At times the situation there was pandemonium, especially on Motion Days, which then used to be Fridays. A battle would take place between barristers, pushing their way out and solicitors, forcing their way in. Each member of the Bar going out shouted Four, Seven or Eight, to indicate the number of the court he was going to. Simultaneously, Paddy was expected to write down, as Campion did, those numbers on the sheet. Paddy could never get this right and, to make himself busy, would shout names at random, particularly that of his old pal, Henry Moloney. Or he would yell to people, 'Ah, give me a chance, will ya?'

Eventually, things got him down so much he started to shout, 'Leave me effin' alone,' and at times abandoned the Door in midstream, leaving it to be taken over by one of the younger boys. He eventually retired with his 'nerves'.

I said I practised on the Eastern Circuit, although it was not fashionable. Posh people used to go on the Leinster Circuit, embracing Tipperary, Kilkenny, Carlow and Waterford at that time. You had to apply to join that Circuit, and for a year the aspiring applicant was called a 'probationer'. Once he had dined a certain number of times in two or three towns, he was elected. A strict code was observed. Attendance at dinner was compulsory and punctual. Absence without cause incurred a fine, usually 'presentation of wine for the cellar'. There was nothing like this in the eastern counties.

When I was a junior barrister, I'd travel around the circuit by train or bus. I remember staying at the Glenview Hotel and the owners had eight children. Every wedding anniversary they conceived another child.

People like me who had to get to Wexford took to using the bus, but a journey of some seventy miles could take about five hours. Haltings took place at many public houses on the way, organized, I suspect, by the proprietors bribing the bus crew. Each hostelry was bleaker and filthier than the one before. Still, once we got to Wexford, we got a great welcome at White's Hotel and a splendid dinner. The only problem was Jimmy, the porter, who would come to the bus terminus, collect the suitcases and brief bags in a handcart, greeting us all and thanking us very much, presumably in anticipation. One of his jobs was to clean the shoes, and once we'd retired, he would noisily collect all the shoes from outside the doors at any time of the night the spirit moved. He trundled them down to the end of the passage, where he banged and thumped with his brushes throughout the still hours of the night. His task finished, he tramped down the corridor and slammed the shoes down outside each bedroom to make sure that if he hadn't already wakened the occupant, he would do so then.

One thing I learned as I got more experience is that members of the medical profession play an important role in litigation. In most cases where damages are claimed for personal injuries, they can be seen on the plaintiff's side giving forceful evidence of permanent disability resulting from the injury, and then for the defendant, of complete and absolute recovery. In my time, Mr Arthur Chance, an orthopaedic surgeon attached to Jervis Street Hospital in Dublin, was very sought after for insurance companies. He was strikingly handsome, with silver hair, silver moustache, immaculate blue pin-striped suit, and he consulted his notes with the aid of a monocle. He was a most formidable man to cross-examine, because he never answered a direct question – he gave a little lecture as if he were addressing students, and the result was long and ambiguous. It was reputed that insurance companies paid him great fees during the war to travel to country places for the day. A counsel appearing for the employer in a Workman's Compensation case might get five guineas, but it was said that Dr Chance got a hundred guineas, and a car to bring him to the courthouse.

On one occasion he went to Thurles, in County Tipperary, instructed by an insurance company. The case was a Workman's Compensation review, meaning that the man having been awarded a weekly sum for the original order was thought by the employer to have recovered, wholly or partially, and was fit to do some work again.

Opening the case, counsel for the employer told the judge that Mr Chance had thoroughly examined this man and he was satisfied that he was absolutely recovered and could return to his job. Taking the oath, Mr Chance consulted his notes. 'This man, aged thirty-five, told me that he hurt his back lifting a bale of straw two years ago. I examined him thoroughly, during the course of which he said he was no better – the pain was terrible. I remember asking him to bend forward and he winced with pain. Asked to touch his toes, he couldn't get his hands even near his knees. When I palpated his back, he jumped in agony and asked me to stop "for Jasus' sake".

'However, I had asked him to undress for the examination, and although he didn't know it, I observed him closely. To take off his trousers, he had to pull his braces from the shoulder, undo his belt and bend down to remove the trousers as he still had his shoes on. His back movements during this were free and perfect. The same applies to when he dressed again.'

'What was your conclusion?' asked the judge.

'In my opinion, this man has completely recovered and no objective reason could be found for his pain. On undressing and dressing, all movements of his back were full and painless.'

The employer's barrister beamed and sat down. His solicitor smiled and the insurance company man in the back of the court gave a smirk.

Ruefully, the workman's counsel stood up.

'I am calling his local general practitioner, m'Lord.'

There could not have been a greater contrast between the dapper Mr Chance and the local doctor with his dishevelled suit, untidy hair, greasy tie and strong rustic accent.

'What,' asked the judge, 'is your opinion of the applicant?'

'I know this man well. He can't work, he's got a bad back, he's a genuine character and an honest man. It's my own view he'll never again be fit for full labouring work.'

'What did you find wrong with him?'

'Ah, he must have strained his back, the weight was too much. All his muscles and vertebrae are sore. I know all his family and they're all genuine. Workers to a man and woman. He was a rare fellow until he got this injury.'

The employer's counsel got up to cross-examine him.

'You say he hurt his back. What muscle did he strain?'

'Ah, one of those muscles that's attached to the spine. The lumbar muscle – they're all over the back.'

'Didn't you say on one occasion, the last time we were here, that he had a pain up near his neck?'

'Sure,' said the octor, 'he had. It was all over his back. Everywhere.'

'Now, Doctor, you're on your oath. Don't you know this man is a malingerer?'

'Faith, he's not. He's genuine and cannot work. He might try a job for an hour or so, but then he's had it. 'Twould be the bed for him for days.'

'Did you pay attention to Mr Chance's evidence?'

'I did.'

'You heard Mr Chance say' – dramatic pause – ' that he could undress himself without pain, managing his trousers, both dressing and undressing. Have you any comment to make about that?'

'Yes.'

'Well, what do you say?'

'Now,' said the doctor, 'you won't get any work in this town pulling down and pulling up your trousers.'

The man's compensation was not cut off and he and his doctor went happily to the nearest pub.

~ ✿ ~

I always had a reputation as a very good judge – very good with juries. I was a good barrister, too. Very co-operative. I specialized in will cases, murder and matrimonial. I'd give annulments at the drop of a hat. The view of canon law is that a person must have due discretion to marry. I like to see four years' separation

Patrick Mackenzie with his daughter on the day of his retirement, March 1982.

before a divorce goes through – it gives the people a chance to get together again.

Then I was very sympathetic in rape cases. There are a lot of unreported cases. A tremendous number of girls are the victims of date rape. The High Court and Central Criminal Court deal with murder and rape and the circuit hears the rest of the cases. There's a special court for dealing with firearms. Three judges and no jury. In civil cases, it's one judge alone. There's a jury in each civil case, although the insurance companies agitated for the abolition of juries. Juries are made up of a real cross-section, and very rarely was a jury decision upset. If you employ a clever barrister, he'll be experienced in the dangers of the court and generally juries ignore a smart alec and listen to the judge.

It has been known, however, for juries to go against a particular judge. Some of them can be partial. In one case, out of 700 questions put to the plaintiff, 300 of them were asked by the judge.

A judge I often appeared before when I was a junior barrister was Michael Comyn. About him nothing wrong could be said. He was on the side of the underdog and oppressed, mostly. Judges have prejudices which they try to suppress. They might not like someone who pursues a particular occupation, like a publican or a bookmaker.

Michael's prejudices were different. He might dislike a Kerryman, for example. On the other hand, he was partial to the travelling people. He did not, however, condone sexual crimes by the travellers. He once tried a case which was vigorously defended by the accused on the basis that he really did nothing to the young girl who had charged him with molesting her.

When cross-examined about his activities, he eventually admitted that although he had not had intercourse with her, he may have given her 'a flick of the boss'. Michael relished this, and repeated it. The man was found guilty by the jury and Michael asked him to stand up. 'Tim Connors,' said he, 'I'm sentencing you for the offence of which you have been found guilty. Three months for yourself and three for the boss. You will serve six months in all.'

There usedn't to be much crime – I'd put that down to the character of the Irish people. Petty burglary, stealing TV sets, rowdyism in the streets, that kind of thing. That was most of it. There is certainly more crime now.

Fishing at Waterville, 1984.

The saying that ten per cent of the lawyers get ninety per cent of the work and the other ninety per cent share out the remaining ten per cent between themselves, I'd say it's true. A lot of them are sitting around waiting for work. When I went to the Bar, there were 110 barristers and twenty Senior Counsel. There are over a thousand now. There's a lot of commercial work, too.

Once I was a judge, I stayed aloof. I never went back to the Law Library to chat with the others. It's a rather lonely position. As a judge you have to act a bit – put on a suggestion of sincerity.

For any judge, the most unnerving and irritating thing to put up with in court is noise, whispers, snuffling, sniffing and coughing. What can one do?

One day, a friend of mine, a judge, having put up with a great deal of disturbances, nearly blew up when he saw a man chewing gum at the back of the court. He wasn't even moving his jaws silently, but making great sucking noises. Unable to stand it any longer, he called an elderly garda, the custodian of the court, to approach the bench.

'Yes, Justice.'

'Do you see that man there, third from the end in the second last bench, wearing a grey jacket?'

The garda looked over. 'I do, your Honour.'

'Well, get down there quickly and tell him to stop masticating.'

His face a mask, the garda duly made his way to the back of the court, touched the man on the shoulder and said in a loud whisper, 'The justice says to take your hands out of your pockets and keep them out.'

～ ∾ ～

There are loads of characters in the law. What we called the Library Lunatics. The Law Library is a terribly gossipy place. A lot of the barristers would take holidays together, play golf together, that kind of thing. There's no clerk system in Ireland as they have in England. You have to do it yourself. You had a little seat 3 feet wide – more of a shelf. And no telephone. You got a standard fee – the fee was marked on the brief.

People are very ignorant of the law – they don't know what a barrister is. That's why they put up with the junior counsel – paying for him. But it's impregnable. Most politicians have a background in law. There are at least ten barristers among our TDs at present.

When I look back at the great characters I knew in my time, both judges and barristers, I see that with their passing a great deal of tradition was lost. Their duty to the court and the duty of the barrister to his client was the first and foremost thing in their minds. Their incomes were low, the fees were miserably small. What they were paid was in no way commensurate with the earnings of the Bar today. They laboured without the benefit of modern machines, they worked day and night, with no pension schemes, and life was precarious indeed.

Mona Henry

born 17th September 1924

Snug in her little house, one of the so-called artisan's dwellings south of the Liffey, Mona Henry was born and brought up on the north side of Dublin, which makes her, many would claim, a true Dub. She is irrepressibly enthusiastic and energetic, and greatly involved in all the activities of her community. She has the great gift of seeing the good in everything and everyone.

I FOUND THIS, and I thought that you'd like to hear this composition, this essay, I was asked to write on my life as far back as I could remember. It actually was written in 1992 and it's called 'Me'. I never thought there could be so much meaning and life in that little word. And as I wrote it, I said, 'What now?' And after reminiscing and laughing and crying, I'm back at 'Me', so here goes.

'I, Mona Henry, née Walsh, was born one of six children: Pat, my brother, was the eldest, my sister Anna, me, my sister Carmel, my sister Kathleen and my young brother Seán, rest in peace.

'My childhood days were very happy days; mostly they were not long enough. I remember my young brother Seán being born at home and the nurse coming with her little bag. We gave her a hundred pieces of silver, which we had been saving up for the baby.

'My father was the taxi man, so I suppose we were fortunate that we had a car. Every Sunday in the summer, we would go off to Donabate. Mam would bake a big brown cake, a soda cake, a currant cake and an apple cake, and we would have the primus stove for the tea. They were great days and we were always able to take some friends with us, as the taxis in those days were the big old-fashioned ones.

Sometimes, during the week, after school, my mam would have a billycan full of tea and some sandwiches and Daddy would drive us up to the Furry Glen and leave us there and call back for us in the evening. *It was great.*

Left to right: Anna, Carmel, Sean, Kathleen and Mona Walsh in 1935.

'We lived opposite the People's Gardens in the Phoenix Park so we done most of our playing in the park.

'When I was young, I had no granny. I would *love* to have had one. All my pals had them and they were always visiting them and getting lovely presents from them. My parents were the youngest of big families, so I guess their mothers were very old. I played with the same girls from about seven till I was fourteen. I never remember having rows or arguments – we always seemed to agree. None of us had very much, but anything we had, we shared.

'And I remember lots and lots of happy days and events, but although I was a very happy child, I was also very bold. I was what you call a tomboy, or worse. There was not a day I didn't get a hiding. My mother would say, "The day is not ended yet, and you will get a slap before you go to bed." And, sure enough, I would. I never minded getting a hiding. Sure, it was over in a few minutes and then you could go out. But after a while my mother decided that smacking me was no good, so she decided to keep me in after school. This was disastrous. The first time I was kept in was for two days. My pals and I were sitting on the coalman's car and someone frightened the horse and it took off round the block! Everybody was looking at us and my pal was crying and I was speechless with fright. And as we turned the corner, a man stopped the horse and there was mother. I was murdered! She thought I had done it on purpose. She never gave me a chance to explain.

'The next time I was kept in for a week, which was to finish on a Sunday. I remember it well, because it was the Whit weekend and we were planning a hike. Mam went out for the messages and Anna gave me my tea upstairs in the bedroom. I shouted down I wanted more bread and she said I had had enough. But I kept shouting and she threw the loaf of bread up the stairs. I threw it back down and it split into two pieces. At that moment, Mam came in and said, "What is that doing on the floor?" Anna said Mona had thrown it down, but she didn't say how it had got up the stairs!

'My sister Carmel and I were great pals and did everything together. Carmel got polio when she was three years old and had to wear a steel on her leg till she was fourteen. I always remember thinking, "God, I wish it had been me that got it," because I was so strong and healthy.

'My father's two sisters were nuns and my sister Anna was so quiet, my mother used to say, "Oh, she's like John's sisters. She'll probably be a nun." And I thought, "Well, here's one that won't be!" My sister Anna might have been quiet but she was very bossy and she would polish the floor, and she would make us slide up and down on it. It would be like a mirror. Then she would make us sit on the sofa. She was very houseproud, and still is, but I love her.

'The one day, I don't remember what I had done, but my mother said she had had enough of me and she was putting me into the Sacred Heart home. She gave me a bath and put on my Sunday clothes and said Daddy would be home early and would bring me to the home before ten. I sat on the sofa swinging my legs, letting on that I did not care, but I can tell you, I was frightened for my life. The clock struck nine, and then 9.30 and I was thinking, "God! If only I had the courage to say 'Mammy, I'm sorry.'" But I couldn't. So at 9.45 she said, "It's too late now, so go up to bed and your daddy will bring you in the morning at seven."

'I went up to bed and said, "Thank God." Then I said goodbye to Anna and she just said, "Goodbye." And then I said goodbye to Carmel and Carmel said, "Why are you saying goodbye?" And I said, "I'll be gone before you wake up. I'm going at seven a.m." With that, my young sister Kathleen got hysterical, crying, "Mammy, mammy, don't let her go!" And my mam said, "All right, I'll give her a chance." And, believe me, it was the curing of me. I don't ever remember being very bold after that.

Then I was fourteen, and was getting our holidays from school and planning all the hikes we were going to have, when my mother came in this day and said, "I have a lovely job for you starting on Monday, serving your time at the drapery at the little shop in Meath Street." So that was it. No holidays, or choice of what I wanted to do. I loved school and would have loved to have stayed on, but I loved my little shop.

'Well, that was the end of my childhood, but other things opened up for me and, being a tomboy, I played all the games and ended up playing camogie, which I loved. At sixteen, I met Michael and I must say that Michael was the best thing that ever happened to me. He was older than me and when we would be coming home (we had to be in at ten o'clock) Michael and his pal, Pat, would only be hitting into town. He never noticed me, but one night I saw him coming and he had a lovely tweed coat, with a tie belt and a big stand-up collar and down to his ankles. So as he came up, I said in passing, "He's like de Valera." And he just *looked*.

'But eventually I got going with Michael and when the winter came, he wore the tweed coat this night and I said, "I remember when you wore that coat for the first time." And he said he would never forget that the first night he wore it, he remembers the girl saying he was like Eamon de Valera. He said he got a big lump cut off it the next morning. I said, "That girl was me!" And we often laughed about it afterwards.

'I am married now forty-five years and I can honestly say they were all very happy years. Michael fitted into our family like one of us. My mam and dad loved him and Michael always spoilt me rotten. He was not only my husband, he was my best friend and my best pal.

'You could not argue with Michael. I would often be up to ninety, and in the middle of it all, he would say, "Give us a kiss." And I would say, "I know what I'll give you!" And then we'd have to laugh. And that's the way it will always be, please God.

'Now I have left lots and lots of things out and I have had my little cries doing it, and I'm glad to have done it. All the young girls could be my daughters and some of them my younger sisters. I have enjoyed them and I hope they will remain my friends. I am calling this my class of '92.'

It's amazing what I could write. My childhood days *were* happy days. We lived right opposite the Phoenix Park. First we lived in a cottage and I remember when my youngest brother was about a year we moved into a bigger house. (I was eight when I moved and I always think eight is my lucky number.) And we moved into Aberdeen Street, an upstairs one, and I was there until I was sixteen, and then we moved into the bigger house, out on the main road, and that was my mother's house and my sister lives in it now. You might say we grew up there – we were all teenagers there, like.

But the Park, it was lovely. On the Infirmary Road, if you were up in the bedroom you could look into people's gardens and it was beautiful, now. Now, we weren't allowed to go into the top gardens – only allowed to stay in the bottom gardens – and if your mother was making the bed and she saw you (naturally, of course, you went where you weren't supposed to go) – and she would see us.

But we were very happy. They were poor times. They were poor times and everyone shared. A lot of people round there worked at Guinness's and they were considered good jobs, them and the tobacco factories, Players and Wills – they were good jobs and they were pensionable jobs as well; they had their own doctors and things like that. Ah, when we were small, there was an awful lot of TB around at that time. And families were wiped out. Now, *families* were wiped out. And as a child you don't think of that, you know, but when someone your own age dies, it makes you think. I remember there was one family, Floods, and they had three children, teenagers, and three of them died, you know. The father died. It was very sad. That was only one of hundreds.

I remember my mother would wash us on a Friday night, your hair was washed then, and on a Saturday night you got your bath. A big bath in front of the fire and as you were going upstairs you got your clean vest and your clean pants and you got those going up. No such thing as a nightdress – you slept in your vest in those times. But everyone did!

I had a friend and people had what they called in those days lodgers, and that was to supplement their income, you know. And I remember this girl – she was the youngest of her family and I used to sit beside her in school. Carmel Devereux. And they had a lodger and he was mad about Carmel. And every day we'd go down to meet him and he would give her twopence. Now, twopence was a lot of money. And she would buy a tin of NKMs. Now, a *tin*, not just...of NKM sweets. Now, you could get a halfpence-worth of sweets, but twopence for to get the tin. And she'd open it, and when she'd open it, instead of eating it first, she'd hand you one. She was lovely.

Now, at Christmas, you didn't get much at Christmas. You got a big stocking, hanging down and there'd be cinders in the end of it and then you'd have an apple, an orange and a banana and a shiny new penny, and two new hankies with Daddy Christmas or Little Bo-Peep – you know, those little things. Whatever you got, you were happy with it.

I remember Carmel, he bought her a scooter, and a scooter in those days! My God Almighty! But you'd be only out and she'd give you a ride on it. She shared everything and it was like having your own scooter, you know. And Christmas would come. You'd write the letter to Santa but sure... You'd say, 'A pair of skates.' And say, 'Santa, even *one* skate!' But you never even got *one* skate. But whatever you got, you were happy with it on the day you'd wake up, you know?

And I remember then, my brother, as we got older, he wanted a drum and my mother got this drum and there was a dinge on it, and it was put at the end of the chimney. And Mammy said Santa couldn't come down – he just threw it down the chimney and that's how it got the dinge. You know, just simple little things.

But I was, I suppose, very lucky to have the parents I had. My father was a lovely man. He died when he was sixty and it was a shame, because we were all grown up and he was just able to sit back and enjoy himself. He was never sick. I was married at the time, married when I was twenty-one. (In those days that was very young, you know.) But, however, he lived for the family. He was never outside Ireland, my father. Never outside Ireland. And he lived for us.

My mother was a very hardworking woman, too. In those days, now, you came in on Monday from school and it was washday. The big bath would be up on this thing, boiling, and it was all cotton – had to be boiled, blued, starched. Even your curtains, now. When you think, you just rinse them out. My mother, in our big house, she had cotton curtains, you know. You'd be pulling them with her, you know, trying to get them even. Oh, all this sort of thing. Like the work was hard, and they worked all day, cooking and then they'd have to darn your socks – your socks were wool. My father used to mend the shoes. We had a last and he'd get the leather and you'd have to sit in when he'd be doing the heels. And I remember when you'd get new shoes he'd send you up to the shop for this card and they'd be Randall's and he'd put one on the side of your heel and one on the side of your shoe and one at the toe, and there'd be sparks flying when you'd be running! But, you see, they saved your leather for so long, and he done all the shoes, now.

And my mother was a great cook. We were fortunate. She'd make a meal out of nothing. She'd make a meal *out of nothing*. If you'd come in to my mother at any stage, she'd be talking in to you and next thing there'd be hot scones in like that. She had a very open house. Anyone could come to our house. All my friends, now, would come on a Sunday for their tea. We'd go up to play the match and Mammy would have scones on the window, and brown bread. She'd bake every day, and you'd never think of that when you were a child – you just accepted it. When you think – she must have worked all day.

It was a very open house and on a Tuesday night my aunt would come. My aunt was a great character. I remember when I was a teenager we'd walk into town. (You wouldn't have the money, and you'd walk. You'd only have the money from Friday to Sunday and then it was gone.) And my mother, she'd say, 'Your Aunt Biddy'll be there – we'll go up tonight.' We'd be listening to something on the radio – there was no television – it might just be only on for half an hour. And we'd have great fun. You made your own fun. You'd have a game of Ludo. You made games and you improvised for everything, because you hadn't got anything. You hadn't got toys or anything. I remember you'd spin a top and you'd have a lash. (I don't know if you ever heard of it?) You'd lash it around the block and you'd colour it and stick silver paper on the top and your top'd be nicer than somebody else's. And the fellers'd have the bicycle wheels with a little stick and they steering them around. And the day wasn't long enough for you.

And then you'd play in the night-time, as I say, and it was very safe for us. You'd get out after tea in the winter and you'd play Chase the Fox – did you ever play that? That was great. One fellow has a chalk and he puts an arrow and off he goes, and you have to follow the arrows. Oh, it was great, sure. You'd be all night before you'd catch him, you know.

Oh, and we used to go off on lots of hikes when we were children, now. We'd go off to Leixlip – out in the country it was then – it's not country now at all. Dublin. And a big estate in Lucan, we used to picnic there and we'd get a boat out on the river. Now, we'd send the biggest one up for the boat. And nobody could row, and we'd go from one side of the river to the other. And we'd say, 'There's primroses!' When you couldn't get them on one bank of the river, you'd get them on the other. We had great times and I think it was about sixpence for the boat and we'd all give a penny each.

You'd also get the tram to Lucan village and you'd have to walk up to Leixlip, to the lane – about three miles – and we'd pick the cowslips and that was for the May altar. And we'd be walking back and we would be exhausted and there'd be twenty, thirty of us – everyone'd have the one idea. And we said, 'God, if someone stopped the car and said, "We'll give you sixpence for that bunch," would you sell them?' 'Oh, no!' We wouldn't sell them after all that. We'd have them for the May altar.

We were a very happy family. We were blessed with the parents. My father was a countryman and my mother was Dublin. My father was from Laois. He had three brothers and two sisters and they were nuns. They went to Spokane in America. Sister Monica, she was lovely. Now, she would write letters home and when she'd be writing, 'Give my love to Anne and Pat' and then next year, 'Give my love to Mona' and we were all mentioned as we came along. We were all mentioned in the letters.

She came home. Actually, my father's brother, he was nineteen years older than my father and my father was only young when he went to America, so my father never knew him. And the year I was getting married, Uncle Richard, he was coming home – not for my wedding, but just as it happened. He was coming home and he couldn't understand having a younger brother he'd never seen and his daughter getting married. And they were real Americans and we used to sit up all night listening to him. Talk about a *seanchaí*! He started out on the Panama Canal, then they pioneered the land that he's on in America, himself and this man, Martin Green, from Galway. *He* came home as well, and he was at the wedding, too. It was very funny, the house was so crowded and we'd a very big landing in my mother's house and everybody getting dressed, and there was the two of them shaving one another. On the landing!

But he gave us great stories. He lived in Twolake – that's in California. His neighbour was Martin Green from Galway, he was on the next bit, and he used to go out on a horse to him. If they visited once a week or once a month, you packed your own stuff and brought it. That's the way it was then. But I remember he said they were caught by the posse. They'd gone over the border – I can't remember what for – and anyway, he was arrested. And my uncle said to the sheriff, 'Look,' he said. (Martin saw what was happening and Martin set fire to the shack.) 'Look,' he said. 'I have these papers there worth a lot of money. Would you let me go and get my papers?' So the sheriff said, 'All right,' and let him go. Course, once he got over the border, he was gone flying!

But anyway, they pioneered this land between them. And they got two crops a year over there in America. And he'd a son and two daughters. His son was called after Roger Casement, and he's a lawyer. He was the District Attorney of Seattle. And his two daughters were schoolteachers, as was his wife, a Corkwoman. And when they went out first, when they pioneered the land, there was Indians and they were put up on the reservation. And she used to teach the children there, like.

We used to listen to him talking about all that, and he'd a way with him – you could nearly see the posse coming down and all. It was marvellous. Chief Eagle something was the chief of the Indians and all that. You could listen to him!

My father had two sisters who were nuns who were lovely. My father had three sisters in all. He had this sister Annie who never married – she stayed at home. Sister Elizabeth was the first one to go to America and Sister Malachy wanted to go and the priest said, 'Now, I think your place is with your mother.' My grandmother was after having my father and I think it was a change of life baby. So he says, 'It's with your mother.'

So she stayed with her mother until Seán made his First Communion and then she went off. And she was telling us the story afterwards, and she said that although it took you seven or eight years to be a nun, going back then, didn't that all change and it only took two years. So the years that she stayed with her mam, she was still a nun in the same amount of time, you know.

Two years after I was married she came home, back with Uncle Richard, and she was lovely. She'd a great sense of humour, too. I remember this butcher here in Dolphin's Barn, his sister was out there in America with my aunt, and she had promised to visit him. So, anyhow, we were chatting after a beautiful dinner there, and he took out his cigar and he passed the cigarettes round. And Sister Malachy, she took the cigarette and I said to myself, 'God! They're really free in America.' And she put it in her mouth and when he came round with the match, she just put it down on the table. She'd a great sense of humour. I'm going back now, fifty-four year. At that time, you didn't think nuns had a sense of humour, for to do anything like that. And if she'd actually lit the cigarette, I'm sure we'd have fallen on the floor!

My mother was a Dub. She had three sisters and she had three brothers and her brother worked in Guinness's. One of her sisters never married, my Aunt Katy, and she stayed with us for a while, and she died very early. She died of TB, you know. An awful lot of people did; it was like the way cancer is now. You mentioned it and everyone was scared. And then the conditions in some of the places were so bad.

Sure, people had their babies at home, they all had a baby at home. You couldn't afford doctors. You'd see this little nurse – she was very tiny – you'd see her little case and you'd say, 'Oh, someone must be getting a new baby.' It'd never strike you, even though you'd be ten and eleven, where babies came from. In those days, like, you know, you were told nothing. I don't know how we ever got married! Your mother told you nothing!

But you'd see her coming up with her little case and the next thing, the baby... But everybody had big families in them days. My mother had six, but the friend that I palled with, Dymphna, her mother had fourteen. And I remember Dymphna saying, 'My mother is going to get another baby. Look, every time she's going to get a baby...' and she pulled the shutter back by the window and there was a pillowcase with all the little baby's clothes washed. It was hidden behind that. But it would still never strike you where all the babies were coming from.

But they were very lucky. Her father worked in the Civil Service and he'd a good job and he was paid every fortnight. And it was very funny – one week all the boys would get pants and little black shoes, runners, and the next week the girls would get the little knickers and the little white shoes. And that's the way it went every fortnight. You'd only get a fortnight out of those little canvas shoes, you know.

She was a lovely little woman, the mother. Oh, she only died a few years ago, over ninety. She was a lovely little person, now. If you were playing on the street and Brendan or somebody hit you, you'd go over and Mrs Middleton would say, 'Oh, fight your own battles.' And that was that. But if you came to my house and said, 'Mona's after hitting me,' Mammy said, 'Come in!' Which was dreadful. But with Mrs Middleton, you were friends immediately and that was that. But if somebody else seen you getting a clip in the ear, it was demoralizing for a child, like.

But they all done very well, all those. Her mother lived down the road, and she took the eldest two. And they just had two bedrooms, but they'd pull out two beds in the night-time, and none of those boys ever slept in the girls' room. She was able to do it. She managed it, like. You might say she'd only twelve, because the granny took the two eldest.

Now, the youngest of them is fifty-five. I was at a twenty-five wedding anniversary of my friend, and her youngest brother married one of the Middletons. I hadn't seen this girl for over twenty years. And she came over to me and she said, 'I believe you were a friend of my mother's.' And I said, 'I am indeed. Many's the time I changed your nappy.'

You left school at fourteen. Nobody had the money to go on in school. You went in school till you were in your fifth – seventh class, and you were usually fourteen at that. And the teachers were very good. And in my school, if you wanted to go on for to do the Service [*Civil Service*] – you didn't do your Leaving [*school certificate*] in those days – she'd have what she called an extra class. You stayed back after school and you'd get these extra lessons. But it would be only the brightest that would be picked for that. If they were able for to do it. Or you could go to Emerson's College or that. And that'd be twelve-and-six a week, and that'd be an awful amount of money a week. An awful amount of money. I remember my friend now, Annie, saying that her father would have the money out every week for her. She was the youngest, you know. Then he was a Guinness's man, like. He had it, you know. But most people left, and you went to work in a shop or a factory or whatever was there. And you had no choice!

I would have to say I had a brilliant teacher. And my principal would come every year and say, 'I have something good to tell you. You have the same teacher.' But the knuckles would be taken off you! But you done everything through the medium of Irish, and you done English. You just could not say, 'I can't do my lessons' or 'I couldn't do my lessons.' You'd be caned! And I got plenty of caning. But I never got it for not knowing my lessons. I got it for talking or something like that.

I'd have to say, when you think now of th'education. There was fifty-two in my class. A huge big thing, with your desks, and all of the teachers were dedicated. They all were strict. You wouldn't say, 'Boo!' Oh, you wouldn't say, 'Boo!' Miss O'Toole was the principal and she'd put me in charge of the exercises. I would count them and bring them up, and my friend said, 'Put an extra one in.' (She hadn't done her lessons.) Which I did. Twice I done that. And this day Miss O'Toole, she said, 'I was sitting last night, and I was thinking, and Maureen Powell came into my mind and I said, "I haven't had an exercise from her."' Oh, my heart nearly sank, and I was taken off the job, naturally. Which I learned a lesson. Never, even for friends, I'd never do something that wasn't right, after that, you know. To have a little job like that – there weren't many of them in schools. Somebody'd collect the books and somebody'd get the sewing bags. There was only about four jobs. I met Miss O'Toole afterwards and I said it to her. 'I learned the lesson the hard way.' And she said, 'That's the way you learn the lessons.' And it's true.

In the school you had half an hour for catechism – you'd only do a certain amount – a little penny catechism. And it's beat into your brain – you'd never forget it, like. And you'd go down to the church after school and do the Stations – oh there'd be a little snigger as well as that, you know. We used to have religious examinations, maybe every two, three years and this priest used to come into the school. (I remember he had this big birthmark, and, oh, he was a lovely priest.) The big folding doors'd be put back, and three, four classes would all be in that, maybe a hundred girls. And you were put alphabetically. I was Walsh, so I was down near the end.

The day before the examination, anyway, they were practising and we'd got cooking apples, and I had a big lump of apple in my mouth, and the teacher says, 'Mona Walsh', and, of course, I couldn't say a thing. 'Well, now,' she says, 'if the priest comes tomorrow and you don't know your catechism, the school'd fail.' I knew that I knew, but I couldn't say because I'd get caned.

Anyhow, the next day the priest came, and he just brings ten up around the table. He didn't even ask us and he gave out four rosary beads, one for each class, for to raffle. It came, anyhow, to me and Diana Moloney – she was a brilliant pupil, teacher's pet – but, anyway, I won it! 'Oh,' she said, the teacher. She was very mean, and she said I didn't deserve it, but I told Mammy I'd won them and she was delighted.

So, the next morning, I brought the beads in, little blue beads, and left them on the desk. And she came round – we'd be writing. (She used to put the pencil in between her teeth and she'd do your knuckles if you weren't doing it right.) She said, 'What are those beads doing on the table?' 'Oh,' I said, 'my mam said if I didn't win them honestly that I wasn't to keep them.' 'Put them in your bag!' Now, my mam never said that! If my mam had known! How I had the courage to say that to the teacher. 'Put those in your bag,' she said. 'You won them.' And that was that. It changed me. I'll never forget it! For to have the courage for to say that. Because you've no idea. She was mannish, she was very big. But I have to say, she was a great teacher. She was really a great teacher.

Maybe it's your parents, too. Because when we would be doing our homework at home, sometimes you wouldn't ask Dad because he'd go off and he'd tell loads and loads about it. And on Sunday, when he'd bring us out, he'd bring us up the mountains and he'd say, 'That's Red Hugh O'Donnell's grave.' And he was always trying to tell you history. I remember Poulaphouca. It was only being made, then. It was a huge big dam, and he'd bring us out and he said, 'When you grow up, this will be a reservoir, and you can always say you saw it when it was nothing.' But you don't be that interested when you're a child, you know. But it'd stick in your mind. You'd ask him about history, and he'd go into detail and you'd like to do your eccer and get off and then play a game.

He was really a family man, now. He was a mechanic and he worked in the – the bus company, I suppose. (It was the tramway at that time.) While he was out sick they came out on strike, and he never got his job back when the strike was over. So he got a taxi, his own taxi, and one time, my father got rheumatic fever and he went off to the hospital in an ambulance. So this man, Dobbin was his name, he was supposed to be doing the taxi while my father was in hospital, and my mother gave him money for the petrol. But when it came to Friday, he had no money for her. He had drank the money! I mean, you wouldn't have money from last week, like that. She'd had to try to give him the money for the petrol. Oh, it was dreadful, now.

I was about eleven, twelve, you know, and I knew what was going on. When he came out of hospital, he was in bed and he gave me the money to go and pay the ESB bill, because if it wasn't paid, you'd be cut off and it wasn't a matter at that time of ringing up – there was no phones in the houses. I remember going in on the bus for to pay that bill, because it'd be more to get it put on again than the actual bill. Electricity was cheap at the time. And I remember when we got the gas in the house. We used to have these lights – the mantles – and the paraffin oil. We'd a huge big round table and a big tablecloth, and two big lights for doing our exercises, and when the exercises would be done, one would be blown out and we'd just the one, and the gas mantle up on the thing. And if you only puffed, sometimes, they'd break, they were so fragile.

And then we got the electricity! And, God! that was marvellous! The *difference* in the brightness was marvellous. And then, when we got electricity, we got th'electric iron. Until then, you were heating the irons on the fire; we'd three big irons. My mother was a great washer and starcher. I remember in school, they said, 'D'you ever say thank you to your mammy for keeping you so clean?' She kept Anne and myself and Carmel the same, always dressed the same. We'd three coats and three little hats the same – everything was the same. Anna's would be passed on to me, but mine could never be passed on to Carmel. So Anna and Carmel always got the new things. I was like Second-hand Rose! I was so hard, I was an awful tomboy. And Anna just grew out of them, but Anna was always much bigger than me and then when I came to twelve, I overshot

Anna, and it was great! Everything had to be new for me! It must have cost a lot for to keep us so nice, but people were very proud.

Carmel was three and a half when she got the polio, and in those days we used to take a place down in Portmarnock, and my mother was washing Carmel this night and – I would be five and a half at that stage – and she couldn't stand! And my father raced her into the hospital. It was infantile paralysis in those days, that's what they called it, you know. Oh, she was in the hospital for a good while and then when she came out she had a steel on her leg, a brace on her leg, you know. But she used to fly round with it – *fly* round with it – it made no difference to her. She wore that until she was fourteen, and then they brought her in and I think she got seven operations to lengthen every sinew in her leg, so that her heel would hit the ground.

But all the time during those years, from when she was four until she was fourteen, summer and winter, my mother used to rub hot olive oil into that leg, so when she brought her back – it was Dr Chance – he said my mother should have got a medal. He said if my mother hadn't have done that, her leg would have been wasted and would have been much thinner. But no matter what happened – you can imagine, with six children, now – wasn't she marvellous? Olive oil that was up and down, up and down. But it didn't stop Carmel. Carmel was very pretty.

Now, we were all dark, and Carmel was blonde. She was the only one that was fair. My mother was very dark. My mother was like a Spanish person – she'd brown eyes, and none of us... My father had very bright blue eyes, so I presume it was my father's gene. But she'd jet black hair and she'd loads of hair, and when we were children we used to love to brush it and she used to put it up in a bun and put it up different ways. But she'd lovely brown eyes. We all had the sallow look that she had. But Carmel was fair. But she played camogie and she played everything.

But I often say if the bubble burst, the Liffey wouldn't be big enough for all the people. They couldn't improvise, the people today. During the war, everything was rationed. You couldn't live on it. You'd be drying the tea for to try and use it again. *Everything* was rationed. Butter was rationed. And if you got a bit of lard! Oh, God, to get a bit of lard!

I remember we were all working and my mother went into hospital and Carmel was at home and my Aunt Bid came over and showed

Carmel. We never had to buy bread because my mother done it all.
You see, the bread was rationed, too. Can you imagine it? Just getting
two slices of bread. When you know you can't have it, you want
more! And Carmel used to make the big cakes. They wouldn't be as
nice as Mammy's, but it'd do, you know.

And then the pipes would freeze because they were only lead
piping. I remember coming down one morning and got my breakfast and everyone was saying the pipes were freezing and they
couldn't get any water. And I said, 'We had no trouble. Our water
was all right this morning.' And Mammy came home and said,
'Kathleen, our water was all right, wasn't it?' And she said, 'Yes, I
took the water out of the hot water bottles and made the tea.' So
talk about improvising!

The gas was rationed. We had a great glimmer, though, because
we were between all the hospitals. We were surrounded with hospitals, where we lived. My mother was boiling everything on it and
she said, 'No one is to answer the door, if a knock comes to the
door.' And, of course, my father being a taxi man, people would
ring. And this day, my father went out to the door and wasn't it the
glimmer man! My mother was taking the pots and running about,
but he just came up and threw some water down on the pipe and –
psssttt. You see, the pipe was hot! So, anyway, we were cut off. Oh, it
was disastrous.

But we'd a big range in the kitchen anyhow, and we'd have hot
water in a big iron kettle boiling on it. Outside, we had the primus
stove and sawdust. And my mother would hang a pot on it from
about half nine in the morning – a big pot with the potatoes for
eight of us. It would take that long to boil. Once it would boil, it
wouldn't take so long.

And there was a man lived behind us in Montpellier Gardens, and
he was a big shot in the thing. And mother wanted him to get the gas
back for us. 'Well, I will,' he says, 'but I couldn't at the moment.
You'll have to be penalized a little bit.' But after about a fortnight, he
got it put on, but that was a big concession. You see, they'd cut the
gas off, but there'd always be a little glimmer. And if there was a
black-out, we'd never have a black-out because we'd the barracks all
around us. We had McKee Barracks and Collins's Barracks, Clancy
Barracks. Then you had Stephens's Hospital and the Mater Hospital.
We'd the best of both worlds that way.

But the glimmer man would go round on his bike and at that time the gas company would have what you call an orange bike – painted orange. And everyone would say, 'Oh, the glimmer man's around.' Well, the blinds'd be pulled on the door and no door'd be open. He was bad news, in other words. Anyhow, we were caught and they never let my mother forget it. They used to say, 'Oh, Mammy, here's the glimmer man.'

But she made do. It's amazing if you had to. We always had potatoes and always had vegetables. She was a great housekeeper. We never had to buy jam – we'd have home-made jam. And we all had to help with the jobs. Carmel's pal, she'd come round on a Saturday morning and she'd get stuck in and then you'd go off to Cassidy's and buy a little blouse or whatever you could afford and off to the dance that night. You'd be coming home, cycling or walking home – you could in those days! The dance halls'd be in Parnell Square, and you'd be hoping for a pass for the next night. The rookies – the guards – they'd be training up in the depot, and most of the girls up around there, they all married guards. Oh, loads of them married guards. But you'd go up to the dance – we know a good few policemen now, and we laughed after – the stockings'd be tore off you with their big boots. They were so awkward. They couldn't dance, half of them, and in those days, fifty years ago, it wasn't the way they have brains now. It was brawn. They were all huge – six foot, six foot-four – they'd be like a pump, going like that with your arm.

And you would walk home through the Park without a bit of bother. No fear. The only thing you'd see was maybe a flasher, and those type of people, you'd say they'd never do anything to harm you anyhow. You were all right.

But, going back to my mother. She was marvellous, you'd have to say. When you got up, the fire was always lighting and she was up first, and my father would get up and meet the early train, and he'd come back up and get the breakfast for us. My mother, she usedn't to sleep so well. And he'd say, 'Your mam is going to sleep when everyone else is getting up.' Now, the Department of Defence was on the other side of the road and they had a clock. It was a quarter, a half, three quarters, always striking. This'd be every night she'd be sitting there and *bong, bong, bong.* Dad'd say, 'Ah, if you can't sleep, count the sheep.' And she'd say, 'I'm counting sheep all the time.' And he'd say, 'Well, count them backwards.' But this night she said, 'John, John, quick! There's a sheep in the garden.' And he says, 'Woman, would you get into bed!' But right enough, wasn't there a sheep in the garden! There was a drover and there was something wrong with the sheep. There used to be a cattle market in Dublin every Thursday, and they'd bring the animals up on the train on a Wednesday. And they put it in the garden. You know, my dad said, 'Only that I seen it, I would have said your mam was going mental!'

Going back to the jam. We used to go down to the market. We used to get a basket, a chip, from the Daisy Market. There was a huge big fruit market and you'd get fruit slightly damaged and you'd be picking out and you'd get it cheap. And we would do blackberry jam and every sort of fruit, whatever was in season. We had friends, they were caretakers in the Royal Hospital – they were lovely people, they were Protestants, and she used to make the chutneys, because all the gardens were full of fruit and everything, and he would come over with a sack of potatoes and cauliflowers and apples from the orchard, and it was like manna from heaven. Something you would never taste, you know, let alone eat!

And my mother used to grow vegetable marrows in the garden. Now, I would never eat a vegetable marrow. They grow in the manure part of the garden – they grow underneath, you know. And my mother used to cook that with a white sauce – anything you had, my mother always had the sauce, whatever sauce had to go with it. Nothing was ever a bother as far as her cooking.

My mother went into service. In her day there'd be nothing else, you know. She went out to work when she was twelve, because her mother had died. But she worked for this doctor, and she always set a lovely table, and our table was *made* in the kitchen. It was a huge big length, and there were drawers each end of it and we'd a form in on that side of it and the three of us used to sit on the form. There were two of everything on the table, otherwise you'd always be saying, 'Pass the sugar' and 'Pass the milk'. As we were getting bigger, mother'd make an apple cake and a ginger cake and you could bring your friends in on a Sunday, and she would have the butter in little patties, little criss-crosses and little balls of butter. And she had the white tablecloth, a lovely linen tablecloth. I can see all that – brown cake and currant cake and soda bread – that was *nothing* because we had that every day. And then she'd do scones and the scones'd be risen that high – they'd be lovely. She done that every day and never used anything to measure it – she threw everything in.

I remember when Cathal Brugha Street opened, the catering college, we went and done two years there. I remember doing the apple pie and we were putting the little leaves on it, pastry leaves, and this girl, she put three slits in it. The teacher came round and she said, 'Why did you put the slits in it?' And this girl says, 'Oh, mammy always does this.' 'Oh,' she says, 'Mammy's not here now. I'm teaching you,' she says, 'and you've let the steam out of it,' she says 'and the apples might not be cooked.' So you learn all the time.

For an extra half-crown you got a second subject, and we picked embroidery. We got this tea cosy. I have it, actually. (I must ask Carmel where hers is.) I would be fifty-four years married, so that tea cosy must be fifty-four years. And it was ecru – it would eventually wash white. And the teacher said, 'Thread your needle with green thread', and by the time she got round to everyone, the bell was gone and it was over. The next night, she said to do stem stitch, and by the time she came round again – there was about forty in the class – it was over again. So there were these two little girls, about fourteen, and we were waiting and one said, 'I'll show you how to do the thing.' So now I have it here. Just a big tulip and bits of grass growing. I said at the time, 'I'll keep that, it's an heirloom.' So, needless to say, I never did finish it.

It was a beautiful vocational school. But when we were going the first year we just done the Christmas cake, you know. The first year you don't ice it, you do mostly basics. But the second year, we said to Mammy we were doing it, and we couldn't get it for to stay up. The icing was too soft. So we kept scooping it up in hills, and we put a cherry on each, and it was like the Seven Hills of Rome! When we done that the next year it was so simple!

I remember Mammy would mix butter and sugar with her hand – we'd do it with the wooden spoon. She'd have it done in no time. Her sponges used to be that heighth. With the jam, oh, they'd be lovely. And if anyone was sick around the place, she'd whip a sponge up and she'd send it up to them. In those days, everyone shared.

Going back to the war years. Everything was rationed. *Everything* was rationed. Petrol was rationed. We used to have to get the tea on the black market. Twenty-five shillings for a pound of tea and a pound of butter would be a pound, money. It might only be three-and-six, but you would pay a pound, which was a lot of money then.

In the war you'd hear the bombers going over. You had a curfew and you had a black blind. I was just fourteen, and Ireland, they had this ARP, you could join it, and my friend and myself went along, she was a year older than me, I let on I was fifteen, and you had to be sixteen for to be a warden. But we were what you called EC messengers. But, anyhow, there was a big parade coming off, and my brother was in the Local Defence, and people were being fitted for their gasmasks. And we would be fitting them – when you think I was only fourteen! You'd put the mask on them and there was this little round thing, and you'd ask them to breathe and if there was suction and that'd hold it, then it fitted. I remember in our house, at the window, where you pulled back the shutter, there were all the gasmasks in a cardboard box.

Anyway, they were holding this big parade, and I got my armband with EC on it, and ARP, and a helmet. And we went on the parade. And my father said to my brother, 'Well, you're a year in it, and you're an adult, and here's your sister coming home with a uniform.' He was walking in the parade but he'd no uniform, and here was me with my armband and helmet! And you'd feel so *important*, you know. And then in the ARP they would have these mock things – you'd report to a place down in Blackhall Street and you were told to go out to a certain place – it could be Manor Street, and you'd be standing at the corner and the next thing an ambulance would come up and you were supposed to be injured. Like, it was supposed to be a bomb. And it could be your leg, you know, and your leg would be all done up and then you'd be brought down in Brunswick Street and after that you'd be let out and you had to walk home – that was the awful part of it. The other was great – it was exciting.

You would hear the 'planes going over in the night-time and one night, the night of the North Strand – that was a dreadful bombing, now, a dreadful bombing. There was a lot of people killed, and we had a butcher, Fitzpatrick, in Manor Street and his head was blown off. Oh, it was *dreadful*. But then there was another night, there was a bomb, and where was it, only in the Park, right next to us. And the noise of it! We were in bed at the time and we all got up and were hanging out the window. Now, it was at the dogpond, and there was a house there and half of it was blown away. There was a man and a woman and a child in it and there was a bed blown up on to a tree in it, and yet there was no one killed! And whatever way the blast would go, you could be standing here and you were all right, and there, you'd be blown to smithereens.

Oh, my brother was out of the bed, of course, and my father, too, but no way would he allow me out – I was only a child in his eyes. But they all went up to the Park, but they never thought about the Zoo. The animals, they could have been all over the place! The bison was knocked out – they had four of them – and the railings were only – not for the animals but for to keep the people out. And the dog-pond was directly opposite that. And the authorities, they had a plan; if something happened, all the animals would have been gassed. But my father and my brother only realized afterwards how stupid they were to go up to the Park, because once the bombs dropped, the 'planes were gone. But they never thought – they could have met a lion on the way!

And then the 'planes bombed the South Circular Road and we used to say they were after the Jews, because all the Jews lived along there. That was their quarters, and they had a church and all the rest of it. They all moved out to Rathfarnham then, a lot of them, during the war, and moved out to Bray, too. Well, the Meath Road, those beautiful bungalows, they built them. Actually, the Jews, you might say, *made* Bray, because they all went out to live there – 'twas a lovely seaside place. And they bombed Bray, so we really think they were trying to hit where the Jews were.

And then I remember that other man – where was he from? Galway, was it? He was on the radio; he used to broadcast from Germany. Lord Haw Haw – Joyce was his name. We used to hear him on the radio. We'd be sitting waiting for him to come on! 'Twas a big thing. Well, we'd no radio for years and then we had a radio and on a Sunday night Joe Linnane would be on with *Question Time*, and we'd all give twopence, and whatever number you'd draw, when *your* person would be on, number two, you'd say, 'He should have got that! Oh, how stupid!' Because whoever won would get all the twopences and you'd maybe get a shilling and that was a lot of money, you know. That was your amusement. But we'd be waiting for Lord

Haw Haw at ten o'clock, and my father was always in for that. And you'd hear a pin drop. And then we would say the rosary – everyone said the rosary – and we'd be giggling and we'd be all ready for bed, and somebody would maybe drop a marble, and next thing, if Daddy thought it was you, he'd say, 'Mona, *you* start the next decade.' And you wouldn't know where you would be – he had a way of catching you out, you know.

As regards religion – my age group, our religion will never go because it was bred into you. And when you think of all the people who have died who thought they were dying in sin! Sure, there's no such thing as sin. Sure, we'll all fly up to heaven!

I want to tell you, you would know everyone in Dublin. Over where I lived, over in Infirmary Road, those houses which you call Montpellier Gardens, they were only being built when I was eight, so there were three fields at the back of our houses, and cows would come in for the market on Thursday, and we spent our time in these fields. We used to get a penny pocket money, and Anna, who was two years older than me, got twopence. But we used to go down to the fields and the people would throw out the jam jars and the whiskey bottles, and if you brought them down to the place, you'd get a half-penny for them. And that would get you into the pictures, because the pictures was twopence on a Saturday.

Now, my friend's father worked for Guinness's and he was a bit fond of the whiskey, and he used to get the little baby Power's, and he'd have them under his pillow, the empty ones. And there used to be a queue on the stairs, all the kids trying to get the bottles, because they couldn't take them when the father was asleep!

Everyone done that. *Everyone* done that! And that's how everyone got into the pictures. If you did go on a Sunday, one paid sevenpence and you'd get another seven in for fourpence each, and you could go in the cushions, but if you only paid twopence, you went to the wooden seats. Everyone was in the same boat.

People were so obliging. If you wanted something done, Mammy'd say, 'Get Bill Noone', and he'd come and you'd give him a packet of cigarettes and that was it. My mother or my father, if they could do something, they'd do it. Years ago, people done everything for you. It was a lovely way. Oh, it was a lovely way. There's so little of it now.

But you knew everyone in Dublin. You'd see Brendan Behan walking down the street, and Alfie Byrne, the Lord Mayor. Alfie Byrne, he wasn't very popular with us, because the three fields at the back of us, they were left to people who went to Australia and couldn't be found. And Alfie Byrne confiscated the land and he built flats on them, and it ruined the whole area.

We lived off the North Circular Road, we lived in a cul-de-sac, and you had all the big people, the wealthy people like the Hickeys, and they all had nurses in the grey uniform and they'd wheel the children out and they had maids, staff in each house. The children would be walked up in the Park every day. All those houses, they went into apartments. Now it's different – people are buying up the houses now and they're all whole again, but in those times it did bring the area down and we never forgave him for doing that.

But when he would come, they'd have the Park Races on and that was a great day. They would have the jarveys with their cars, lining up from our house all the way up and the people would get off the tram and they would be brought up to the Races. In the Zoological Gardens, twice a year they'd have a dinner, and the chauffeurs would let the ladies in with their furs, and then we would line the pavements. You'd be surprised at all the people we saw. Schnozzles. D'you remember Schnozzles? Jimmy Durante. He came, and the men would have their tails and the big black shiny hard hats and the women would have gloves up to here, and we would be up there from about half seven till about half nine of a summer's evening, looking at them going in, you know.

And on the front road, we'd the President's house, where they would have all wood slats going in for garden parties. And we would be looking in at them, too. It was like *Upstairs Downstairs*, you know. Then all the presidents would come down our road. You would see them quite often and all the visitors would go to Áras an Uachtárain – they'd come down our road and you'd have a motor-cycle cavalcade up front. I saw the first President laid out, when I was a child. He was like Stalin, a big moustache. Douglas Hyde. He was like a Russian.

I was there, too, with the ladies' club, when Hillery was in. He suffered with his back, and his aide-de-camp, he put a cushion in on his chair, and he came to every table and he knew all about the area! He was lovely, and so was she. And we were there when Mary Robinson was there.

And Princess Grace came and she was beautiful. I remember the time she was coming down Parkgate Street in an open car and she'd have a white turban on her, and she was really beautiful. Then Kennedy, he was lovely, too.

At one time, presidents had to do what the government told them until Mary Robinson – she opened it all up. I thought that no one could surpass her, but Mary McAleese.... Mary Robinson, she was great. When she got inaugurated first, we were at a dinner at the Gardai Hall (the gardai run a dinner for the senior citizens), and the organizer said, 'We've got a surprise for you.' And the whisper went round that it was Mary Robinson. It was her first function, and there were two hundred of us, but she went round and shook hands with everybody. And I thought that nobody could surpass her. But Mary McAleese is marvellous. I think she's brilliant. Now, Mary Robinson was always a rebel, but Mary McAleese goes quietly – she can reach to every level. There's nothing presumptious, pomptious or anything about her, and she's very dignified. Bishop O'Connor, now, going to be made a Cardinal, he was giving out to her for receiving in the Protestant church, which he should never have said. That was an awful thing, like, because we all believe in the one God. Now, they're not going to church here, but it doesn't mean they don't believe. Everyone does believe there must be a God – you'd want to be stupid to believe that's there none. They will eventually come – it'll be the full circle. It's like fashion – everything goes in a circle.

When we were small, we would be put to bed at seven – you wouldn't be asleep, of course. There'd be daylight out. And there were thirteen, fourteen houses up at the back, and we'd say, 'Twenty-two Aberdeen Street.' And one of us'd say, 'Mrs Barnes.' And we'd say, 'Kathleen, thirteen Findlater Street.' And on the pop, she could tell you who lived there. It was a game. You knew everyone.

And apart from that, I played camogie and I would referee a lot of matches. There's twelve on a team, that's twenty-four people would know the ref. Then I went on to play pitch and putt, and I'd play bridge with this friend and she'd say, 'You're like a begging ass – you know everyone.' And that's the way it was. I met this lady when I was playing bridge down the Civil Service Institute and she was very old, and she said her name and I said, 'Did you play camogie?' She said she did and I said, 'Were you in the camogie book?' That book must be 1916 or something like that. She was playing for Dominican College in her long gymslip and she must be ninety. The name struck me. 'Oh,' she said, 'you're very sharp.' Wasn't I sharp?

And we had a new teacher for the craft class, and she was introduced all round and she said, 'You're all southsiders?' I said, 'No, I am north side. I'm a southsider now,' I said, 'but I was from near the Infirmary Road.' 'Oh,' she said, 'do you know Dick Somerville?' And they said, 'Here we go again.' Sure, Dublin is very small.

You cycled everywhere or you walked. You were walking into town, down all those side streets. Years ago you'd know people; you might not know their names, but you'd say to yourself, 'Oh, that woman lives in Church Street', because you'd see her at her door – people would be standing at their doors, and you always said, 'Good morning' or 'Good evening,' even though you wouldn't know a person. Now, everyone is so busy and now you're in a car. Then, you were going on your bike and you'd ask somebody had they a pump if you'd have a flat.

Northside Dubliners were very close and very feeling for one another's family. If there was trouble, everybody felt it. I remember one time my cousin was up from Cork and this knock came to the door and I went out and this girl, Josephine Cahill, was there and she said, 'Is your mother there?' My mother used to lay people out – she was great. At that time, you washed them from head to foot and you sent them back the way they came into the world. (I don't know the way they do it now.) Josephine said, 'My father's dead.' And I came out in floods of tears. And there was my cousin, and he said, 'What's wrong with you?' I said, 'Oh, her daddy's dead.' And that's the way I felt, we were so close. He couldn't understand me crying for someone else's daddy.

Mammy would go up – that's a calling you have. But my father was hopeless. She came down, and she said, 'John, come up. I want you to shave Mr Cahill.' 'I will not!' he said. 'I will *not* shave Mr Cahill.' So she got the razor and she shaved him. We had this big sideboard, satin walnut, four big drawers and a big back on it and a big mirror. My mother, she was great for bed linen, always had loads of linen. And if anyone died, she'd lend them the four sheets for to put on the walls, and the white quilt. I hated going near that thing – I called it the death drawer, because anyone that died, they got the big white honeycomb quilt and that would be put on the bed and the corpse would lie on it, then it would be laundered and put back. And they used put white sheets and pin them up on the four walls and a little black bow on each one, and the whole room'd be covered with the sheets.

I said a lot of things about the good times, but as we get older, we're inclined to forget the bad things, or maybe bury them. But there was a lot of hunger, too, and a lot of people with nothing. Dublin, the inner city, was full of tenements and we just lived on the outskirts of town, and the country was next door to us. But in town, the houses were four or five storeys high and people would have huge big rooms and at that time people had ten, twelve, fourteen children. And then they were brought to their houses in Cabra. They didn't appreciate it for the simple fact that they were used to the big room and they could have three or four beds in it and the kids could sit on the beds. And when they built the little houses, they gave them just two little rooms upstairs and the one room downstairs and it wasn't like the big room they had. They couldn't put twelve chairs in it!

I don't think there was any social welfare then. I remember Eddie Begley, living next door to us, he'd had TB, and I was only eight and I thought he was old – he probably wasn't all that old at all. But he wanted shoes and he went round to the priest, and he was asking for a voucher for shoes and the priest said, 'Well, when I want shoes, I have to go out and buy them. I haven't got any money to give to you.' 'Well,' said Eddie, 'if I go up to the Protestant minister on the North Circular Road and he gives me the money for the shoes, *that's it.*' Which he did. Went up and he gave him a voucher, so that was the last of his religion. That was true for lots of people. The priests in those days were very pompous. If you met a priest in the road, you'd bless yourself and genuflect. You had them up on a pedestal. And they weren't close to you. (You'd genuflect and bow your head, but that was in case they had the Sacrament in their pocket.)

Now, the gasman used to come round about half three on a winter's day and he had this long stick and he'd light the gas lights and they were lovely. (They have some of them up in the Park now, ornamental, with bulbs in them.) He would come around all the people and the coalman would come with sacks of coal, come twice a week, and put it on his back and bring it in. Everything was brought to your door. The vegetables was brought to your door. He'd collect the money of a Friday. The fellow who came with the veg, he'd come round again in the afternoon, and all your waste was kept separate and that was called swill, and they collected that for the pigs.

There was little pig places all over Dublin. I can honestly say since they were taken away from Dublin, the bacon has never been the same. Because they only fed the pigs on the leavings of your table, which was cabbage and potatoes and carrots and all. But now, don't ask me what they get down the country now, some sort of nuts, which they feed them. In my days, when you'd go to Holy Communion, when you'd come home – you only had a fry on a Sunday morning – the smell of the rashers as you were passing the houses coming home! You'd be weak with the hunger! But you'd put a rasher on now and you wouldn't smell it.

Then the big thing was bikes! You didn't get a bike until you were fourteen. You had to go to work to get a bike. Sometimes a person would loan you a bike because it was the only way of transport, and you could not afford a tram, even though it was only a penny or twopence. But when you were fourteen, your bike lit a whole new life for you. A crowd of us used to go out every night after work. You'd have your tea and off out to Seapoint. About ten of us. And you'd cycle out and if the tide was out at Blackrock – it'd go out a good bit there – then it was Seapoint. That was the way. On a Saturday after-noon we'd cycle out to Portmarnock, one of the nicest beaches, all the beautiful sand, and we'd great times on the bikes. We'd go for a spin in the night-time and we'd go up to the Park or we'd go to Leopardstown. You knew your Dublin. You knew every street in Dublin. No problem to leave your bike. In town, they had these things in the middle of the road, and you'd just lean your bike against it and you didn't have to chain your bike, not at all. You went up the Park and you threw your bike on the grass and you'd play your camogie for two hours or three, then you'd get your bike and that was that. It was only in later years you couldn't leave a bike.

They built Cabra then. All the inner city went out to Cabra and we used to sing, *'Oh, they're tough, mighty tough in the west. And they've lots of curly hair upon their chests.'* They were like aliens to us. In our school they only took two in one class and two in another. I suppose there wasn't room. Like, we'd say, 'They're from Cabra.' They were different. They talk of racism now! It was there then, and we were only children. We thought we were above these people. Isn't it amazing, now?

Well, when you'd get your bike, there was this man in Cabra and you'd go up and just sign the form, and you paid five shillings a week when you worked. That took you two years to pay it off. You had to be fourteen to sign the form, and your bike was like your motor car. You had your basket in the front for putting your handbag in it, and your back bag. It was your whole life, your bike. Everyone had them.

But drink never came into it. You could go off for the night for a dance, you'd be walking home down to Bolton Street, and at the section of Bolton Street and North King Street there was a milk bar. And you went in there and the fellows would get a pint of milk and you'd get a slice of that cake with the pink icing – snow cake, they called it. And that would be twopence.

But one time, I was probably eighteen, and my sister would be twenty, and we were going to the depot and we said, 'If we had a bottle of sherry!' I was going with Michael, now, and we just got the taste for a drink. And we sent Michael in for it because you wouldn't dream of going into a pub. Oh, God, if you went into a pub, you were queer, now. There was Ryan's, there was loads of pubs – there was six pubs on Parkgate Street, because we were near the end of the town and you could nearly do the bona fide out to our little place. (There was what they called a 'bona fide' – if you went outside the city, you'd get a drink when the pubs in town closed. Let's say the pubs closed at two and didn't open until five. But if you went out two miles you could get a drink in those hours because you were a bona fide.)

Anyhow, we got the sherry and the glasses and we were in the sitting room, sharing it out – only a small bottle – Sandeman's. (We got the best – we were afraid to get anything else.) And my friend was hiding the bottle from Mammy with her coat, only you could see it in the mirror! Mammy found the glasses and she said to my young sister, Kathleen, 'What are these doing?' And, fair play to her, she didn't tell. You couldn't tell a lie to my mother – you'd never get away with it. She said, 'Were you drinking?' We said, 'No,' and we were staunch, now. She said, 'Well, I'll give you the benefit of the doubt. The two glasses could be left from Christmas.' She sensed something was wrong. But I

Mona's first camogie match playing for Dublin in the All Ireland, 1949.
She is on the right.

suppose, with two teenager daughters, she was ahead of us in things like that. And she was psychic. She could tell the cards. This night, she told the cards and it came true and she never told them after that. We said, 'Oh, make the wedding bed for us.' But she'd never.

～ ∾ ～

We were a sporty family. My brother played and my sisters Anna and Carmel played camogie, and we played for this team, Owen Roe. We went all the way from junior to senior and myself and my friend Nancy, we were picked for Dublin, which was a great honour. It was our first senior year, playing at Croke Park, and my father used to go with the car and they all picnicked out, but I'd go with the team in the bus. I'd rather have picnicked – they had a better meal than us; we'd maybe only have a bowl of soup before the match.

And we had polo in the Park. Oh, it was beautiful. Tuesday, Thursday and Saturday. Magee down on Arbour Hill, he had the horses, and all the local fellows used to make the few bob, because they'd have to ride the horses up for the polo. At the back of the President's house there's a stables there. There was a fellow in the pavilion and he'd have to whiten the balls, big wooden balls.

Oh, they were all big shots. And in winter they'd go out to India and play the polo in the warm country. And they'd have the *chukkas*, and you'd want to hear the curses of them! So, they'd have what you call a *chukka* and that'd go on for ten minutes and then they'd change the horses. The pavilion they had was white and they had all those lead windows with the little diamonds – it was quaint. And on Saturday they would have teas and a few of the locals would be waitresses there. There was work! And twice a year they'd a huge big gymkhana thing. And you'd get lemonade and they'd be throwing little cakes out to you. You'd get the crumbs, you know.

We had some good times, but these were the things that lit up your life. Otherwise there was nothing to do. During the war there was no coal and you would be using turf, and I remember my father bought some and the turf was *wringing*. You'd be putting it on the fire and you'd hear it hissing, and the bellows would be going and the ash from it was going all over and you'd want to be on *top* of it for to get a bit of heat.

But everyone was using it, and up the Park, all up the main road, two miles up the Park, they had it stacked, big stacks of turf, and it'd be higher than the house, the both sides, and they had watchmen in case it'd be taken.

Our dog, it had pups and my brother came in from a dance and she was after having pups, and the last one, it was nearly dead. And we put it into the oven, because there was only a glimmer and the heat brought him round. We called him Lucky, and we used to bring him up the Park. He was a pointer and he'd run up on the turf and he'd dislodge it, and the watchman'd be going mad, saying, 'Who owns that dog?' And, of course, we didn't own him!

Brendan Behan, he was in the tenements first, and then he moved out to Crumlin. All the tenements moved out to Crumlin and Drimnagh. They were in heaven. I had a friend, Kathleen, and when she got married first, she was in a house in Buckingham Street, at the top. And in the morning George used to have to get two buckets of water and bring them up the stairs to the top. Everyone had to do that. All from the one tap. And then they were building these corporation houses and they had a draw twice a year, say January and August. You put your name down for a house and on that day, you'd all go down and you might be lucky and, oh, the excitement!

I remember Kathleen got this house in Ballyfermot – it was a small house and they were made for newly-weds. It was a great lift. If you had a family later on, then you would get a transfer to a bigger house. But these ones for the brides! There weren't loads of them, only a block here and a block there. I think they should have something like that now for newly-weds. To have a draw. It's the fairest way. Years ago, you'd have to have so many children to get a house. You'd never get one if you only had one child. In Cabra they gave them baths, but they put the bath in the kitchens. (Of course, it was for the space.) But they used the baths for the coal – they were so used to these huge big rooms. But they'd loads of gardens, the length of the avenue. Great privacy.

Today, young people, there's no way they could afford a house. There's no incentive today. I know now they're all educated and if you're educated you should be able to stand on your own feet, but even with two of you working, you still can't buy... When we were married in 1946, Michael's wage was £7/10s. The children are getting that for pocket money now! You lived according to your means. You were happy with nothing.

Getting married, you gave a party for the people you worked with and the wedding was the big thing. When I got married, I was twenty-one and I was looking for a flat, and I'd look in the paper and then I'd meet Michael from work and there'd be queues of people. We kept looking for flats and I was getting one up in Phibsborough but my mother said, 'I wouldn't let you into that. It's filthy. There's grease on the walls – you'd never get that off.' So I went in to Mammy and I was with her for a year and a half, and then I got a self-contained flat at the end of the road on Conyngham Road. A lovely flat in a big house, and I was there for fourteen years. But I played camogie in the Park, and all the players, all the hurlers, would come down to my house. They used to say, 'Oh, you can't leave this house.' We'd a huge, big, tiled kitchen, and this house I'm in now would fit into that kitchen!

When I got my flat, I bought this bedroom suite and it was £200, and my mother said, 'You must be mental.' They were the good old days for the furniture. That was living when you had a full bedroom suite!

And this night a man came round and they had an association for the artisans' houses. And he said, 'You should be in an artisan's house. Why aren't you?' And I said, just like that, 'I was never offered one.' Which I had been, but I never wanted to move. The next night he came and said, 'Why didn't you tell me the truth? You were offered three places.' 'Oh,' I said, 'I forgot about it. That was a long time ago.' So, didn't he get this one, and Carmel came over with me to see it. But I kept thinking of my big flat. I was self-contained with a bathroom – a bathroom, in those days, you know! And we'd a long garden and we'd everything sowed in it, flowers on one side and carrots and everything all on the far side. But Carmel said, 'Take it. Pay the rent. It's cheap and you can always change your mind.' What you usually done was, you done two years and then you'd put your name on the list and you'd go back over to the north side. So we took it and the lads came over and papered it and I had to get rid of all my big furniture. And I came in and I loved it. I'm here ever since, and I'm involved in everything in the parish, and I wouldn't leave it. I could go over to my mother's and I had the bike and I'd be backwards and forwards.

This friend of mine, she and her husband were all Owen Roe, and when you were with a local club, the fellows had a football team and a hurling team and they ran dances. And the dance would be in Parnell Square. You'd look to see if Jimmy Smith was on, because he'd let two in for nothing. He'd let the four of us in for five shillings. Now, although he was GAA, it was céilí and old-time. They didn't call it Owen Roe because you couldn't have the old-time. (It had to be céilí with the camogie.) Michael my husband was a soccer man – he was Rovers – and we used to go out on the bikes, hail, rain or snow. We used to cycle out Dundrum way. If Jimmy was on the gate, he'd let us in for nothing. That was the only way we saw these matches. And if you'd go to Croke Park (and if we had a penny for all the times we went to Croke Park!), all the matches used to have a sideline, all round the pitch, about four rows.

We'd get Mass in Phibsborough and we'd bring the sandwiches and we'd go down and Croke Park'd open at twelve. The match wouldn't start till about half one, maybe two, and we'd be sitting there and there'd be accordions and everything, all playing and singing until the matches would begin. But you had to come early.

If Wexford or Kilkenny were playing, we'd say, 'Who'll we shout for?' And whoever it was, we'd give it our all. There was this girl, she was from Tipperary, a real fanatic, and this day Tipperary were playing and we'd be shouting, 'Oh, for God's sake, referee, are you blind?' And she'd turn round and be looking at us. And I'd say, 'Don't be starting anything – we'll have to finish it!' She was real tough, she was a huge big girl, you know.

Sometimes, we'd go to Croke Park in the morning and play a match ourselves and in the afternoon we'd go to watch one, and at half seven, eight, there'd be another match down in the Civil Service ground. That's how you spent your Sunday. And it was real exciting. If Croke Park was put off, we'd cycle off to one of the soccer matches, because they played in all sorts of weather. We were sports fanatics.

Even though the GAA wanted you to speak Irish, you didn't speak Irish, really. My mother was very good, she'd say, 'Now, speak Irish.' And it was terrible funny at the table. *'Tabhair'm píosa aráin.'* ('Give me a piece of bread, please.') And she'd be looking to see what you were missing. *'Tabhair'm spúnóg.'* That was very obvious, she'd know that. ('Pass me a spoon.') And *'Tabhair'm bainne'* ('Pass the milk') and *'Tabhair'm im'* ('Pass the butter'). Now, they hadn't a clue, my mother and father, but they were very good like that.

At the camogie, once a month we would have the referee's reports in Irish. And when you wrote out the list of your team, the names had to be in Irish. So at least you were writing all the names all the time. I was *Móna Ní Bhreathnach* ('Mona Walsh'). I refereed, and the week that that would be on, there'd be no complaints. Normally, I'd say if the teams would be rough or whatever, but that time, no, just the bare thing. List of teams attached, *mise le meas, Móna Ní Bhreathnach* ('I remain, your truly, Mona Walsh'). There was a few who were very fluent, but the Irish you learned in school, they changed the spellings three or four times. I'm seventy-six years of age, and anything in the room I can tell you what it is in Irish. But you couldn't speak it. Yet it's lovely to hear it spoken.

Anyhow, in the camogie, we decided to have a seven-a-side, and you had to speak Irish. They was trying to promote the Irish. We had great fun – we'd be practising and we'd say, 'Oh, *buaill ea.'* ('Oh, hit it!') 'Oh, *go hana mhaith.'* ('Oh, very good.') You had to speak it and Caroline Kennedy, the goalie, she pucked out the ball and didn't it hit Judy Doyle in the ankle and she said, 'Oh, *I osa Chríost!'* ('Oh, Jesus Christ.') You couldn't say that! I never enjoyed anything as much. You'd be surprised where the Irish came from. You'd think you'd forgotten it.

We done that a few times. But then, we had to finish up in 1974. The girls wouldn't come out. They had all these other games in school – they had badminton and so on. And they didn't want to come out in the rain. Mostly, with the GAA, you played in the winter. Which is stupid. They're trying now for to get the matches played more in the spring and summer, which would be much better.

My friend sent me a card. She said, 'Mona, I've joined a pitch and putt and you'd love it.' And she sent me a form and four of us joined it, over in Phibsborough, and she was right – I loved it. One year we went to a dinner and they were all getting their trophies and my friend said, 'We'll have some of those next year.' We were so determined, and as it happened, I got 'Player of the Year'. I've got all the trophies up there and I've given loads of them away. When anyone used to come in, they'd say to Michael, 'Do you golf?' and he'd say 'No, they're the wife's.' I loved it, and we started the golf, then.

I'll tell you what, people in an area of Dublin, like up here in Rialto, all know each other, and you'd need to be so careful. Michael was in the pub and he was talking and he said, 'He's a kind of strange kink, over there.' And the fellow he was talking to said, 'That's my cousin.' He said, 'I want to tell you, you'd want to be very careful. You're new here, but there'd be brothers and there'd be sisters and there's cousins and they're all related.' In the artisans, you didn't get a house unless some of your parents were in the artisans already.

Dublin is very small and it's very friendly. *Very* friendly. It used to have all these characters! There was Hairy Lemon. Oh, he was very hairy. We were afraid of our life of him. We said, 'Here's Hairy Lemon!' and everyone would fly in and the doors'd be shut. The poor man'd be coming round begging. And then there was old Johnny Fortycoats. And he'd loads of coats on. He could hardly walk, but he was very nice and we met him one night we were in a chip shop down in Berkeley Road. He was in the corner, and we said, 'Oh, there's Johnny Fortycoats.' Anyhow, next thing he smiled over at us and we were talking to him, but he was very cultured. He'd a lovely soft voice and wasn't stupid or anything like that. And we just said that you can't judge a book by its cover.

Then there was another fellow on the Oxmantown Road, and when he come out, he'd run backwards! He couldn't walk – he had to run.

Now, he wouldn't be flying, but he'd come down to the shop and he'd come in backwards. I suppose the brain was just twisted. Other than that, he was all right. He wasn't mad or anything. He'd never fall.

Then we'd a little fellow, Tommy. Oh, he was only that heighth [*indicates about three foot, six inches*]. Very powerful, the same age as my oldest brother. Now, the busmen loved him. He lived in Oxmantown Road and the bus used to stop at the corner and he used to be talking to the busmen. He was so small, he kept growing up with all the kids – he'd be with kids of seven or eight, because he was only that heighth. But didn't the busmen buy him a car? With a battery in it, because his little legs was too small to... Oh, a beautiful car. Just the nearest thing to being real! All his sisters were the normal heighth, beautiful-looking girls, and the fellows, too, but he'd all his faculties. Whatever freak of nature it was.

And then there was Bang Bang. He went to the theatre that had all the cowboy pictures, years ago, and in those times the buses was open at the back with a pole on the platform. And he'd be hanging out the pole going down George Street, and he'd be going, 'Bang! Bang!' like you'd think he was on a horse. When he was passing by, you'd say, 'How are you, Bang Bang?' Like he was *called* that!

Eddie Mulvihill

born 23rd February 1926

Despite some ill health, Eddie Mulvihill's spirit is as fiery and romantic as ever it was. He has, and always has had, a wonderfully dramatic way of speaking. Great booms, followed by pregnant pauses, then a hissing whisper are just part of his repertoire. But he is no old ham – he means what he says and he has an original cast of mind. His passions are Ireland, Irish culture and history, and he has a genuine love of poetry. His other passion is for a cigarette and from time to time he enjoys a drink of Scotch whisky. For a scantily educated working man, his love of Lord Byron and his ability to quote great passages of verse are remarkable. Naturally witty, with a great line in invective and a tender heart, Eddie is a real one-off.

YOUR FATHER'S UNCLE, Davy Hickey, got jailed at eviction times. He suffered in it. He was supposed to have pegged this harrow at a policeman. He'd be more than a policeman – what they called that time an Emergency Man.

Tommy Larkin was arrested – the people used to all flock at evictions, they'd be shouting and ballyragging, if you like. This young lad, th'ould bailiff struck him with the butt of his gun, and Larkin was there and his blood boiled. He was a big strong man and 'twas reckoned he broke the bailiff's jawbone with a single box. There's a song:

> *When the bailiff struck my child a blow,*
> *My darling Larkin soon laid him low...*

I like poetry. We had no wireless those times, but there was a programme on a Thursday night and we used to go down to Hickey's. I think *Around the Fire* was it. Storytelling and a bit of dancing, too. I could dance in my time. I loved dancing – I went all over the country. There was a big new place opened in Limerick called the Zetland, and I went to Kiltormer, Ballinasloe.... Ballroom dancing and set dancing, I could do that too. I used do the tango.
[*An elderly lady, leaning on her walking stick overhears this and interrupts.*]
[*Elderly lady:*] The tango! What kind of lepping would you do to that?
EM If I got the right music, I'd chance it with you now.

245

[*Elderly lady, laughing:*] By God, I can hardly walk! The tango was it, or the tangle?

EM I danced it a thousand times in my time. A lot of womenfolk was much better at it than others – you'd meet one with two left feet and what could you do?

Pat Slattery, sure he's a knot of oak, that's what I call him. Tom, his brother, I knew him since he was a boy. 'Twas I taught him to drive a tractor – he was a great young lad, always was.

I have a good house out near Shragh. I'm anxious to keep that house in middling shape, middling, mind you.

In September '87 (now I'm talking about 1887), a mighty eviction took place in my home place. My mother, she was the only daughter and her brother died a young man, Eddie Kelleher. He made a living by buying turf and putting it in a boat and selling it in Killaloe. He had no engine on his boat, only sails. You had easy going down river, but you learned to go against the wind as well as with the wind and the current. You could gather the wind in your small sails and your big sails, 'twas a great art in it, and *'twas* done.

You've heard tell of Clonmacnoise. Now then.

> *How solitary she now sits by that great river,*
> *That once-throng'd city.*
> *She was the nursing mother of our saints*
> *And the teacher of our highest learning*
> *For a long six hundred years.*
> *Yet in olden times she was a queen*
> *And the children of many lands came to do her homage.*

That great river was the Shannon, of course. I think that was James Clarence Mangan.

Pateen Whyte. Did you ever hear tell of Pateen Whyte? He was in America for years and years. There was boats, turf boats came up the river and he was on them. He used to play cards with them up in Boher.

You had to be good to get into the Boher school. And one time someone was playing and Pateen said, 'He's erratic and erronic, dominated by his quest of greed, which is very embarrassing to his partner.' Oh, they were very intelligent people – they were all scholars in their own right.

I started smoking very young. My grandmother was eighty-eight when she died and she used smoke a pipe and I used get the job at home of minding her. She'd big long skirts down to the ground, and for fear she'd get on fire, I'd fill this pipe and light it. I've been smoking for seventy years. Never seemed to do me any harm. Gerry Brooder, he smokes them Gold Flake all the time, he never changed.

This foot and mouth, now. I remember long ago, we had two clutches of bonhams expected to make a good price for them. Next thing we had to do was open the gate and let them out into the field.

I remember old Joe Slattery, God rest him, he bought two or three bonhams for £1 apiece. They should be at least £4 or maybe £5, according to the strength they'd be. Ah, they'd be big, because they'd gone past being sold. You had no fair to go to. Only people would hear about it and they'd come to the house.

I have a little one, 'tis appropriate for this time. I learned it from Paddy Brooder. God rest poor Paddy. In 1942.

> *If you showed a pig across the road*
> *Or moved a clocking hen,*
> *'Twould immediately be diagnosed*
> *As foot and mouth disease.*

I seen a lot of fairs. I went all over the country nearly. I sold hundreds and more than hundreds of suck-calves. I bought them from Kerry and County Limerick. Bring them to Woodford and Killimor and bring them to Ballinasloe. Going the whole time. Early in the morning and very early in the morning and late at night. 'Twas a job with a lot of hardship to it. And spend one night or maybe two nights a week with no bed. Didn't take any effect on me till I got that cursed stroke. I had a van. I had a lorry in later times. You'd sleep in that. Tommy Hanley would tell you about driving round the country.

It's a pity you never met old Thomas Hanley. He was a hive of information. He had words at will. He had great speaks of his own that no one else had. Something that'd be small, and people arguing about it. 'Will you make two halves of a cherry?' he'd say.

They were great old people then. They were brainy, I must tell you. Harmless, nice people but very brainy people. After a fair night in Woodford, they'd sit round and recite and tell stories.

I remember the coming of de Valera to Woodford, and we had a big banner. Two men painted this on it, a big banner across the street. 'Historic Woodford Welcomes Their Leader.' Eamon de Valera came that evening to Woodford. They wanted people riding a white horse out to meet him, and Gerard Brooder had an ould brown pony. Sports was high that evening, I'm telling you. De Valera, 'twas he formed Fianna Fáil in 1927.

I must ask Hanley where is that banner. Mark Maughan and somebody else painted words on a big white banner across the whole street of Woodford, anyway. Woodford is steeped in history, as you have heard tell of it. Look at all the priests that came out of Woodford parish. I have a brother a priest myself – he's in Canada. He's a Monsignor, by the way, right now. He was the youngest of us. He was a scholar, too.

My mother taught school in her time. Not a fully qualified teacher, she was a JAM, a Junior Assistant Mistress. The teacher at the time, Mrs Broderick, she nominated my mother to take her place – was she on maternity? And my mother never got a shilling for it. No favours. 'Twas Mrs Broderick would have to pay her, you know. People didn't want much them times. And they were happy. Happy, happy days. And will never come again.

I will go back to Owen Roe O'Neill. Conn Bucock O'Neill, I think he was a brother or a step-brother. Eoghan Ruadh O'Neill. Ruadh is Irish for 'red'. There's a *Lament for the Death of Eoghan Ruadh O'Neill* written by Thomas Davis. And then there's another poem.

O, mourn, Erin. Now he is lost, he is dead,
By whom the proudest flag was borne.

And then there's

Proudly O'Neill to our aid is advancing
With many a chieftain and many a clan.

It's very, very easy learned, Irish. But Irish grammar is very, very tricky. You'd need to be a scholar to pick that up.

There's an old man in Woodford, he's not expected to last the night. Josie W. I ran foot races with him, and I was never able to catch him. I'd stay with him for three parts of the race but in the last part he'd lose me. I couldn't catch him. The poor fellow is dying tonight.

Great woman of Three Cows, a grath, don't let your tongue thus rattle.
Oh, don't be saucy, don't be stiff, because you may have cattle.
I have seen - and, here's my hand to you, I only say what's true -
A many a one with twice your stock not half so proud as you.

Good luck to you, don't scorn the poor, and don't be their despiser,
For worldly wealth soon melts away and cheats the very miser,
And Death soon strips the proudest wreath from haughty human brows.
Then don't be stiff and don't be proud, good Woman of Three Cows!

That's James Clarence Mangan, too. That's going back now.
And I have a nice little short poem.

I see his blood upon the road,
And in the stars the glory of his eyes,
His body gleams amid th'eternal stars
His tears fall from the skies.

Isn't that nice? I think 'twas Joseph Mary Plunkett. I'm nearly sure. My mind is fairly good, only for the knock-out I got.

I never wrote any poetry. I like it but I lack the technique, if you like, to write poetry, you know. My favourite poet. I'm sorry to tell you he was an Englishman. [*Lowers his voice*] Lord Byron. You read some of Byron's poetry? I'll give you quotes from it. I loved it. My mother, God rest her, loved it. She died quoting some of it. She did.

Adieu, adieu, my native land
Fades o'er the waters blue.
And offer up to me and thee
My native land, goodnight.

That was *Childe Harold*.

I'm only going to hit in spots here and there, now. I'll give you the good parts.

Come hither, hither, my little page.
Why dost though weep and wail?
Why dost thou dread the billows' rage
Or shiver at the gale?
For if I thy guileless bosom had
I'd laugh to flee away.

That's a part of *Childe Harold's Goodnight to his Native Land*.

I had one sister. There were six of us entirely. She died. I remember well th'evening she died. The fifteenth of August, at eight years of age. But the doctor, he was coming every night for a week and he did-n't know what she had. The finish of it, it turned out to be meningitis, and it killed her. It killed my poor mother, too. She was the only girl she had. There was five brothers in it.

I want you to meet Tommy Tuohy. I will tell you quietly [*lowers voice*], Tommy Tuohy is a scholar. We did a lot of plays. You ask, did we put them on in Portumna? We didn't leave Shragh. We did stage them in Woodford. Too many aristocrats in Portumna what would criticize us. In the end they *wouldn't* criticize us, because we were better than them.

Eddie Mulvihill and Tommy Tuohy in conversation

Tommy is a fresh-looking man who used to be the postman in and around Woodford. Alert and fit, he is an Irishman through and through, despite identifying himself as an Irish-American. He loves Irish music and singing, and at the end of this conversation he did me the honour of reciting a poem he wrote, his voice vibrating with the most profound feeling for this part of the world, its history, its heroes, its battles and campaigns.

TT I retired about five years ago, I suppose, and doing a bit of farming now.

EM There was none of us dry that night!

TT We had two big turnouts. They gave me a hell of a send-off, first down at the Community Centre in Shragh, the people below, I can never forget the people below. Nor I can't forget the people up in Woodford, at Moran's. Two nights! Two nights! I didn't feel too bad the next day. I got through it anyway. They were really wonderful. I never appreciated anything as much in my life. Because I didn't expect anything like that. Presented me with a beautiful television and a few more mementoes. Michael Moran, in Moran's lounge, that's where they had the big …

EM He engineered it all.

TT I didn't know it was on at all. A Friday night. They were all in from here and all the surroundings. Oh, four o'clock in the morning I think we broke up. Daylight. A band, all kinds of music. Father Conroy!

EM Can I say something? [*In conspiratorial whisper:*] Tommy Tuohy, the best-respected man in the parish, I would say.

TT Oh, well now. That's going a bit, a bit…

EM I brought that out of an old play we done, Tommy and myself one time, and we had a few more in it. A little old play we done for Father Cuffe, God rest him. I gave you a speak from it.

TT We served for fourteen years in a drama group below, for Father Cuffe. All the houses you see round Looscaun [*site of the church and the priest's house*], the walls and the turfsheds and all, all the equipment that goes with the house, all that came out of that. The first plays we done was with our teacher Master Doyle, a Corkman. He was great, we had the regattas, and sports and swimming and singing and hurling and football. He was great.

EM Do you know, and we going to school. Oh, but, sure, this man was years and years and years ahead of his time. He brought us at his own

251

expense to hurling matches and... Now they have school tours, visiting all those places. And if he got a few more years in our part of the country, he would bring all the scholars to a place like Clonmacnoise. 'Twasn't from him I learned that speak I gave you. I learned that at home from my poor old mother. She taught school in her time.

TT She taught school in her time. A learned lady. But our teacher was twenty-five year ahead. Not like Master Canning, the first teacher, he was trimming all round him. Idling lads was all he was doing. But Master Doyle, he could trim you and give you a slapping all right, but he could teach all them things outside the school curriculum. Hurling, jumping, gardening, swimming, singing, all kinds of sport, and he used to always say, 'Always be your own man. Never talk down to your shoes! Talk to the wall, hit the wall with your voice. And take criticism, if 'tis constructive criticism, take it. But if 'tis destructive, kick it out of your way.' He used to tell us that. He was great! He was teaching boys and girls. A Corkman. A real Gael and an Irishman to the core.

EM Irish to the core.

TT By God, there was no backsliding with him. He was national-minded, you know.

EM Oh, we have Irish. Tommy and myself could strike up a conversation, and we could hold an hour and we wouldn't speak one word of English.

TT The young ones that's out now! Th'outlook has changed. They have no love of country, no love of language nor no love of culture. 'Tis U2 and you, me, and big bands and all that kind of stuff. Pops and...

EM Lookit! I will tell you what the famous Patrick Pearse once said. He once said, 'Nothing good ever came out of America', and I'm beginning to believe him now.

TT They ruined the Irish music and everything. You've Galway Bay [*a local radio programme*] and from morning till night and nothing but pop. Nothing Irish. Clare FM is all right.

EM Christ, come here till I shake hands with you! I'd run and turn off th'ould thing.

TT On Radio One they have Ciarán MacMathúna on of a Sunday morning at half-past eight when no one's listening to it. The culture has changed and the people has changed. I may tell you the schools is adding nothing to it either. Not a thing.

EM I will tell you and I will speak for Tommy as well. We fought to get that school and that little hall there. We fought it hard amidst great opposition.

TT Once your schoolhouse goes, your identity goes. But 'twas built. 'Twas built! There was great community effort in that.

EM The Lord have mercy on your cousin, a famous man, John Slattery, and Tom. They came to us and built it and we went and mixed the stuff for them and we went in the evenings. And we kept at it. And then we had to have a fundraising crowd as well to try to keep the finances a bit right. And mind you, we paid for it according as we went along!

TT No debt! Our present bishop that we have now, he played cards with us. He used to come down to Connell's in Clonmoylan and he came down one night with a suitcase and packs of cards, ten or fifteen packs. They used to have Twenty-five then, weekly teams; they put up two trestles, you know, what they'd be using for plastering, put boards across it and make a table, and he played many a night, Bishop Kirby. He used to be a priest then, down Ballinasloe. That happened!

EM Kirby's of Baylough, Athlone. I knew it well. And – would you believe it! – I knew [*portentously*] the bishop's mother! I did. I met her. He wasn't a bishop then. He was – wait till I tell you! – he was an only son, and they had a famous place in Athlone – Baylough, Athlone. And he didn't, wasn't a bit interested. Went away, went to college and turned out what he is today, a bishop. So now for you!

TT By golly, he played cards there with us, to raise money, and we building that! So.

We had fourteen years as drama society for the church. Do a play every year for the church, the surroundings and all that. Comedy mostly.

EM We have good speaks from it. Tommy'll give you a good speak. Me and himself had to hit the boards. Someone in the audience shouted, 'Ah, good lads. 'Tis easy knowing you were on the boards before!'

TT We done one big three-act comedy. The best one we ever done was *A Will and a Woman*. Three acts in it. I'm not able to tell you now who wrote it, but 'twas a great thing. A few of them dead now, too, that took part in it. Me and my man was two bachelors, which we are today. Two bachelors, as such. And Hanley was a strolling fiddler – Tommy. No one knew who he was, only a strolling fiddler. Anne Glasby, now, Martin Flanagan's wife, she's dead. Anne Flanagan. She was the leading lady, she was the Yank that came home. Who else was in it?

EM 'My God!' she said. 'Do those fellows ever wash anything?' And I had to answer her. I said [*puts on a respectful voice*], 'We washes our face at Christmas, Ma'am.'

TT 'If anyone wants any more washing than that, there's a pump down th'end of the yard!' So now! The pump down th'end of the yard! Well anyway, now. The whole gist of it was, anyway, my man was going to marry her and I was harassing him on and doing him up for the wedding and Hanley came in as a strolling fiddler and he was the man. He was married to her before!

EM She had property and hadn't she it left to a cats' home! And we kicked up hell over it, Tommy and myself.

TT The lad said, 'We'll get married tomorrow morning,' he said, 'and we'll come home and me and you can sleep down th'far end, like we always did.' 'Twas the best job on earth! 'Twas a great story. He [*Eddie*] was the leading light. Hanley was the man appeared out of the blue and upset the whole apple cart.

EM Hanley was a great community man. God, he was great. He joined in all them things.

TT And he joined us for the Comhaltas, the music. For the Stephens's Day thing, the féile, Hanley was the first man, thirty-two years ago, stood above in the street of Woodford with a lorry.

EM He brought up his lorry! He brought up his lorry and parked it here in the street in Woodford. Took off the creels and carts and took everything off it and made a dancing flag out of it, if you like. Oh God, he did.

TT That's what started the Mummers' Féile, thirty-two years ago. Originally they started it, May Fogarty and Patricia Eames and Vincent Farrell. I'll give you the kingpins of it, now.

EM Master Fahy, he slipped in then, from Ballinakill. And Master Ryan.

TT That's who started the Mummers' Féiles. We were thirty-two years in it and it's all the time. We run the Comhaltas here, the big day for Stephens's Day. That's the only fostering of the music – we're trying to keep it alive, anyway.

The last group that came, this last year, they were from Ennis and Killeeneena. They were great! The best of a group. They were out all day and they gave all their proceeds of the day to Hospice. They got £600 of a prize from us for winning the act, d'you see, and they had £1,400 or £1,500 and 'twas all to the Hospice in Clare. Weren't they a good group! They were in Moran's and they done all the pubs.

EM Three or four years ago, now, we put up that time a thousand pounds and a group from the County Cavan won it!

TT We went back to Killeeneena to present the prize to the leading pub. I can't think of the name.

EM I can think of nothing, since I got this stroke.

TT The Tulla lads was in it. Met P. J. Hayes, myself, there that night. He's Martin Hayes's father. [*Martin Hayes is a famous fiddler who plays traditional Irish music.*] The old Tulla Céilí Band was in it. They gave us a great night. A big night, and they were in it from Ennis. 'Twas a real Irish night, I may tell you.

EM We'll put it into a nutshell for you. They came from far and near!

TT They haven't one mummers' group in Woodford! Isn't that bad! We had two junior groups, a little group in from Derrygoolin and three out of one family and two out of another and I was delighted to see them and they got first in the junior groups. And there was another one from Killeenadeema – they got a prize, too. They were the juniors, you know. 'Tisn't easy keep the music going!

TT Davy Hickey was only sixteen when he was jailed in Galway Jail for his part in the Land Wars.

EM Activities in the Land Wars!

TT Himself and another man, by the name of Pateen Whyte. They were jailed.

EM They were known as Fenians, that time. That's how Pat Slattery got his nickname, 'the Fenian'. 'Twas ould Thomas Hanley, God rest him, a grand old man, that christened Pat, and a young lad, 'the Fenian', and it's on him still.

TT Davy Hickey was in a house, a namesake of my own, Tuohy's, himself and three or four more. They attacked, the military and the whole lot of them. They were well equipped, you see, the powers that be. Davy was such a small boy, they put him up in the loft, which was in every house. And they attacked, anyway, and the redcoat cut a hole down through the roof with his bayonet and they had a harrow up in the loft and my man came down, legs first through the thatch, coming in overhead to catch the boys down below. And Davy up with the harrow and pinned him again the roof. He could neither go up nor down. He was only sixteen, a small fellow. Sure, they massacred the lad! Forks and shovels and all, whatever they had.

EM To touch one of the forces of the Crown at that time, it meant jail for life, sure.

TT He got four years anyway, and Pateen Whyte was another one. He had to do the four years. In Galway Jail, where the new cathedral is now, that's where it was. And the judge, when they brought him to court, here in Woodford, the infantryman said that Hickey flung a harrow at him. And the judge said he couldn't understand how such a small youth could peg a harrow at a man. Begod, he got the works, anyway.

EM Little do you know about British rule in Ireland in them times. Do you know what I heard it compared to lately? 'Twas just as bad as what Hitler done to the Jews in the last World War. Now for you! Now for you!

TT Well, after them times, there was the Black and Tans and it was holy hell. Holy hell.

EM I don't know whether Tommy has that song for you. In that time, or a bit after it, the four lads that got shot on the bridge in Killaloe. 'A dreadful news through Ireland ran, it ran from shore to shore.'

I knew the man, he's dead now, God rest him, that was with them. He was with them but he wasn't active. It was proved after that he wasn't active. They caught him and they made him walk on the bodies. They made him step from one to the other on the bodies and 'their blood flowed with the Shannon, convenient to the town'.

TT Michael-Joe Tarpey has that song. He has it. Then after that, they had the truce. They split over the Treaty, one wanted to accept and th'other didn't, and they split and Lloyd George gave them guns to fight one another.

EM He gave them rope enough to hang themselves. He knew 'twas going to happen.

TT That's what ruined Ireland. They broke up in disorder and built the boundary in the North, the six north-eastern counties sliced off. A festering sore then and ten times worse now.

EM Ten times worse now. Festering ever since.

TT Every decade there's a rising there.

EM A planter lived in my house for nineteen years. My poor mother had to go to school from the side of the road. The planters living in her house. We had a slate house in Shragh in 1887. We were put back for eviction until a year later. When I think, it puts me in mind of what my poor mother went through. The planters were no gentlemen, I'll tell you that. I'll give you the names. You had Walker, and Nesbitt and Jackson and Johnson and Buchanan. They took over the houses of the people. They picked the best houses. They wouldn't pick an ould wreck. An ould thatched house and it all rotten, they wouldn't go in there.

TT A lot of them is gone. A few of them blended in and that was it.

EM You see, the people went out and they shouted at the planters if they went up the road, if they were going to a fair or.... They'd boo them, in other words.

TT They were thirty years out, you know. That's a long time. It's a good part of a lifetime.

That covers the Land Wars, anyway. Tommy Larkin lost his life in the Land Wars. He was defending a house and he was an only son and he was taken prisoner, twenty-one years of age, and convicted and put in Kilkenny Jail. He resisted most terrible, he was a big, powerful man. He resisted. But anyway, he was convicted and he gave the policeman such a trimming, they landed him in Kilkenny Jail and they gave him four or five years. And he got sick!

EM 'When a bailiff struck a child a blow...'. The youngsters'd be out, you see, booing them and shouting them and this ould bailiff, he couldn't take that and didn't he, with the butt of a gun, didn't he hit this young lad's child! A good, hardy child. He struck him with the butt of a gun and knocked him. And Larkin was there and seen it. Larkin. A strong man. He broke his jawbone with a box of his fist. And, of course, he got Kilkenny Jail, 'that living hell, where they starved my darling in a narrow cell'.

TT He got sick anyway, and they didn't treat him properly and he died. After hunger strike and all the rest of it.... Water was the one thing that killed him; he wasn't supposed to get water and they pumped buckets of water into him. Dysentery, you know. Killed him pure dead. He's buried below in Abbey. Abbey Cemetery.

EM Next time you come and you've more time, we'll bring you down. You'd like to say you visited. We put a headstone over Tommy Larkin in Abbey.

TT There's Tommy Larkin's headstone now in the photograph. Sean MacBride unveiled it. Famous Sean MacBride, Maud Gonne's son. A Celtic cross. Cost £1,000. We collected it locally. There's the date on the back of it. August 1986.

EM I'll give you a speak he said that day. Sean MacBride. He read it out of a book. 'The fools, the fools, still live our Fenian dead.'

TT There's Looscaun church, where forty evicted tenants were given land. The church let them in that time.

EM I'll give you a phrase from the song about Tommy Larkin.

> *Not a finer man you e'er did pass*
> *In the town of Woodford, going in to Mass.*
>
> *A bailiff struck a child a blow*
> *My darling Larkin soon laid him low.*

TT He died on hunger strike and he was brought home and buried in Abbey. There was thousands of people at that funeral. When his father and mother came home to Gurteeny, they found an eviction order on the door. They were to be evicted the following Monday. That was when Ireland was Ireland and England was England. That was Clanricarde. But it was the goddam Irish that was working for him.

EM Th'Earl of Harewood.

TT Th'Earl of Harewood. That was the last royalty that was in it.

EM Steeped in history, this place. It is. As well as Woodford. I seen a time, I was just about more than a boy at the time. And de Valera came to Woodford and they had white horses out Rea, welcoming him in along.

TT They had sods of turf on pitchforks, steeped in paraffin oil, lighting his way.

EM I seen – he was only a boy then, Gerard Brooder, Maddy's son. They didn't happen to have a white horse, but he had this ould brown pony and by God, they put Gerard up on her, welcoming de Valera into Woodford and he having a big tricolour, holding it up over his head. He was only a boy then.

TT Me and Eddie went to school together.

EM We were very nearly self-educated. But the master, he found out we was interested.

Did you ever read a book called *The Great Hunger*? By Lady Woodham-Smith. I read it twice. Any amount of our people dying by the side of the road. Oh, God, wouldn't it make you cry?

Terrible things. My mother was evicted. She was Callaghan.

TT I'm a blow-in! I'm an Irish-American. I was born in the United States. I came home at six and a half with my parents.

EM More Irish than the Irish themselves.

TT Oh, that was the tradition I was reared up in.

This is a poem, now. It was meant to be put to music, but it wasn't. The first time it was heard was in 1998 at the Mummers' Féile, in Woodford. A new poem or a song, that was one of the items, like, you had to compose a new song that nobody ever heard.

The title of this song now, is 'Slieve Aughty's Mountain's Brown', and it was composed in Christmas, nineteen hundred and ninety-eight, for the Mummers' Féile in Woodford, by me, Tomás Ó Tuataig. Now.

Last night I had a magic dream, I stood on Ard Aoíbhinn,
The gem in Slieve Aughty's crown. Derrygoolin in the valley down below I saw.
I crossed Ulick's Mountain on a magic wind that brought me to Lough Atorick.

Lough Atorick, the place you will find seanachaí and bodhran players in days
*   of yore,*
Birthplace of Seán Ó'Haoda, champion all-Ireland bodhran player, gone from
*   us today,*
go ndéeanafaidh Dia trócaire ar anamacha na marbh.
[*May God have mercy on the souls of the dead.*]

I passed Aileen Dara and Upper Forge and landed at the bay in Woodford
*   beside the town.*
I saw the statue of Our Lady in the grotto, guarding the place and the valleys
*   down to the Shannonside.*
I stopped in the street. I thought of the brave people who stood there at
*   midnight,*
meeting in 1886, and defied the British Empire proclamation.

On that magic wind, I took the road to Rea. There I saw the stone circle,
Dating back to other days, twelve thousand BC.
I crossed Rock Hill and Lough Isle and I stood on the hills of Cappa and I
    viewed the valley down below,
I took the road to the branch line, past Drimnavee and Bolag and
    Drumnamuckla, too,
On my way until I came to the point of the wood beside Clonmoylan Bog.

I met some men I did not know; they were standing on the bog
And one of them, in his ghostly hand, he held a slane and a sod.
One spoke to me and said, 'We are the ghosts of former days who fought
Hard for the rights of which you hold today.
Do not sell out your bog for Euro Judas gold.
Do not sell out your bog for Euro Judas gold.'

'A chara [friend],' they said, 'we will sing you a verse of a song to help you on
    your way.'
'Just one verse,' he said, and this is what he sang.

> 'The purple heather is the cloak God gave the bogland brown.
> From primrose dawn, a lovely range to sunset's farewell fire.
> No morning bells have we to wake us with their mellow tones
> But the winding call of duck and quail awake us to our labour undone.
> We clean the sodden shelving bank in sunshine and in rain
> That men by Christmas fires may thank the wielders of the slane.'

They said they were on their way to Moanakeeba Bog, and they vanished out
    of sight,
Holding their slanes high in the air and with the shout, 'Do not sell out! Do
    not sell out!'

I turned down the road at Power's Cross, passed Clonmoylan and Bauntia, too.
I stopped a while at the cross of Shragh. I saw the schoolhouse on the hill
    where I learned my ABC,
How to play the hurling, Gaelic games, football and how to swim at the castle
    in Clondergoff
By our own teacher, Seamus Doyle, who came from rebel Cork.

There today stands the hall built by voluntary men in the year of seventy-nine.
I saw Cloonoon on the hill. This is my native place that I hold dear to my
    heart, my native place.

I travelled down Rossmore, past the Cruacán [dwarf or hunchback]'s fairy
    hill. I saw the place
Where the fairies play, hurling not far from Piper's Hill.

I saw Kylenamelly, the place of the bees and honey, and Kylenashee, where
    lives the Fairy Queen.
I found myself in Douras; I passed by Rosstullis, too, and to Bawnmore,
The place you'll find good horses and strong men, too.
I passed Clooncoe and Drummin and Oghilly. I stood at the cross of Gurteeny,
At the corner of the grove, where many a tale of love was told in the gloaming,
    long ago.

I saw Gurteeny on the hill, birthplace of Tommy Larkin, who gave his life for
    Ireland in the year of 'eighty-six.
Gurteeny, famous for its singers, dancers and musicians in the days, long, long ago.
I saw Deroober on the hill, Coos and Slaughty, too,
Sheltered by the breezy hill of Clare.

I took the road out of Flesk and awoke from my ghostly dream
In Lowertown, not far from the Earl's Chair.

There is one request when my earthly journey is over.
Lay me down to rest in the golden sand of Gortaganna,
Beneath the shadows of Ard Aoibinn and Sliabh Aughty's mountains brown.

EM Your friend Pat Goherry, he gave me the elbow. 'Christ! How does he think of it!' Christ, Goherry! I thought he'd knock the place, clapping for you.

TT That was at the féile, at the fléadh. And after, I didn't get the prize! 'Twas some lad down in Banagher. But 'twas like political life everywhere. There's a sleaze everywhere.

EM And he reading out of a book!

TT And he reading it out a paper, you know. I put that all out of my head that day. The whole lot. The whole lot. But it didn't happen.

I learned this from an ould friend of mine, a County Limerick man, in Lisdoonvarna.

> *'Twas a jolly fine song and jolly well sung,*
> *Jolly good company, every one.*
> *If you can do better, you're welcome to try*
> *But always remember, the singer was dry!*

Voices

This final chapter is devoted to shorter pieces – snatches of reminiscence, brief lives, anecdotes.

Austin O'Toole

I first glimpsed the tall, imposing figure of Austin O'Toole at a cattle mart. He was wearing a wide-brimmed hat with a short peacock feather in the band, and as soon as he spoke his distinctively gravelly voice left an indelible impression. His innate courtesy, plus a romantic leaning toward poetry and learning, have not been blunted by the life and hard times of a cattle dealer and farmer.

My father was an islander, from Inishturk, off the coast of Westport, and he came out from there about nineteen or twenty years old and joined the RIC, which was under the British Government, and he was sent to Craughwell and then on to Killimor, where we're living now. My mother happened to be living there at the time – she was a very young widow. She'd married an RIC man from Roscommon and he died suddenly on a New Year's night before her baby was born. So that girl is alive yet – she's eighty-five gone now, and she's like a hen pecking oats – she's all go. She's a nun. All pep. But I do say to her now, 'Why don't you throw in that old job, sure, and come home and retire here?' No, no, she's dedicated yet. I'm delighted for her that she is that fond of it, because I think an awful lot of them got lured into it, now, into the church. There were no vacancies. Nothing else. Or else get your match made for some hairy ould farmer that could be your father – that went on, too, a lot.

The British, for all the harm they did, but they brought great architecture – lovely houses. And the canals and railways. We've to thank them for that, no matter what you say. They done the railway. We

262

talk about the British and what they did, but they did that to their own, too. At one time a chimney sweep could hire children of three, four years of age, and if they got lost up one of these big chimneys, well, it was just an accident. A lot of them got smothered.

Because my father was an RIC man, he was always called Mr O'Toole, which he resented. They didn't call him Austin. People had a slavish attitude. Anyway, my mother was a teacher in Killimor and he bought the house where I live now, and he wasn't popular for that either, because there were people with more money than him wanted to buy it. The reason was there was an auctioneer in Ballinasloe and he and his wife were living the high life – they were all Protestant people – and he was setting the house to another Protestant horseman, and he was putting the money in his pocket, telling the solicitors in Dublin that he couldn't set it because it was boycotted. The local people had put in big bids on it, £1,500, they tried to make it a convent, which was a good idea. And he didn't declare that to the solicitors.

So my father resigned from the police – he refused to carry arms (this would be in around 1928, 1929), and when the gardai started, he joined them and he was a sergeant in Mullingar. Well, when Eamon was born, he came home for the birth and he was talking to a woman in the pub (she was a publican), and she said, 'If I was a young woman, I'd go over the auctioneer's head and go up to Dublin to buy that place.' So he said nothing, and the next morning he took his bike at six o'clock and he cycled into Ballinasloe and caught the train to Dublin and bought it. It was sold unknown to the auctioneer and all the interested parties. Politics entered into it then. He, as a gard, should have had permission to buy. He got the option to resign or sell. And he did neither. So they took his RIC pension off him – shows you how bitter people can be.

He was a farmer's son, so he did a bit of farming and my mother taught school, but times were very hard. Oh, Jesus, would you stop! There was no money, no social services, no support of any kind. Times were very hard.

I went on to deal in cattle, and I took a lot of cattle off the station in Drumree, County Meath, where my heart was. I was interested in the County Meath, I loved the people. I used to bring cattle for a fellow making a big farm near Tara. Do you know Dunsany? Dunsany Castle and Killeen Castle is very close by, which is a rare thing with castles, to be close up. Do you know how that happened?

There were Plunketts – Blessed Oliver Plunkett would be descended from them. In fact, some of his vestments were got in Dunsany Castle one time. But 'twas a huge estate and they decided to divide it, two brothers. So that night, probably had a drop of wine, they decided they'd go on horseback in the morning, and whatever a man could cover, he could have.

So the Dunsany man was up first, and he'd a lot of it covered, and he was coming close, and the Killeen man said, 'If you come any further, I'll shoot you!' So, he built his castle there, where he took position. 'Tis quite close, less than half a mile, from Dunsany Castle. I think Blessed Oliver's head is in Drogheda.

It's not the gift of the lover, it's the love of the giver. There's a joy in giving. I enjoy it.

When I was going to school, I was murdered! The master used to kill us all! He'd bring in three or four sticks at a time and beat the devil out of people, and there was nothing about it at all. He got away with it! You were supposed to be wrong if you was beat. But my father once…

The teachers would swap classes for singing and I wasn't in the singing group. But a good, fine day the principal, he was a savage, he'd bring us out, and before he'd go out he'd rise the window just like that, and he'd put out the sticks, the way people wouldn't see him carrying a stick. And he'd bring the class round in the sun. Anyway, he beat me and he gave me a good box and I hopped off the wall and, sure, the roughcast all tore my face.

And my father was a real policeman – he didn't want us fighting or trespassing on people's land and we'd to come home strictly on the right side of the road. No fooling. And I came home with the scarred face. 'You were fighting!' 'I wasn't,' I said. 'You were!' 'I wasn't!' 'What happened your face?' So I had to tell him, although my mother had told me not to say anything about it. Well, he was going to go in to the teacher and he was going to do the devil and all.

So, there was another teacher that was very great with my mother, she taught down in Quansborough school, and she used to call the odd evening to have a chat and a cup of tea. She was there this evening and my mother was so peace-loving, she was teaching in the school and she didn't want any annoyance with this teacher. She was a fool!

But anyway, Maggie was leaving and my mother left her out as far as the gate, and I was watching as my father shaved and got ready. He was going on his bike to see this teacher and I was delighted. But I was watching round a big beech tree and he went to the gate and the two women were standing there and, begod, didn't they persuade him it was the wrong thing to do. He turned back. So my case was lost then. But I was very disappointed. He got away with it.

So I ran away out of school as quickly as ever I could. The compulsory tillage came in – we were getting into tillage, and I thought 'If I pick stones, I'd do anything rather than be in school.' I left at thirteen years and nine months. Sure, jobbing around the house, working horses and doing farm things, doing anything. Sure, that's all right when you're a gossoon, you don't know the difference! But I regret my education, very much I regret it. I do.

I love poetry, now, and we have a session in town, there, I go to. I wouldn't have high-flown stuff, but I like it. Bits of old poetry. I'd have only simple old ones. There was an old fellow called Pat Buckley, he died, the poor fellow, and he was a singer and he could recite, and he'd great stuff. I used go see him. The next thing, Pat went into hospital and Pat was dead. A loss. But anyway, he'd let you out the door, and no matter what you'd mention, he'd chime in with something that would go with it, you know. Some little bit of poetry. But he gave me 'The Vacant House'. 'Tis an English poet, too, I think.

The Vacant House

Whenever I walk a-suffering, along the winding track
I pass by a poor old farmhouse, by its shingles all broken and black.
I suppose I've passed it a hundred times, but I always stand for a minute
And I look at that house, that tragic house, that house with nobody in it.

Now, this house on the road is suffering, needs a dozen panes of glass,
And someone ought to weed the path and take a scythe to the grass.
It needs new paints and shingles, and the vines need to be twined and tied.
But the most thing of all it needs is some people living inside.
Now, if I had a lot of money and all my debts were paid,
I'd put a gang of men to work with brush and saw and spade.

I'd buy that place and do it up the way it used to be,
Then I'd find some people looking for a house and I'd give it to them for free.

But a house that has done what a house should do, a house that has sheltered life,
That has put its loving wooden arms around a man and his wife,
A house that has echoed to a baby's laugh and held up its stumbling feet,
Is the saddest sight, when left alone, that your eyes could ever meet.

So whenever I go a-suffering along that grassy track
I always stand for a minute and I take a good look back,
And it grieves me to see the crumbling roof and the shutters flying apart,
And I can't help feeling that poor old house is a house with a broken heart.

Isn't that nice? It's true, you know.

Jack Lambert

Despite his years, Jack Lambert, from County Wexford, retains some very boyish qualities, a mixture of shyness and a delighted mischievousness. Hunting and its attendant social life have been of great importance to him always.

I've hunted since I was thirteen. I was a follower, and my uncles used to hack to the meet, from Enniscorthy to Gorey. My grandfather was killed by a horse. He was fifty-five years hunting with the Killinicks. There was no wire that time, blind ditches, and you depended solely on the horse. A feature of this part of the world is that you get a ditch built up on both sides. I can't understand why.

I love the Irish draught horse. The brains of the Irish draught. There's a bit of Connemara in them.

Years ago, the Master would get half-crowns, they'd throw them on the counter of the pub where you'd meet. A horse was never made before he got a drunken ride. A lot of masters are fond of the bottle. But with the horse, you had a partnership. Of course, you had to have a bit of natural, it had to be in you.

I had a mad mare one time – she won two point-to-points in the same day – the first and last race. But she was mad. I was out this day and we were in a run and I saw this one, she was jumping the bank, and – she was secretary at the time – a real old lady, having it real quiet and steady. Didn't my one pull her way in on top of the bank beside her and just brushed off her! But she galloped after me and she whipped me. So now, when we stopped by the gate, 'Now!' she said, 'Give me the half-crown!' I hadn't paid her at all, and I would have got away with it only for upsetting her. The cap money, that was.

Marley Lace, that was the mare. She had four foals before we broke her and when she missed, my father said to me, when she didn't go into foal the fifth year, he said, 'What are we going to do with her now?' Said I, 'We'll hunt her and we'll sell her that way.' So we hunted her then, and I was interested in the point-to-points. I was kind of riding in them.

We're set for this coming Saturday and Sunday. The Hunt Steeple-chases, semi-finals and finals this weekend. We think we stand a chance. We're not going up for the good of our health. There'll be sixteen teams from all over Ireland, by invitation. There are four on a team: a lady rider, an ordinary member, a hunt official and over fourteen stone. They're the four – you must have those qualifications. You compete against another team. It's in Dublin this year, but we travel all over Ireland.

That's our hobby round here – all the farmers' hobby. About ninety per cent of the farmers go fox hunting.

Matt Roche

This man is something of a legend among the hunting fraternity on account of his cheerful endurance, for he went out as Master in County Wexford for decades, regardless of weather, and admirably performed the equally essential duties of entertaining the company after the hunt.

I'll tell you something, now, that happened a long while ago. This man's father, he bought a horse. He was a calf dealer, and every fair within thirty miles, he bought away and he'd bring them home, or he'd bring them to another fair. One night, his wife got a brain haemorrhage and so he went to the priest, a famous priest, but he said he could do nothing. But this old farmer, he said, 'You can make her well if you want to. You cure her, I don't care if every animal on the farm dies.' And three months after, he brought the wife home and the last animal on the farm died the same day. The mare even died. The farmer was standing on the steps of the door, and he said to the priest, 'You can do it if you put your mind to it.'

I've hunted with three packs: the Killinicks, the Wexfords and the Bree. Five days a week. I once did nine days without stopping. I'd hack over to the meet, about twelve, thirteen miles. Over to Rosslare. Then hunt from twelve till four, or a bit later. Then you had to have a few drinks. It's not so bad if you haven't to hack, if you have a horse box and a jeep.

I'd go in all weather. The only thing would be a snowfall or you couldn't travel with the horse.

We can get big enough crowds. One meet there were forty followers on a holiday. One of the biggest at the time. And we often had eighty or ninety out.

I started off riding on a pony, no saddle. There was no riding in the family. But we had a neighbour and he'd hold me on while he'd be breaking them. The Master, he was my idol. Paddy. He started at £200 a year and he hunted for twenty-one seasons. At the end he was getting £800 a year – I started at that. Times have changed.

Tom Murray

For some unknown reason, the muse visited Tom Murray late in his life, and he wrote a good deal of verse straight from the heart before she suddenly departed and, for now, he writes no more.

About ten years ago, I took the idea one day that everything could be written in poetry. I never wrote before and I don't do it any more. But here is one I wrote, called 'The Reason Why'.

> *Paddy and Billy were two little boys*
> *Who lived in a Belfast street.*
> *They were happy and gay while they played with their toys*
> *And they smiled when they happened to meet.*
>
> *But as they got older and went on to school*
> *That smile quickly changed to a frown,*
> *For Paddy went up the road every day*
> *And his little friend Billy went down.*
>
> *This caused the two boys to wonder and think*
> *What that could be all about*
> *Even now, after many long years,*
> *They still haven't sorted it out.*

For Paddy he was a Papist
And Billy, he was a Prod
Though they went to different churches,
Both knew there was only one God.

Paddy was taught to say his prayers
And go to Mass in Ardoyne,
While Billy heard tales of the gallant king
And the battle he fought at the Boyne.

To separate and to segregate
Was a normal way of life.
This brought about an atmosphere
Of bigotry and strife.

No one ever really tried
To heal this awful crime.
The rift between the parties
Got wider all the time.

Any help that ever came
From either Church or state,
It seemed to be too little
And always came too late.

Those who held the wealth and power,
They wouldn't cede an inch,
Until the underprivileged
Were forced to feel the pinch.

The Troubles really started
In nineteen sixty-nine,
With Civil Rights building fights
And hundreds dead or dying.

Now we can see the outcome
Of long and bitter years,
Of misery, death, destruction
Broken hearts and tears.

Of those savage, cruel murders
All done in freedom's name,
It's enough to make an Irishman

Hang his head in shame.
How different things may well be now
If we hadn't been so silly,
Like explaining the simple facts of life
To Paddy and to Billy

That God gave everyone the right
To live in his own way,
Ireland might very well
Be a happier place today.

I wrote that in 1990.

When the Pope came to Ireland, I wrote this poem. I didn't give it a title.

In the year of seventy-nine, the world it was bad,
Strikes, prices and depression had people sick and sad.
Then in July, the message came and filled us all with hope
Ireland was to be honoured by a visit from the Pope.

I've seen many popes, but my favourite is John Paul. His smiling face, a noble Polish face. He's a man who knows the facts of life. A sportsman and a scholar.

His message rings throughout the land from every church and steeple
Love your God and love your neighbour is his prayer for all the people.
When he came to visit us, all the world could see
He got an Irish welcome from Ireland and Ó'Fiach.

Down through the years, many famous men have come to our fair shore
But the equal of John Paul II I never saw.
He kissed the children, blessed the sick and filled us all with hope
God love and bless our Pope.

I don't know what it was. A little phase came into my life and went away again.

Bridget Dirrane

Mrs Dirrane is a most alert and formidable old lady. Kind and courteous, yes, but her great age has not softened her. It is clear that throughout her long professional life she was used to being in command.

On one visit, I remarked on her painted fingernails. 'I don't like it. One of the nurses did that. They've been painted these last three weeks. Everybody knows it's artificial. Plain nails – you can shine them and that's just as good.'

I was born Bridget Gillan on 15th November 1894, the youngest and smallest of eight children in the townland of Oatquarter, Inishmore. My brothers and sisters were Pat, Mary, Julia, Joseph, John, George and Margaret Anne. I can still rattle off the birthdays of each one of them although they are all long since gone, *go ndéana Dia trócaire orthu* – God rest them.

Irish was our native tongue; we had it from the *cliabhán* – the cradle, although we spoke English in the house, too. Both my father and mother could speak English, which was unusual on the Aran Islands in those days and we were encouraged to speak English at school so that we could get on well if we left Aran. *Tá neart Gaeilge agam fós* – I have a power of Irish in me yet. It was always my favourite language and I often spoke Irish in Boston afterwards.

In my childhood on Aran we had plenty of fun, getting great enjoyment out of simple things that cost little or nothing. The game we liked best was Rucco, something like hurling or camogie today. We played it with sticks cut from trees to make a kind of hurley and we played with a sponge ball. Handball up against the gables of the houses was very popular, too, and I remember that we used to go running on a moonlit night and the first of us to fall into the sandpit in Kilmurvey was the winner. My cousin Martin Walsh and my brother Joe were excellent at rock-throwing, which was a real test of strength. Football was very popular, and we couldn't afford real footballs so we made our own from balls of yarn or old clothes.

People used to play cards, especially in the winter, and my mother, God rest her, was a great card-player at either Twenty-five or Forty-five. The players used to gather in different houses and the prize was a boxty cake [*a cake made from potatoes and flour*]. The losers had to make the cake and give it to the winners.

While I was growing up, I was taken to Galway by boat a number of times, so when Dr O'Brien in Kilronan asked me to go to Tuam [*on the mainland*] to look after his son's family there, I had no fear of leaving the island. I liked Tuam and it was there I received my first ever bouquet of flowers from a man who obviously liked me. I was a wild young thing that time and didn't take him seriously, but getting the flowers was nice.

After a few months there, I went to work for Father Matthew Ryan, the parish priest in Knocknavilla, County Tipperary, very much a rebel county. Father Ryan had been jailed during the Land League agitation long before this, and he was a great follower of the nationalist movement, so it was very fertile land for me to join Cumann na mBan, the women's branch of the nationalists. This was around 1918.

Our main aim at the time was to help out young men on the run. In all, there were about eighty of us in that branch of the Cumann, and we prepared food for the men on the run and often took great risks in bringing it to them. We knew where to leave it among the rocks and the heather or in a little house hidden in the bog. If we had any spare money we gave it to them also. It was a tough time. There was very little conversation if we happened to meet. It wasn't always the same men and there were seldom more than four or five of them together. Some died, many were arrested and it was a great privilege for us to help them in any way. All decent men, the finest this country produced. In all, I spent two years as a housekeeper for Father Ryan. He often told us, 'When you talk to these men, tell them to call to my house if they wish me to hear their confessions.'

The Black and Tans were the scourge of Ireland at this time, creating terror every place they went. They were loathed by the people. Their uniform was a regular black suit with a yellow-orange stripe down along the side of the pants and also on the hems of the jacket. Hence the name.

They came in big lorries, pillaging and looting, not caring who they shot. They would shoot into the air to create fear and some of their deeds were dastardly in the extreme. In Tipperary they shot a young lad in the back, after telling him to run home. Around about this time, too, Father Griffin in Galway was taken from his house in Sea Road and murdered. I'm glad that men like Father Griffin are remembered, with a road in Galway named after him and a football club in the city called the Father Griffin's. Men and women who suffered and died for Ireland will always be remembered.

In 1919, I was in Dublin, training as a nurse. One day I was reading a letter received from Aran from my cousin, Coleman Dirrane, informing me of activities on the island, when I heard a knock on the door. When I opened the door, a whole swarm of Black and Tans fell in on top of me like a plague of locusts. I ran to the kitchen to get the letter which contained some information of IRA movements and managed to put the letter in the fire in time. This incensed the Tans. The officer in charge began to question me and I answered him *trí Ghaeilge ar fad* – through Irish all the time. He was furious and said many a person was shot dead for less. I answered him defiantly. 'I have only one life to give, but if I had a thousand lives to give, I'd give them for the same cause.' I told him to go ahead and shoot. He put the revolver down by his side and said, 'Get over there and put your coat on. You're under arrest.'

At that point I didn't care whether I was shot. I saw many a young man being shot after he was tortured. My life was worth very little compared to the lovely young men who were shot or hanged. I got my coat and was loaded into a lorry. I was taken first to the Bridewell, then transferred to Mountjoy Jail. While in the Bridewell, I sang all the Irish songs I knew and danced away to my heart's content, making the officers furious. They were glad to get rid of me. Mountjoy was very clean compared to the Bridewell. There was no trial.

I continued to be troublesome in Mountjoy and went on hunger strike there. Countess Markiewicz [*an Irish patriot and the first woman elected to the House of Commons, although she never took her seat*] was in Mountjoy at this time. Looking back now, I don't know how I survived. Eventually, the Mayor of Dublin sent in a good meal to all of us and I gave up the hunger strike for that. Shortly after that I was released.

Once, Countess Markiewicz came to my rescue when, after I had escorted Maud Gonne MacBride home late at night, I was pinned down by gunfire from a lorryload of British troops. The Countess knew I was shocked and escorted me back to Saint Ultan's Hospital and insisted on my being put to bed to ease my nerves and get some rest.

In 1927, I emigrated to America, Boston to be specific. Boston is the place where so many Inishmore people before me had gone and where so many of my relatives and friends lived. When I was growing up, nearly every household on the island lost one or two of their family to America. Their departure then was like a funeral. Some of them never returned home. Worse still, some never lived to see America. Going away was easier by the time I left in 1927. I set sail from Cobh, or Queenstown as it was known then. Even at that stage we hadn't shed the English influences in so many areas!

The ship was very comfortable. It may have been the *Franconia*, which I certainly travelled on once. The fare across cost me £12, a fair amount of money in those days. It wouldn't get you very far today! On arrival in New York, emigrants from Ireland were subjected to a very thorough medical examination. If you failed the test you were sent to Ellis Island where you were kept in quarantine until you recovered. If you didn't improve, you were sent back home. Although I was seasick on the voyage, I got through the medical with flying colours.

When I came to Boston I took up a nursing job in a hospital, and I joined the Galway Middle Club where young Irish people gathered every Saturday night for music, set-dancing and tea. A céilí band provided high-class Irish music for us. We used to attend Mass at 2 a.m. on our way home from the dance. The Mass was held at that hour to accommodate the Irish workers.

These were the days of the Depression in America and times were tough.

I was living in Dorchester, a great Irish neighbourhood, and I met Ned Dirrane, my future husband, at his aunt's house. Our marriage took place in the month of November 1932 in Saint Thomas Aquinas Church in Jamaica Plains, and we went to live in Third Street, South Boston, renting an apartment from a Connemara man. All we had was a kitchen, bedroom and small dining area, for which we paid him 70 cents a week. I was nursing at the hospital and Ned worked in a local wool store. He worked hard and had long hours, starting at 8 a.m., and was paid 22 cents per hour, which improved in time to one dollar per hour. It was very difficult to make ends meet but we got by, leading a very simple but happy life. Things weren't to get better until Franklin D. Roosevelt came into power.

I admired the Kennedys greatly, especially John F. Kennedy. I valued every hair on his head and was lucky to be in Boston for the Kennedy era and proud to have canvassed for him door to door. I was always well received and at times when I knocked at doors it was like as if I was at home in Aran or Connemara. Practically every home had Irish connections, the majority of them coming from the west.

Boston really supported the Kennedys politically and a fine team of helpers and canvassers got involved in JFK's campaign. I sent him a special good luck and Mass card wishing himself and his family every success in his venture and I still have his letter of acknowledgement in my possession.

President John F. Kennedy visited Galway in June 1963. His visit was received with scenes of wild enthusiasm and, in his speech at Eyre Square, before he received the freedom of the city from the Mayor of Galway, this is what he said:

Mr Mayor, members of the City Council, Prime Minister, Ambassadors.

If the day was clear enough and if you went down to the bay and you looked west and your sight was good enough, you would see Boston, Massachusetts. And if you did, you would see down working on the docks there the O'Dohertys, Flahertys and Ryans, and cousins of yours who have gone to Boston and made good.

I don't know what it is about you that causes me to think that nearly everybody in Boston comes from Galway. They are not shy about it, at all.

It is strange that so many years could pass and so many generations pass and still some of us who came on this trip could come home here to Ireland and feel ourselves at home and not feel ourselves in a strange country but feel ourselves among neighbours, even though we are separated by generations, by time and by thousands of miles.

The Kennedys do not forget either – even a humble person like myself who canvassed for JFK almost forty years ago. Jean Kennedy-Smith, sister of JFK, visited me in St Francis's Home, Galway, recently and we were photographed together. She also visited me in my home – Cliff Edge Cottage in Oatquarter. One day, a young man knocked on my door. With an American accent he asked, 'Is this Bridget Dirrane's house?' When I said, 'Yes,' he replied, 'My name is William Kennedy-Smith. My mom, Jean Kennedy-Smith, will be here shortly. She is on her way by bicycle.' I couldn't believe my ears. She arrived shortly afterwards, and yes, it was the American Ambassador to Ireland. Teddy, the youngest of the Kennedys, also visited me in Aran with his son.

And I eventually came home to Aran. I never lost touch with home during my thirty-nine years in the States. Back in Aran after all my wandering, I found myself living with my brother-in-law, Pat Dirrane, in his house in Oatquarter. Pat was no stranger to me. I knew both him and his brother, Ned, from my childhood days in Inishmore. I was now in my early seventies, Pat in his sixties, and since we had always been great friends, we both decided it was best to get married to protect our good name, maintain respect in the community and show good example. As I say this, it sounds very cold and proper. To put it simply, we got on well and it was the natural thing to do.

Next morning I was up to our parish priest, Father McNamara, to tell him of our decision and ask him to help arrange a quiet wedding and marriage ceremony for us. He was very supportive and contacted the Bishop of Galway and arranged for us to be married on 27th April 1966. It was a very private affair. Nobody in Aran knew what we intended doing and we both wanted it that way. I bought a nice navy outfit in Ryan's of Galway and Pat purchased a new suit, too.

It is very unusual to marry two brothers. They were so different in many ways. Pat was a lovely man, so humorous and full of fun and loved dancing. When I think back now and remember the nights in Cliff Edge Cottage – our home – when we danced the night away together, it brings a tear to my eye. We got on like a house on fire.

Unfortunately, Pat's poor health gave me quite a lot of concern, especially in his latter years. He was never demanding and I nursed him right up to the end. He died peacefully on Ash Wednesday 1990, as we recited the rosary at the bedside. I was very lonely then and am lonely for him still. He is buried in the family plot in Killeany graveyard and when my time comes that's where I'll be buried, too.

I bonded my wedding rings together as a token of my love for the two Dirrane brothers, Ned and Pat, and the rings travel with me wherever I go.

On 18th May 1998, Bridget Dirrane received an honorary degree from the University of Galway, presented to her by Hillary Rodham Clinton.

I was given an academic gown to wear: a dark green cape over a black cloak with bright blue borders. And I had to wear one of those things on my head – a mortarboard. It was a wonderful day, and Hillary Clinton is a real lady. She has a lovely smile, and I wish her very well in her life.

I was really well looked after. One of the nurses stood behind me and sheltered me with an umbrella. I didn't just get the degree, all written out beautifully in Latin, but everyone made a big fuss of me. My friends in the Aran Islands presented me with a crystal clock in the shape of a Celtic cross. And I was given a Galway crystal bowl, and then I got a Tara china plate. All inscribed. Everyone was very kind.

And I loved the flowers I got. I love flowers. Daffodils, roses they give life to a room.

EVENTS FROM 1600 TO 1900

Below is listed a series of some of the major events that shaped the political, social, economic, cultural and religious life in Ireland in a period spanning three centuries. Only the bare facts are given, but even such sparse information reveals a story of struggle, oppression, injustice and misfortune met with undaunted courage and a blazing ambition for freedom. The reader is advised to consult a history of modern Ireland for a fuller picture.

1601 Battle of Kinsale: The English defeat Irish rebels and their Spanish allies, who were determined to dethrone the Protestant Elizabeth.

1603 James I comes to the throne. Lord Mountjoy, Lord Deputy of Ireland, crushes Irish rebellion. Hugh O Neill and other rebels leave Ireland to take refuge on the mainland of Europe (the Flight of the Earls). Much of their land is confiscated.

1606 Settlement of Scots, loyal to the Protestant monarch, in the Ards peninsula (in present-day Northern Ireland).

1608 onwards The Plantation of Derry: confiscated lands are taken by English and Scots settlers, through the offices of the City of London (hence the city's new name, Londonderry). The settling of 'planters' continues in adjacent counties.

1613 Opening of Parliament in Dublin.

1625 Charles I comes to the throne.

1641 Catholic-Gaelic rebellion for return of lands. 59% of land in Ireland held by Catholics.

1642 Outbreak of English Civil War.

1644 The Battle of Marston Moor marks the beginning of a succession of defeats for the Royalists at the hands of Cromwell's Roundheads.

1649 Execution of Charles I. Oliver Cromwell arrives in Ireland as its civil and military Governor. There are massacres in both Drogheda and Wexford, and one of the most important rebels, Owen Roe O'Neill, dies in November.

1650 Kilkenny surrenders to Cromwell, who then returns to England. Catholic landowners are exiled to Connaught (the most westerly province).

1653 Forfeited Irish lands are surveyed and allocated to those who have rendered service, the so-called 'planters'. Cromwell becomes Lord Protector.

1660 Parliament is restored in Dublin. The Restoration of the Monarchy, as Charles II is proclaimed King.

1685 Accession of James II

1688 Birth of James, heir to James II, pushes the claim of Protestant Mary, James's daughter and wife of the Dutch prince, William of Orange, into second place. William of Orange lands in England at the invitation of the English parliament. James escapes to France. Gates of Derry shut against James's troops. 22% of land in Ireland held by Catholics.

1689 James arrives in Ireland, raises an army and lays siege to the city of Derry, where thousands of Irish Protestants seek refuge. The besieged city is relieved.

1690 William arrives in Ireland. James is defeated at the Battle of the Boyne and escapes to France. William fails to capture Limerick and leaves Ireland.

1691 The Battle of Aughrim sees James's forces routed and the Williamites victorious. Limerick surrenders.

1695 The 'Penal Laws' come into effect, which basically restrict the rights of Roman Catholics to education, to bear arms or to possess a horse worth more than £5.

14% of land in Ireland held by Catholics.

1697 Roman Catholic clergy outlawed by Act of Parliament.

1701 Act of Settlement establishes Protestant succession.

1702 Queen Anne comes to the throne.

1704 Further Penal Laws restrict how much land Roman Catholics can own and imposes 'tests' for public office.

1713 Jonathan Swift becomes Dean of Saint Patrick's, Dublin.

1714 George I comes to the throne. 7% of land in Ireland held by Catholics.

1727 George II comes to the throne.

1728 Franchise removed from Roman Catholics.

1760 George III comes to the throne.

1782 Catholic Relief Acts allow Roman Catholics the right to own land outside parliamentary boroughs and also restore some of their rights to education.

1791 Young Dublin barrister Wolfe Tone publishes *Arguments on Behalf of the Catholics of Ireland*. Foundation of the United Irishmen in Belfast, formed as a 'union of Irishmen of every persuasion in order to obtain a complete reform of the legislature, founded on the principles of civil, political and religious liberty.' United Irishmen formed in Dublin.

1792 Catholic Relief Act allows Roman Catholics to practise law.

1793 Roman Catholics regain restricted franchise.

1794 Roman Catholics allowed in principle to attend Trinity College, Dublin. United Irishmen in Dublin suppressed.

1795 Wolfe Tone leaves for America. The foundation of the Orange Order, its avowed purpose the maintenance of the Protestant ascendancy.

1796 Wolfe Tone travels to post-Revolutionary France to elicit support for an Irish uprising. United Irishmen in Belfast arrested. Habeas corpus suspended. Wolfe Tone arrives with a French fleet on the south coast.

1798 Martial law is imposed. Rebellions in various parts of Ireland, from Wexford to Ulster Wolfe Tone arrives with another French force, but is arrested and commits suicide in prison.

1799 At Westminster William Pitt recommends Parliamentary Union between Britain and Ireland.

1801 Irish Act of Union: Ireland becomes part of the United Kingdom. The Irish (College Green) Parliament is dissolved.

1803 Robert Emmet incites a rebellion but is arrested, tried and executed.

1813 First 'Twelfth of July' riots in Belfast

1820 George IV comes to the throne.

1823 Daniel O'Connell's Catholic Association is founded.

1825 Catholic Pro-Cathedral opened in Dublin.

1828 Daniel O'Connell elected MP for Clare.

1829 Catholic Emancipation Act allows Roman Catholics to enter Parliament and hold civil and military offices.

1830 William IV comes to the throne.

1837 Victoria comes to the throne.

1841 Census gives population as 8,175,124.

1842 The newspaper *The Nation* is founded by Thomas Davis and others.

1843 Inspired by Daniel O'Connell, a 'Monster Meeting' is to be held in Dublin, calling for the Repeal of the Union. It is prohibited.

1844 Daniel O'Connell is convicted of conspiracy and sentenced to a year's imprisonment; this decision is later quashed by the House of Lords.

1845 First signs of blight in the potato crop. Prime Minister Sir Robert Peel orders the import of Indian corn (maize).

1846 Trevelyan opens depots for the sale of Indian corn but closes them later in the summer. Repeal of the Corn Laws, to allow the import of cheap corn. Lord John Russell replaces Peel as Prime Minister. Public works started to provide relief, but stopped in expectation of the new autumn harvest. Total failure of the potato crop. Public works resumed. First deaths from starvation reported.

1847 Soup kitchens established. Fever epidemic. Responsibility for distress thrown on local rates. Ireland left to 'operation of natural causes'. O'Connell dies.

1848–9 The worst years of famine.

1848 A news-sheet, *The United Irishman*, is set up, but its editor quickly sentenced to transportation.

1850 Irish Tenant League founded.

1851 Census gives population as 6,552,385.

1852 First Saint Patrick's Day parade in New York.

1854 Catholic University opened in Dublin.

1858 In Dublin, James Stephens founds the organization that will become the Irish Republican Brotherhood.

1859 Fenian Brotherhood founded in the USA.

1861 Census gives population as 5,798,967.

1862 Harland & Wolff shipbuilders founded in Belfast.

1867 Execution of the Fenian 'Manchester Martyrs', following the shooting of a guard during an attempt to rescue the head of the IRB from a police van.

1869 The Prime Minister, Gladstone, disestablishes the Protestant Church in Ireland.

1871 Census gives population as 5,412,277.

1874 A general election sees 60 candidates in favour of Home Rule returned.

1875 Charles Stewart Parnell elected MP for County Meath.

1879 Foundation of the Irish National Land League. Evictions are carried out, at the demand of absentee landlords.

1881 Census gives population as 5,174,836. Parnell arrested. Land League outlawed.

1882 Chief Secretary Lord Cavendish and Under-Secretary T.H. Burke are assassinated while driving through Dublin's Phoenix Park.

1884 Foundation of the Gaelic Athletic Association.

1886 Irish hierarchy endorses Home Rule. Gladstone's Home Rule Bill is defeated at Westminster.

1887 *The Times* publishes a letter supposedly linking Parnell with the 'Phoenix Park Murders'.

1889 The letter proves to be a forgery. A divorce petition is filed, in which Kitty O'Shea's husband cites Parnell as co-respondent.

1890 Parnell re-elected Chairman of the Irish Parliamentary Party but by the end of the year there is a split in which Parnell is defeated.

1891 Census gives population as 4,704,750. Parnell dies in exile.

1893 Foundation of the Gaelic League. Second Home Rule Bill passed by the House of Commons but defeated in the House of Lords.

1894 Irish Trades Union Congress formed.

1899 Yeats, Synge and Lady Gregory amongst others help found the Irish Literary Theatre.

EVENTS FROM 1900

The following series of events had great impact in Ireland in the first half of the 1900s. Even though all the men and women who tell their stories in these pages lived to see the twenty-first century, this first half of the twentieth provided the formative years in their lives.

1900

January After its split ten years earlier over the Charles Stewart Parnell–Kitty O'Shea affair, the Irish Party is reunited under John Redmond.
The British defeat the Boers at Spion Kop.
March The relief of Ladysmith is announced.
April Queen Victoria visits Ireland for three weeks.
May Mafeking is relieved.
October The Conservative Party wins the British General Election.
November Oscar Wilde dies in Paris.
December Limerick City Council offers the freedom of the city to ex-President Kruger of the Transvaal and to Maude Gonne.

1901

January Queen Victoria dies. A vote of condolence is rejected by Dublin City Council by 42 votes to 35, but eventually passed with abstentions.
September The United Irish League calls for a strike.
October The Pioneers (Pioneer Total Abstinence Association of the Sacred Heart) holds its first annual meeting.
December In Newfoundland, Marconi receives the first transatlantic signals, transmitted from Cornwall.

1902

April W.B. Yeats's play *Cathleen Ni Houlihan* is first performed.
May The Boers surrender to Britain.
July Balfour becomes Prime Minister.
August Edward VII is crowned.
December A conference of landlords and tenants begins in the Mansion House to settle the land problem.

1903

January Following the conference, a report recommends that tenants be allowed to buy their land with loans from the Treasury.
March St Patrick's Day is made a bank holiday.
July King Edward VII and Queen Alexandra arrive on an official visit.
August Pope Pius X is elected.
The Irish Land Act becomes law, allowing tenants to buy out their landlords.
December The Wright Brothers make their first successful flight.

1904

January The Motor Car Act lays down a speed limit of 20 mph.
February J.M. Synge's play *Riders to the Sea* has its first performance.
March All pubs close on St Patrick's Day at the behest of the Gaelic League.
April Edward VII re-visits Ireland.
September Sir Antony McDonnell, Under-Secretary for Ireland, publishes a report which becomes the programme for the Irish Reform Association. It suggests a form of power be devolved to the Irish administration and votes £6m from the Treasury to the Irish Financial Council.
November G.B. Shaw's play *John Bull's Other Island* is first performed in London.
December The United Unionist Council is established.

1905

December Campbell-Bannerman forms a Liberal government in Britain.

1906

May Arthur Griffiths publishes the first edition of *Sinn Féin*.
August The Waterford-Rosslare-Fishguard line is opened.
December The law banning the opening of pubs on Sundays is made permanent.

1907

January There are riots at the Abbey Theatre at the opening of J.M. Synge's play, *The Playboy of the Western World*.
May James Larkin begins a series of strikes involving the dockers of the Belfast Steamship Company.
July Edward VII and Queen Alexandra visit Ireland.
The Royal Irish Constabulary goes on strike in Belfast, protesting about conditions and pay. Soldiers and the RIC from the south take over.
August Riots on the Falls Road, Belfast, are suppressed by the British army, killing four civilians.
October Marconi's wireless telegraph opens for transatlantic press telegrams at Clifden, County Galway.

1908

January The political party Sinn Féin wins 15 seats in the Dublin municipal elections.
The Municipal Gallery of Modern Art opens in Dublin.
April Asquith, a Liberal, becomes the British Prime Minister.

1909

January The first old-age pension is paid, to people of 70 and over.
December Asquith tells Parliament Ireland must be given a measure of Home Rule.

1910

January The general election results in a hung parliament, with the Irish Party holding the balance of power.
February Edward Carson becomes leader of the Ulster Unionist Party.
May Edward VII is succeeded by George V. The Abbey Theatre refuses to close in mourning for the dead king.
Halley's Comet is visible in Dublin.

1911

April According to a national census, Ireland's population is now 4.39 million.
The Home Rule bill is introduced to the House of Commons.
July George V visits Ireland.
August The Women's Suffrage Federation is founded.
October A monument to Charles Stewart Parnell is unveiled in Dublin,

1912

April Asquith introduces the Home Rule Bill in the House of Commons.
The *Titanic* sinks with the loss of 1,490 lives.
May It is announced that there have been more than a million pledges for teetotalism in Ireland since 1905.
September Nearly half a million Unionists sign the Ulster Solemn League and Covenant against Home Rule.

1913

January The Home Rule Bill is rejected by the House of Lords.
The Ulster Volunteer Force is formed, to oppose Home Rule.
September The Provisional Government of Ulster is formed by the Unionists.
November The Irish Volunteers are formed.
The Irish Citizen Army holds its first drill.

1914

April Carson welcomes Winston Churchill's proposal to exclude north-east Ulster from Home Rule.
June Arch-duke Ferdinand is assassinated in Sarajevo.
August Britain declares war on Germany. The Home Rule Act becomes law but is suspended indefinitely.

1915

April Irish regiments are among the first to arrive at Gallipoli.
May The *Lusitania* is torpedoed off the coast of Cork, at Kinsale, with the loss of 1,502 lives.

1916

The Compulsory Service Bill, allowing for the conscription of men between the ages of 18 and 42, excludes Ireland.
April Sir Roger Casement, who hopes to land a cargo of arms, comes ashore at Banna Strand and is arrested by the police, who were tipped off by an informer.
24 April: The Easter Rising takes place in Dublin.
25 April: The Lord Lieutenant proclaims martial law in Ireland.
29 April: Padraic Pearse, one of the leaders of the uprising, surrenders to the British. Three thousand people are injured in the fighting and 450 killed.

May 3 May: The British army begins executing leaders of the Rising. Padraic Pearse, Tom Clarke and Thomas MacDonagh are shot by firing squad.
4 May: Joseph Plunkett, Edward Daly, William Pearse and Michael O'Hanrahan are executed.
5 May: John MacBride is shot.
8 May: Eamonn Ceannt, Michael Mallin, Con Colbert and Seán Heuston are shot.
9 May: Thomas Kent is shot in Cork.
12 May: James Connolly and Seán MacDiarmada are shot by firing squad. Asquith visits Ireland.
June Sir Roger Casement is put on trial in England and found guilty of treason.
July There is a massive offensive at the Somme.
G.B. Shaw writes an article in the Manchester *Guardian*, asking for Sir Roger Casement to be treated as a prisoner of war.
August Sir Roger Casement is hanged in Pentonville prison.
Greenwich Mean Time is introduced into Ireland in place of Dublin Mean Time, which was 25 minutes behind GMT.
December Lloyd George becomes the Prime Minister of a coalition government. James Joyce's *A Portrait of the Artist as a Young Man* is first published.

1917

March A revolution in Russia leads to the overthrow of the Tsar.
April The USA enters the war.
June Republican prisoners, including Countess Markiewicz and Eamon de Valera, are released from jail.
July Eamon de Valera is elected for Sinn Féin in the East Clare by-election.
October Eamon de Valera is elected President of Sinn Féin.
November The Bolsheviks take power in Russia.

1918

February The Representation of the People Act gives the vote to men aged 21 and over, and to women aged 30 and over.
March Russia leaves the war.
November An Armistice is declared on the western front.

December In the post-war general election, Sinn Féin wins 73 out of 103 Irish seats. Countess Constance Markiewicz becomes the first woman to win a seat in the House of Commons.

1919

January Sinn Féin establishes Dáil Eireann, the Irish Parliament.
The Anglo-Irish war begins.
April Eamon de Valera is elected President of Dáil Eireann.
June Alcock and Brown land in Galway after the first transatlantic flight.
December Republicans attempt to assassinate Viscount French in the Phoenix Park, Dublin.
Lloyd George's government attempts to introduce two Home Rule governments – one for the six counties of north-east Ulster, another for the rest of the country.

1920

January The RIC enrols demobbed British recruits, soon to be called 'Black and Tans'.
June Eighteen people die in riots in Derry.
August Terence MacSwiney, Lord Mayor of Cork, is arrested by the British Army.
October Terence MacSwiney dies in prison, following a prolonged hunger strike.
November The eighteen-year-old student Kevin Barry is hanged in Dublin for his involvement with the Irish Republican Brotherhood.
Enrolment begins in the North for three new categories of special constables: A, B and C Specials.
Eleven British intelligence agents are shot on the orders of Michael Collins. In reprisal, the Black and Tans murder 12 civilians in Croke Park, a sports ground in Dublin.

1921

May The Custom House, repository of official records, is burned by the IRA.
June The Northern Ireland Parliament sits for the first time. Sir James Craig is appointed Prime Minister.
July A truce in the Anglo-Irish war is declared.
The Dáil Eireann meets openly in the Mansion House in Dublin.

December After two months of negotiations in London, a treaty giving the 26 southern counties independence is proposed.

1922

January The Dáil Eireann passes the treaty by 64 votes to 57, leading to the formation of the Irish Free State.
The Provisional Government of Southern Ireland formally accepts the transfer of power from the British at Dublin Castle.
February Pope Pius XI is elected.
May Eamon de Valera and Michael Collins agree a pact for the forthcoming elections.
The Royal Ulster Constabulary is officially established.
June A general election is held in the Free State.
The Free State Army bombards the garrison in the Four Courts, Dublin.
July Limerick and Waterford fall to the Free State Army.
August Cork falls to the Free State Army.
Michael Collins is shot dead. *September* The Dáil Eireann convenes, but Republicans abstain.
November A British general election returns the Conservatives with a Unionist majority in the North.
Erskine Childers, an anti-Treaty Republican, is shot by the Free State Army.

1923

April Seán O'Casey's play *Shadow of a Gunman* has its première at the Abbey Theatre in Dublin.
September The Irish Free State is admitted to the League of Nations.
November W.B. Yeats is awarded the Nobel Prize for Literature.

1924

October A British general election returns the Conservatives, with the Unionists in the majority in the North.

1925

April Some Nationalist MPs take their seats in the Northern Ireland Parliament, swearing the oath of allegiance.

1926

January John Logie Baird demonstrates the television.
Seán O'Casey's *The Plough and the Stars* opens in the Abbey Theatre, Dublin.
May Eamon de Valera launches Fianna Fáil, a new political party.
November George Bernard Shaw wins the Nobel Prize for Literature.

1927

June A general election results in a hung Dáil .

1928

May Women 21 years and over are given the right to vote.
October The Gate Theatre opens in Dublin.

1929

October Stock markets crash in the USA, followed by a worldwide slump.

1931

October The IRA is outlawed.

1932

February A general election results in a minority Fianna Fáil government.
March The order outlawing the IRA lapses.

1933

January Fianna Fáil wins the general election.
Hitler becomes Chancellor of the Weimar Republic.
May The Oath of Allegiance is removed from the constitution of the Irish Free State.
September The political party Fine Gael is formed.

1934

April Lord Craigavon, leader of the Ulster Unionist Party, refers to Stormont and Northern Ireland as a Protestant Parliament and a Protestant state.

1936

May The first Aer Lingus flight between Dublin and Britain takes place.
December In the fighting between the followers of Franco and the Republicans in Spain, there are Irish volunteers on both sides.

1937

May Neville Chamberlain is appointed Prime Minister.

December The Constitution of Ireland comes into force.

1938

April Seánad Eireann, the Irish Senate, meets for the first time.

June A general election results in victory for Fianna Fáil.

Douglas Hyde becomes President of Ireland.

September The Munich Agreement between Hitler and Mussolini agrees to the dismemberment of Czechoslovakia.

1939

January The IRA begins a bombing campaign in England.

W.B. Yeats dies.

February The Department of External Affairs officially recognizes Franco as leader of Spain.

Eamon de Valera announces that the Free State will remain neutral in any imminent war.

May James Joyce's *Finnegan's Wake* is published.

September World War II begins.

1943

June Fianna Fáil wins the general election.

1944

May Fianna Fáil is again elected.

1945

April Mussolini is killed by Italian partisans.

Hitler commits suicide in his bunker.

May Germany surrenders. Victory in Europe.

In his victory speech, Churchill attacks de Valera and the neutral position he took during the war.

June Seán T. O'Kelly is elected President. Seán Lemass succeeds him as Tánaiste, deputy Prime Minister.

July A general election in Britain leads to a Labour victory and Clement Attlee becomes Prime Minister.

August The USA drops an atom bomb on Hiroshima (6 August) and then on Nagasaki three days later.

Japan surrenders, signalling the end of World War II.

1946

July Clann na Poblachta, a new Republican party, is formed by Seán MacBride.

1947

January A bill to make Shannon the world's first duty-free airport is put before the Dáil.

1948

February J.A. Costello becomes Taoiseach, Prime Minister, in the new Dáil, where a coalition government is in place.

December Oireachtas, the Irish Assembly, passes the Republic of Ireland Act.

1949

February Unionists win a majority in elections in the North of Ireland.

April Ireland leaves the Commonwealth.

June The Ireland Act, guaranteeing the status of Northern Ireland within the UK, is passed by the House of Commons.

1951

May Following the general election, Fianna Fáil becomes the largest party in the Dáil and Eamon de Valera becomes Taoiseach in June.

1953

January Samuel Beckett's play *Waiting for Godot* is given its premiere.

March Stalin dies.

June The coronation of Elizabeth II takes place.

Sir Edmund Hillary and Sherpa Tensing conquer Everest.

The Reverend Ian Paisley organizes a protest against Modernism.

FURTHER READING

The books listed below are each of great merit and will give a fuller picture of some of the storytellers as well as of Ireland itself, through all its mutations. And on the subject of age, Ronald Blythe is both enlightening and very moving.

A Dictionary of Hiberno-English Terence Patrick Dolan (Gill & Macmillan)
Ireland A History Robert Kee (Abacus)
The Journeyman Eamon Kelly (Marino)
Irish Folk Ways E. Estyn Evans (Dover)
Lawful Occasions Patrick Mackenzie
Modern Ireland 1600-1972 R. F. Foster (Allen Lane)
A New Day Dawning: A Portrait of Ireland in 1900 Daniel Mulhall (The Collins Press)
The View in Winter Ronald Blythe (Penguin)
A Woman of Aran Bridget Dirrane (Blackwater Press)

INDEX